# *Refusal of*
# *the Shadow*

# *Refusal of the Shadow*

## Surrealism and the Caribbean

◆

Edited by

MICHAEL RICHARDSON

Translated by

KRZYSZTOF FIJAŁKOWSKI

and

MICHAEL RICHARDSON

**VERSO**

London • New York

Published with the financial assistance of the
Bureau du Livre at the Ambassade de France, London

First published by Verso 1996

**Verso**
UK: 6 Meard Street, London W1V 3HR
USA: 180 Varick Street, New York NY 10014–4606

Verso is the imprint of New Left Books

ISBN   978-1-85984-018-4

**British Library Cataloguing in Publication Data**
A catalogue record for this book is available from the British Library

**Library of Congress Cataloging-in-Publication Data**
Refusal of the shadow : surrealism and the Caribbean / edited by Michael Richardson :
translated by Krzysztof Fijałkowski and Michael Richardson.
    p.    cm
ISBN 1–85984–997–0 (hbk.). — ISBN 1–85984–018–3 (pbk.)
1. West Indian literature (French)—History and criticism.   2. Surrealism
(Literature)   3. Légitime défense.   4. Tropiques.   5. Negritude (Literary
movement)   6. Race awareness in literature.   7. West Indies. French—in literature.
8. West Indies. French—Intellectual life—20th century.   I. Richardson, Michael,
1953–.   II. Fijałkowski, Krzysztof.
PQ3940.R44    1996
840.9'9729—dc20
                                                                          95–53309
                                                                          CIP

Typeset by M Rules
Printed in Great Britain by Biddles Ltd. Guildford and Kings Lynn

# *Contents*

# *Translators' Note.*

THANKS FOR THEIR help to: René Bélance, J. Michael Dash, Paul Laraque, François Leperlier.

Thanks also to Terry Hale and to the British Centre for Literary Translation for a bursary funded by the Council of Europe towards this translation.

For permission to translate the texts by André Breton we would like to thank Elisa Breton and Aube Elléouët; Claudie Mabille and Jean-Pierre Mabille for those of Pierre Mabille; Daniel Holly for those of Clément Magloire-Saint-Aude; Laurens Vancrevel of J.M. Meulenhoff, Amsterdam, for that of Hendrik Cramer; Editions Robert Laffont and the author for those of René Ménil; and the authors themselves for those of René Depestre and Paul Laraque.

# Introduction

BETWEEN 1932 AND 1946 a unique series of encounters took place between Francophone Caribbean writers and French surrealists that constitute an important moment in the anti-colonial struggle in the French-speaking world.

The mechanics of this relationship have been little studied, especially in the English-speaking world, even though the importance of the poetry of Aimé Césaire is widely recognized. This book aims to place into focus the issues raised by this relation and to document its various phases.

Some may initially doubt the current relevance of debates that took place half a century ago in the early dawning of the twentieth-century anti-colonialist struggle, believing that they have no more than a historical importance and that, in a post-colonial world, the issues they raise have been confronted and surpassed. Nothing, however, could be further from the truth: contained in these writings are subtle and complex ideas that have rarely been addressed and they continue to raise important questions with multifarious implications for current debates concerning alterity and communication between cultures.

Before considering the specific issues raised by this material, a few words are needed about the nature of French colonialism and the background against which this material took shape.

During the nineteenth century the French colonial myth developed along quite different lines from that of the British. The latter was little more than an apologia for unbridled conquest, and legitimated itself overwhelmingly in the principle that 'might is right', unashamedly using the principle of 'divide and rule' to maintain its power. The British colonial masters assumed the superiority of Western culture

over that of the colonized other and did not in general – notwith-
standing the platitudes of the 'white man's burden' assumed by the
Church – claim legitimation for the colonial adventure in a civilizing
mission which would give colonial peoples access to the 'joys' of
Western civilization.

For the French it was otherwise. Having already lost its colonial
'pearl' in the trauma of the Haitian Revolution, France was far more
responsive to aspirations of the colonial peoples for integration into
the body politic of the 'mother country', making this integration an
element of their colonial policy. This was based not so much on bio-
logical as on cultural racism. The colonial lie was not that
non-Europeans were inherently inferior, but that their culture had
lagged behind in the development of modern society, leaving them
adrift in a stage that the French masters had long ago left behind. For
colonial blacks, the assumption was that they could become civilized,
'French with a black skin', only to the extent that they renounced their
own, supposedly inferior, culture to embrace the values of French civilization. As Frantz Fanon put it, they were led to believe that they
could be 'elevated above jungle status in proportion to [their] adoption
of the mother country's cultural standards'.[1] This game was expressly
defined: it was called assimilation.

Though it may appear at first view that this policy was more generous and enlightened than that of the British, it was in fact just as much
an instrument to ensure the smooth running of empire and contained
within it exactly the same measures of contempt and racism. Indeed, its
effects were more subtle and insidious and it created an identity crisis
with far-reaching consequences still having a considerable impact upon
the present day.

In the Caribbean, the effects of this policy were perhaps more traumatic than in Africa, because it was allied with the memory of slavery
and the persistence of a recollection in the collective mind of an eighteenth-century colonial policy that had no room for the niceties of
assimilation and was based unashamedly upon a naked exploitation
heedless of possible consequences. Slavery had also served the preliminary purpose of separating blacks from their native African cultures.

Equally, the Caribbean offered an example of the risks such naked
exploitation contained in the country of Haiti, which had come into
being in the aftermath of the world's only successful slave rebellion.
The Haitian Revolution represented the colonialists' worst nightmare,
as well as providing an inspiration to anti-colonial struggles that had to
be neutralized for effective colonial administration. The policy of

assimilation was one means towards this end, especially when combined with the foreign policy of all colonial powers, which effectively
ostracized Haiti from the world community while demonizing it as the
'Black Republic'. Supposedly a savage land of cannibalism and
tyranny, it served to exemplify what happened when the norms of
Western civilization were renounced. It was made clear to black people
in the French colonies, in no uncertain terms, that their only salvation
lay in renouncing their own cultural traditions and embracing those of
the white masters. The confidence the French had in their own culture
as lying at the heart of European civilization reinforced this ideology.
If we wish to understand the nature of the revolt against colonialism in
the Francophone countries, we need first of all to appreciate the extent
to which France sought to bind itself culturally (as well as economically, emotionally and psychologically) with the aspirations of its
colonized peoples. In art and literature, French models dominated.
Generally cultural domination created a situation in the French
colonies in which, as Léopold Sédar Senghor put it, 'to merge, or
merely survive as a race, we would have to steal the weapons of the
conquerors'.

But such dominance was dependent upon the confidence exuded
by French culture itself. The First World War would soon dent that
confidence and have a consequent effect upon French relations with the
colonies. And this is where surrealism assumes such importance.

As a generalized revolt against the very foundations of Western civilization and its morality, surrealism was drawn immediately towards
non-Western cultures, and issues of colonialism soon impinged upon
the surrealists' thinking. Above all, the rebellion of the Rif in Morocco
in 1926 both politicized the Surrealist Group and gave a focus for what
would become a determined anti-colonialist attitude within surrealism. In their response to the Moroccan war, the surrealists joined the
communists in giving unequivocal support to the rebels and calling
upon French troops to fraternize. In a declaration, they proclaimed
that 'for us France no longer exists', and in 1929 they redrew the map
of the world to give this statement concrete form and show Paris as the
capital of Germany: as Aragon declared, they were 'the ones who
always hold out a hand to the enemy'. In this famous drawing, not only
France but also the United States has vanished while Britain is reduced
to an inconsequential dot dwarfed by Ireland. Affective considerations
now determine geography: Mexico, Polynesia and Alaska become the
cultural centres of the world, German philosophy dominates Europe,

and Russia and China maintain their positions in the world largely because of political upheavals. Africa is not particularly large, reflecting the fact that the surrealists were not at that time particularly drawn to African art (although perhaps this is a point that has been overestimated, because Africa is depicted as large as South America: it merely seems small in comparison with Polynesia).

The anti-colonialist impulse was restated at the time of the massive 1931 Colonial Exhibition in Paris which sought to re-create, in microcosm, the French Empire in all its glory in the very heart of Paris. The exhibition was an occasion for general euphoria amongst the French bourgeoisie; the surrealists alone were vociferous in their opposition to a celebration of what they called 'colonial piracy', urging people to boycott the exhibition. With the support of the Communist Party, they organized a counter-exhibition entitled 'The Truth about the Colonies', taking for its underlying theme a quotation from Marx: 'A people which oppresses others cannot be free.' Among the exhibits of 'European fetishes' was a black child with a begging bowl.

Three years later, the surrealists published a ferocious anti-colonialist tract in English in Nancy Cunard's important *Negro: an Anthology* (1934). In their tract all forms of imperialism are attacked in such uncompromising terms that it still shocks today. What is most surprising about this document is not the tone, however, but the complexity of the content. Far from being an emotional attack on the manifest abuses of colonialism, it was directed at the psychology of imperialism and especially at those intellectuals who, under the veneer of liberalism, sought exoticism and adventure in 'some mystic Orient or other'. The aspect is emphasized by the title: 'Murderous Humanitarianism'.

It is significant that this tract was signed by two young Martiniquan intellectuals, Jules Monnerot and Pierre Yoyotte (indeed, from the tone it would seem likely that Monnerot may have had a hand in drafting it). Since 1931 a group of Martiniquan students at the Sorbonne (among them Monnerot and Yoyotte) had sought to form a Caribbean Surrealist Group. This never really took shape as such, but they did publish a single issue of a modest journal called *Légitime défense* that was to assume considerable importance.[2] The title, taken from a short book by Breton, announced its surrealist genesis. This was made explicit in their declaration of intent which, invoking both surrealism and Marxism, proclaimed that 'as traitors to [our] class [we intend] to take treason as far as it will go'.[3]

There seems little doubt that *Légitime défense* was the first publication in which colonized blacks collectively sought to speak with their own authentic voices. The tone was unaccustomed and the French authorities effectively banned the journal by making life difficult for the students, suspending their grants and ensuring that distribution (especially in the Caribbean) was blocked and no further issues were possible. Nevertheless, the *Légitime défense* group did function as a genuine collective, quite separate from the French Surrealist Group but informed by the environment of surrealism and receiving the encouragement of the surrealists.[4]

The focus of *Légitime défense* was the anti-colonial struggle, set in a surrealist and Marxist framework. Surrealism was instrumental in providing the students with a point of departure for their critique of colonial society for, in breaking with the ethics of European culture, it offered them a sort of Trojan Horse in which to enter the previously impregnable white citadel. In surrealism they heard white masters with new voices, voices that renounced that mastery. Previously they had been faced with a homogeneous voice of white authority extolling the incomparable values of white civilizations. Now they were hearing white people themselves cogently accusing their own culture of a barbarism that surpassed anything in the history of the so-called primitive peoples. As Jacqueline Leiner has put it, 'Reinvested by the Other, the Black could no longer deny himself.'[5] In this respect, Marxism complemented surrealism in the socio-political judgement it had made on Western institutions.

If, in the immediate term, the publication of *Légitime défense* did nothing to dent the confidence of French imperialism, it nevertheless represented a significant questioning by blacks of the foundations of European culture and the colonial relation.

Among its readers may or may not have been three younger students at the École Normale Supérieure: the Guyanese Léon Damas, the Senegalese Léopold Sédar Senghor and the Martiniquan Aimé Césaire. In 1934 they founded their own journal, *L'Étudiant noir*, also published in a single modest issue. A legend has been built up that this journal laid the foundations of negritude, that it was partly a result of dissatisfaction that *Légitime défense* did not engage with Caribbean and African issues from an indigenous perspective, but appropriated a European standpoint and adopted surrealism and Marxism in an imitative way: according to this standpoint, there was nothing to distinguish its writers from French surrealists or Marxists.[6] René Ménil, on the other hand, considered that the problem lay elsewhere, and that *Légitime défense* failed to avoid reifying black sensibility, so making a mystificatory ideology based upon race possible,[7] an issue we shall return to later. One criticism that Ménil would accept was that *Légitime défense* did not initiate the sort of poetry needed by the colonized, but remained determined by French surrealist models.[8] The first great collection of work in the French colonies to go beyond European models was Damas's *Pigments*, published in 1937 with an introduction by the surrealist poet Robert Desnos. Desnos recognized the great significance of this volume as being that 'Damas is black, insisting on his blackness and on his condition as a black'.

Of still greater significance was *Cahier d'un retour au pays natal* (*Notebook of a Return to My Native Land*),[9] a long poem written by Aimé Césaire, which Breton would describe as 'nothing less than the greatest lyric monument of our time'. This helped to define a specifically black Caribbean sensibility, but also announced a changed relation between black and white in the French colonies: no longer could assimilation be taken for granted as the destiny of the colonized:

> *Listen to the white world*
> *appallingly weary from its immense effort*
> *the crack of its joints rebelling under the hardness of the stars*
> *listen to the proclaimed victories which trumpet their defeats*
> *listen to their grandiose alibis (stumbling so lamely)*
>
> *Pity for our conquerors, all-knowing and naïve!*

The gauntlet was thrown down to colonialism:

> *Accommodate yourself to me. I won't*
> *Accommodate myself to you!*[10]

The *Notebook* also proclaimed Césaire's imminent return to his native land of Martinique, a return that Frantz Fanon would later consider to be of crucial symbolic importance for ideas of Martiniquan identity (it also seems symbolic that the ship that carried him home would be sunk by the Nazis on its return journey: his return announced a definitive break with the values of Europe). C.L.R. James saw the importance of the *Notebook* as threefold:

1. He has made a union of the African sphere of existence with existence in the Western world.
2. The past of mankind and the future of mankind are historically and logically linked.

3. No longer from external stimulus but from their own self-gener-
ated and independent being and motion will Africa and Africans
move towards an integrated humanity.[11]

Back in his homeland, Césaire became a teacher of literature at the
Lycée Schoelcher in Fort de France, and his presence there became
something of a provocation, offering students a bridge to the African
values they had always previously been taught to despise. Césaire's
wife Suzanne was also a teacher there, as was René Ménil, who taught
philosophy. Césaire had the idea of publishing a journal to confront
what he considered the 'cultural void' in Martinique. He believed such
a confrontation especially important since, in Martinique, while there
was an appreciation of cultural issues, the island's society was essentially one that *consumed* rather than actively engaged with culture.
Thus was *Tropiques* born, edited by the Césaires and Ménil, the first
issue of which appeared in April 1941.

*Tropiques* would function simultaneously on three ideological levels:
as a focus for a developing black consciousness in Martinique; as a
covert locus for the anti-Vichy struggle (during the war Martinique
was ostensibly administered by Vichy); and as a journal of international surrealism. Suzanne Césaire was to be very specific about the
attraction and importance of the latter element:

> Our surrealism will then deliver it the bread of *its depths*. Finally
> those sordid contemporary antinomies of black/white, European/
> African, civilized/savage will be transcended. The magical power of
> the mahoulis will be recovered, drawn forth from living sources.
> Colonial stupidity will be purified in the blue welding flame. Our
> value as metal, our cutting edge of steel, our amazing communions
> will be rediscovered.
>
> Surrealism – the tightrope of our hope.[12]

Nevertheless, the editors of *Tropiques* were drawn to surrealism from
different perspectives. For Césaire it was essentially a poetic tool, a
means to use language, and a moral sensibility. Surrealism affirmed
something he had long felt; it was, he said, 'a confirmation of what I
had found through my own reflections'.[13] For Ménil and for Suzanne
Césaire, on the other hand, surrealism was more of a critical tool, a
means of reflection that would provide them with a critical foundation from which to explore their own cultural context. For Ménil in

particular, as a philosopher, it was surrealism's ideas that were most important, and especially its Hegelian basis. Great poet that he is, Césaire is not an original thinker, and his critical writings reveal that he did not fully grasp the philosophical underpinnings of surrealism. His major critical text in *Tropiques*, 'Poetry and Knowledge', while interesting from many perspectives, already gives evidence of a certain theoretical idealism that sits uneasily with his surrealism. Not that this is to imply any discord among the editors of *Tropiques* as to its aims: far from it, as one reads it one is most struck by its unity of tone and by how much the texts respond to one another, almost in a symbiotic way, with Césaire's poetry the starting point for the philosophical and theoretical issues raised.

Césaire's return to his homeland was not to be the only one in this period. Certainly, Wifredo Lam's return to Cuba in 1941 was equally significant, having similar ramifications in the plastic domain to those raised in the poetic domain by Césaire: Lam's *The Jungle*, painted in Cuba in 1942, may I think be seen as the visual companion piece to Césaire's *Notebook*. Pierre Mabille's essay 'The Jungle', which was published in *Tropiques*, brings out this importance. Above all, Lam's work established a means to explore a specifically American sensibility in dialogue with Europe: it opened a means of communication between New and Old World sensibilities to the enrichment of both and in which neither was subsumed to the other.

After the war Césaire and Ménil went separate ways, Césaire to become one of the foremost – if somewhat ambivalent – exponents of negritude, while Ménil would be one of its more trenchant critics. The extent to which *Tropiques* can be seen as a forerunner of negritude must therefore be considered problematic. While negritude did not emerge until after the period documented here, it none the less raises crucial issues, especially in the light of Ménil's later critique, that affect the way we respond to these texts and the questions they raise about surrealism and communication between cultures.[14] For Ménil, negritude came to stand for a political doctrine whose apparent ideological credentials were a mask by which European imperialism used the native petty bourgeoisie to ensure the continuance of a neo-colonialist mentality following independence that would ensure continuing European dominance.

Although the reductive essentialism that came to dominate negritude had been defined in Césaire's poem ('Those who invented neither gunpowder nor compass/Those who never knew how to conquer steam or electricity/But who abandoned themselves to the essence of all things'), it was Senghor who established the ideological gloss. Or more specifically, if we accept Ménil's argument, negritude was established as a political ideology neither by Senghor nor Césaire, but by Jean-Paul Sartre in 'Orphée noir', his influential introduction to Senghor's *Anthologie de la nouvelle poésie nègre et malgache*, published in 1948 and acting as a rallying cry for concepts of negritude. Sartre's crucial role was to give philosophical legitimation to what previously had only been a vague poetics. In the process, negritude's apparently progressive credentials could be assumed as a mask by the native petty bourgeoisie to buttress its class ascendency after independence. Sartre's unwitting role emerged from a failure to see negritude in its own terms; instead he transforms it into something that follows from his own philosophical formulations and was born in some ways from his own negative wish fulfilment: 'The negro in question is a negro who resembles Sartre, a Sartre darkened and sometimes turned upside down, but a very anguished, very existentialist and picturesque negro!'[15] He is a character without concrete reality who has emerged from nowhere, exists outside of all social relations, outside the real world and national contexts. By forming such a character, negritude is led into the error of reifying the view that blacks were colonized because they were black, since the postulates of negritude celebrate an identity based directly upon skin colour. Such identity never existed in reality: the only identity that blacks share emerges from experience of slavery and colonization, and, if one can speak of a specific 'negro' sensibility, one can do so only in relation to a concrete historical situation: through being colonized disparate blacks gained a feature in common. This cannot be considered as a racial trait. If it exists at all it has simply emerged from a common experience.

The terms in which Ménil is discussing negritude here raise general issues about the self/other relation. What is being brought into question is not black consciousness but the whole black/white, colonized/colonizer relation. For though negritude was born of the relation of the black to the West (or more specifically to France), it did not question the relation itself, but capitulated to an 'exotic-for-self' identity (something which, in Hegelian terms, is defined as 'appetitive self-consciousness', the first stage of becoming). But the application of Hegelian terms here reveals that the second part of the process is recognition. Trapped within its own self-consciousness by its ideological straitjacket, negritude is unable to take this step. On the one hand it reflects the European's own inverted image, allowing itself to be defined by an external consciousness; on the other hand it comes to represent nothing but its particular class interests, so serving neo-colonialism. This process also enables us to see how easily potentially liberatory ideas can become congealed and so on the contrary serve established interests. It was Wole Soyinka who pinpointed the way in which this process occurs. He did this when clarifying a notorious statement he was alleged to have made to the effect that 'a tiger does-n't proclaim its tigritude': 'The point is, to quote what I said fully. I said: "A tiger does not proclaim its tigritude, he pounces." In other words: a tiger does not stand in the forest and say "I am a tiger." When you pass where the tiger has walked before, you see the skeleton of a duiker, you know that some tigritude has emanated there. In other words: the distinction I was making [. . .] was a purely literary one: I was trying to distinguish between propaganda and true poetic creativ-ity.'[16] Ideas, then, should not stand still. They need, like the tiger, to keep on the move.

Here complex issues are being brought into play. Césaire is not the focus of Ménil's critique: he makes a distinction between the poetic uses to which Césaire put negritude and the political uses to which Senghor and Sartre in different ways put it. He also notes the crucial role played by humour: Césaire's evocations of negritude are charged with a humorous edge, whereas Senghor's statements are always deadly serious. Nevertheless, we can perceive here a fundamental difference in approach between Césaire and Ménil that touches on how we consider surrealism. Ménil's argument is very much within the central tradition of surrealist criticism, which refuses any abstract formulations of racial or sexual identity (it is, for instance, remarkable how close his argument is to Annie Le Brun's critique of feminism[17]), and it is also interesting to consider it in relation to an article by Roger Caillois, 'Nature à rebours',[18] which was subject to a ferocious denunciation by Césaire.[19] In this article, Caillois particularly criticizes Claude Lévi-Strauss for his relativist anthropological legitimation of other, non-Western cultures. He points out that Lévi-Strauss can only advance his contentions because he takes for granted an inherent Western superiority that is contained within his anthropological project itself: his essential postu-lates are culturally determined. The superiority or otherwise of cultures is invisible to us, since our position within our own culture makes it impossible to attain a sufficiently objective viewpoint to make such judgement. Our points of reference are determined beforehand and the very fact of positing a superiority for a culture other than our own involves a patronizing sense not of one's inferiority, but of superiority.

Césaire's attack in his book *Discourse on Colonialism* completely ignores this argument and bizarrely accuses Caillois of arguing that non-Western cultures are inherently inferior to white civilization, seeing his argument as an intellectual reinforcement of old Christian and colonialist ideas. Nothing of this is in Caillois's article. Caillois is concerned with a critique of the way in which Western intellectuals impute universal values to what are no more than culturally determined precepts and he asserts that 'the only ethnography is white' to emphasize this point. Césaire reads this as a statement of the superiority of Western culture.[20] Césaire's misunderstanding of this essay is very strange and one must wonder whether he perceived in it the implication (in fact from a surrealist point of view) that negritude was itself a Western construct. Indeed the resemblances between Caillois's argument and that put forward by Fanon a couple of years earlier in *Black Skins, White Masks* is striking, albeit from the other perspective.

Certainly Caillois's argument seems to accord with that of Ménil, for whom cultural specificity is the crucial factor. Within these terms, there is nothing within surrealism itself that renders it impermeable to the same process. Thus, as Ménil mentions in his essay 'Concerning Colonial Exoticism', surrealism has also provided one of the means whereby blacks in the Francophone Caribbean have been exoticized for themselves. This is not a critique of surrealism, however: rather it is a surrealist critique of social processes of incorporation and appropriation by which the dominant culture maintains its hegemony, social processes from which surrealism (as a socially determined form) cannot remain exempt. Here a distinction must be made between surrealism as living cultural praxis and as dead cultural artifact.

In another article not included in the present collection[21] Ménil, in a critique of Lilyan Kesteloot's pioneering study of negritude,[22] notes how surrealism can become degraded into an attitude and style in which critical reflection is replaced with mystification. This is something that needs to be borne in mind when reading these texts. Surrealism is a tool of critical reflection and poetic investigation for the surrealists themselves, but it can be transformed into an abstraction based upon anti-surrealist postulates. As Ménil says of Kesteloot, she uses surrealism to make things absolute, mysterious and unanalysable and 'the more obscure the poems are, the happier she is'.[23] Such an approach has a significant bearing on our perception of otherness, not only in a colonial and post-colonial situation, but in a more general sense.

In this context, it is also curious to note Sartre's enthusiasm in 'Orphée noir' for a poetry that is 'revolutionary because it is surrealist. . . . But itself surrealist because it is black.'[24] This statement stands out to the extent that Sartre was hardly an advocate of surrealism for French writers, indeed everything he ever wrote about it in the context of French culture indicates that he considered it to be far from revolutionary. His assertion therefore tends to assume a category of otherness – here a specifically black, 'negritude', culture – in which surrealism becomes an appropriate form of expression. For Sartre this is but a necessary phase through which blacks must pass before being integrated into universal culture when they would, presumably, lose their 'surrealism' along with their 'negritude'. Hardly surprisingly, Fanon considered this a particularly insidious form of emasculation.

Another influential critique of surrealism can also be considered here. The Cuban writer Alejo Carpentier, while admitting his debt to surrealism, considered that it lacked authenticity in Europe: the European surrealist was condemned to a paucity of vision because surrealism was not embedded in society, the European cultural soil being too barren to sustain its richness.[25] Its real domain was Latin America and the Caribbean, where magic remains part of everyday life. Surrealism thus becomes the appropriate means of expression in Latin America, but it is that surrealism divorced from its critical roots and recuperated as a 'real marvellous', or the 'magic realism' that today substantially conditions our idea of an appropriate Latin American literature. But this magic realism is, like negritude, a reification of reality in a particular (exotic) form appropriate to the Other which, although implying a separation from the traditions of Europe, is none the less defined in relation to those rejected traditions.

The crucial intellectual influence on Carpentier was Spengler, whose cyclical view of the rise and fall of civilizations implied a relativity of cultures with their own particular characteristics owing nothing – necessarily – to the universal. Drawn to surrealism, Carpentier was repelled by its monist and universalist basis. The relativity of cultures was essential to his conception of American identity. Yet, while recognizing the importance of cultural specificity and diversity, surrealism none the less fundamentally asserts that this belongs to the realm of appearance and that the universal is the only essence: 'Thought is ONE and indivisible,' as Benjamin Péret put it. Communication is therefore of crucial significance and the differences between cultures can be transcended in the course of the play between self and other. Recognizing the essential duality of all things, surrealism aims at the resolution of the contradictions such duality implies: this is the supreme point that determines the surrealist quest.

Attracted by the appearance of surrealism's practice (especially its sensitivity to other cultures and its assertion of the values of revolt and liberty), Carpentier rejects its Hegelian aspects in order to put forward the notion of an American reality as *essentially* distinct from that of Europe. This conception of what he called 'our America' denies both the Latin and Anglo-Saxon influences in America and affirms a separate American reality, excluding the United States whilst embracing the heritage of both pre-Columbian and African cultures. This presupposes an emergent civilization with its own dynamic owing nothing to European civilization, and possibly coming into its own as the West declines, in accordance with cyclical schemas put forward by Spengler. Communication between cultures is implicitly denied: in our plurality we are all engaged in different quests and any notion of universal values is false. This leads Carpentier to an extremely ungenerous appreciation of the work of European surrealists. He considers, for instance, that André Masson's Martiniquan works merely represent his powerlessness in the face of the Martiniquan landscape; only a Wifredo Lam was capable of revealing the 'truth' of the American landscape. Now, it may be that Masson's perception is entirely European. How could it be otherwise? Nevertheless, his American work is enormously rich and powerful. It may not have the charge of Lam's work, but this is because Lam's work of that period is so original and pathbreaking in its use of landscape that no one can match it. And of course it does present an authentically American perspective, something that Masson could hardly aspire to. Yet Masson's work still represents a legitimate and rich perspective on America.

The problem with Carpentier's conception of an independent American sensibility is that it leaves intact the power relations actually in force in the world. There is contained within it a refusal to engage with the dynamic essential to the way cultures interact. As the Haitian philosopher Jacques Gourgue, criticizing Carpentier, puts it, 'Surrealism and the real marvellous would be intrinsically linked to poorly industrialized countries . . . [and so] justify hazy ideas and illogical actions that one would prefer to leave hidden behind the mountain of centuries. The "irrationalities" that Europeans venerate among us have been combated by them in order to reach the present technical domination.'[26] Are such notions of essential cultural identity – whether in the form of intellectual movements like negritude or 'magic realism' or in forms of religious fundamentalism – anything but rationalized cargo cults serving the escapism of those who feel powerless faced with the inexorable power of international capitalism?

For the writers of *Tropiques*, Spenglerian ideas were also important, sometimes treated in a confused way, but always integrated with
a surrealist Hegelianism. Certainly, Spengler had also been influential
in the development of French surrealism. Most notably, in 1938 Pierre
Mabille published *Égrégores ou la vie des civilisations*, which was basi-
cally a revision of Spengler in the light of Hegel and the class struggle.
What was renounced was Spengler's pluralism and determinism: individual beings or civilizations are not separable from the whole of
creation. Life is a continuum in which all things interrelate. Death as
finality is denied because everything is capable of transformation,
everything exists in a state of latent potentiality, capable of being
realized or activated by desire.

In *Tropiques* these ideas are transposed to the Caribbean context.
This is most clearly seen in Suzanne Césaire's 'Leo Frobenius and the
Problem of Civilizations'. Frobenius, an explorer and anthropologist
whose work paralleled and influenced that of Spengler, was important for the writers of *Tropiques* for his legitimation of the values of
African civilization and thought. But Suzanne Césaire does not allow
herself to be seduced by the immutable relativism displayed by
Carpentier. She interprets the Paideuma (in 'Leo Frobenius and the
Problem of Civilizations') very much in the light of Mabille, as a *ratio-
nalization* of the essence of a culture rather than the actual essence
itself. Accepting the distinction between a Hamite and an Ethiopian
sensibility, she seeks a resolution of the dissonance between them, not
the celebration of one against the other.

The means for such resolution is to be sought in poetry, perceived in
*Tropiques* in pure surrealist terms: as an activity of the spirit that acts
upon the world and transforms life. Concern with poetics permeates
the pages of *Tropiques*, going beyond the frame of poetic understanding specifically to embrace the nature of reality and its perception.
Poetry is a grasping of reality in its pure state. It is always concrete,
emerging from the interraction between form and substance in the very
shock of existential apprehension. As René Ménil insists, it is real
blood that courses through the veins of genuine poetry, because it
exists as a realization of the processes of the imagination. Poetry's
necessity is that of concrete freedom. It leaps with the shocks of life.
Knowledge is thus seen to have a primeval quality and not to develop
in the course of an evolution or progressive unfolding. Through poetry,
one makes oneself one with the world.

This pure surrealist conception is still allied, in *Tropiques*, with a
critical approach towards surrealism. Or rather, the aim is the application

of a surrealism that directly addresses Martiniquan realities. It is not influenced by surrealism; it *cannibalizes* it. As Suzanne Césaire put it, 'Martiniquan poetry will be cannibal or will not be.' This notion of cannibalizing Western culture is a potent theme that has been taken up in more recent so-called Third World discourse, especially in Brazil; it is already given a clear focus in *Tropiques*. Thus, the relation with the West is viewed in an essentially favourable light: 'cultural appropriation, which is a fact of universal civilization, could not in the present case be reduced – prematurely and in a simplistic way – to being no more than a negative colonial phenomenon of political assimilationism.'[27]

Certainly there are, in *Tropiques*, many deficiencies and false paths, as René Ménil makes clear in his introduction to the re-edition issued by Jean-Michel Place in 1978. This is hardly surprising, given the difficult conditions under which it was produced. However, what is more striking is the unity of purpose and resolve to tackle issues in a straightforward way, especially issues of the identity of cultures and communication between them, something that otherwise was barely on the agenda at the time it was published.

The danger of eliding the differences between cultures or of asserting their separate identity is latently present and is something that René Ménil in particular has always been very alert to, something that gives his work an exceptional contemporary quality.

There is, within all of Ménil's articles, a tone that already anticipates that of Fanon and, although Ménil was not Fanon's philosophy teacher, it is clear that he learned a great deal from Ménil's essays in *Tropiques*. Ménil above all insists that discussions about negritude and black identity must be a subject for discussion between blacks and whites. As he points out:

> . . . in the study of negritude, one notes the ambiguous attitude of an emotional type among white (European or American) critics. Their approach is generally affected by a strong coefficient of subjectivity (feelings of guilt, a need for atonement, seeking evasion and exoticism, masochism, etc.). With some we note a reserve, a discretion and a fear of squarely tackling the question: 'It is an issue for Blacks, they are the ones who must undertake the critique of negritude if they think it is worthwhile and say what they think of it.' This is quite natural, but . . . But does it not simply represent a repression of racism not to wish to consider a negro philosophy as one human philosophy among others? Equally, negritude is not merely a matter between blacks, since its object is the relation black–white and it

styles and defines whites correlatively and antithetically in relation to blacks. Finally, negritude situating itself from the start within the framework of progressive and anti-colonialist ideologies, the most liberal white critics have difficulties in surmounting the following problem: how to effect without complacency the progressive critique of a progressive ideology that contains errors? They are afraid that by submitting negritude to such a critique they could be accused of paternalism or even racism.[28]

What is essential, then, is to keep open the paths of communication, while respecting questions of otherness and exoticism.

As we consider these debates today, we need to remain alert to the actual social context in which they were enacted. Martinique, in the eastern part of the Caribbean, was colonized by the French in 1635. As a colonial possession, it was subjected to the slave-based plantation system centred around sugar production (although it was of minor importance to the French Empire compared with Saint-Domingue [Haiti-to-be]). As a response to the slave revolt in Saint-Domingue, and in line with the libertarian policies of the French Revolution, slavery was abolished in Martinique by the Convention in 1792, something that led to much resistance from planters, who openly collaborated when the English invaded and assumed control of the island in 1793. The English restored slavery and the plantation system continued when the island reverted to French control in 1813. Although slavery would be definitively abolished in 1848, the actual system of production remained more or less the same throughout the nineteenth and early part of the twentieth century. Nationalist feeling manifested itself during the Second World War, when the French administration remained under the control of Vichy until 1943. None the less, a plebiscite in 1946 on the future of the island revealed a considerable majority in favour not of independence but of incorporation into France itself. Since then, Martinique has been legally a *département* with the same rights and duties as any in metropolitan France, and has been presented as a model for the French aim of assimilation.

For the people of Martinique things are not so simple and Césaire himself, who was both mayor of Fort-de-France and Martiniquan deputy in the French parliament for many years, reflects the ambivalent relationship of the island to the 'mother country'.[29] Martinique was, along with its sister islands of Guadeloupe in the Caribbean, Réunion in the Indian Ocean, and French Guiana in South America, one of the few colonies to turn its back on independence and willingly accept the maternal embrace of the European colonizer. It is thereby 'an island unfaithful to its roots'[30] which, by voting for incorporation into France, was renouncing the essential Hegelian precondition for self-recognition: the determination to fight for it to the death. It is thereby condemned to a form of simulation in morbidity, as Fanon pointed out. And, as Francis Affergan more recently argued in a fascinating study,[31] the Martiniquan strives for a personal identity even in the process of denying it, thus creating a divided collective personality which, in effect, wants France but not the French. This establishes an amorous relationship based on need rather than desire. The consequence is an extinction of the self rather than the creation of an autonomous sphere of existence, since the object of desire remains unrecognized by the subject. The Martiniquan is in effect neither French nor West Indian, but a disembodied hybrid being unsure of its roots.

These are the consequences of an assimilation that denies otherness and reduces the other to the status of coeval entity. This is based on an assumption of an equality of relations that patently does not exist: Martinique is dependent politically, economically and even culturally on France. In return it pays a tribute, which can be measured partly in financial terms, but more specifically in terms of this denial of difference, providing legitimation for French cultural superiority. This denial of difference reflects a collective psychological need among the French to feel that their culture is still the heart of Western civilization. No reciprocity with others is expected and none is accepted. To be sure this is not only revealed in relation to non-European cultures, since the relationship France has with the Bretons and the Basques follows a similar pattern. It is a situation that is highlighted by the deep trauma that the post-colonial situation has created in France and has great bearing on current racial difficulties within France itself.

In Martinique itself, what has been frustrated is a vision of autonomous development based upon mutual respect. This was the vision that underlies to some extent the impulse behind *Tropiques*. Not that the question of the political or social relationship with France is directly addressed. It hardly could have been in the abnormal conditions created by the Second World War. Nevertheless *Tropiques'* concern with questions of identity clearly reveals the concerns within the island which must have been what led the French government after the war to offer the people the choice of independence.

\*

If Martinique represents one extreme on the scale measuring the fate of post-colonial societies, another Francophone land in the Caribbean, Haiti, represents the other.

As Saint-Domingue, it was for a century the most magnificent colony in history: one of the most fertile pieces of land in the world, during the eighteenth century it was mercilessly exploited to provide untold wealth for the mother country and was the undisputed jewel in the French colonial crown.

The French Revolution, and an indigenous slave revolt in the colony, changed all that. One of the more extraordinary events in humanity's history, the revolution in Saint-Domingue finally led to the establishment of the independent state of Haiti in 1804 when Jean-Jacques Dessalines dramatically tore the white out of the French flag to create the blue and red emblem of the new republic.

Independence was to bring fresh sorrow to Haiti. Internal divisions between mulatto and black were difficult enough, but the people's refusal to engage in anything but subsistence farming, perceiving any attempt to rationalize the economy as a prelude to the reintroduction of slavery, made it difficult for any Haitian government to confront the political and economic needs of the new nation and enable it to compete on the world market. But what really determined the course of Haiti's history was the attitude of the Western powers.

The loss of Haiti had a traumatic effect on the French colonial mentality, bringing with it an urge for revenge. Moreover, the thought of a potentially rich and powerful black republic in such a strategic position in the Caribbean was threatening to all the colonial powers, and to the United States of America. Soon after independence, France imposed an economic blockade, which was not lifted until 1825, demanding payment of ludicrous sums in compensation for the loss of the colony, which the Haitian government would never be able to pay. Britain, and later the United States and Germany, watched the republic through vulture's eyes, each seeking an opportunity to establish their own colonial power, while demonizing Haiti as the 'Black Republic' of violence and cannibalistic practices.

In such circumstances, the possibility of the Haitian people effecting their own development and establishing themselves as independent and equal in the community of nations was virtually nil. Politically and socially Haitian society inevitably became insular, and internal pressures became exacerbated to an intolerable degree.[32] These pressures came to a head in 1915, when the United States invaded; it remained in occupation for nineteen years.

Unmitigated disaster for Haiti though the US occupation was in social and political terms, it did serve as the catalyst for a questioning of cultural identity. For despite its reputation among Europeans and North Americans, the Haitian élite considered itself a uniquely civilized society in the Americas, the inheritor of the splendours of French culture and thus superior to the vulgar Yankees to the north (the US occupation thus caused a crisis of identity among members of the Haitian élite, who felt humiliated by the presence of foreign troops on their soil).

In cultural terms, what the occupation did above all was to spur Haitians to question their own identity and their ties with European culture. As Jean Price-Mars argued in his celebrated 1928 work, *Ainsi parla l'oncle*, the identification with French culture had led to a form of 'collective bovaryism' in which Haitians perceived themselves as other than they were. In effect they had 'exoticized themselves'. Obviously this phenomenon is something very similar to the contemporary situation in Martinique. Two factors, though, were very different. In Haiti, political independence had been fought for and won. And it was only the élite that was tied to French culture. The great mass of the ordinary people had their own popular traditions, based upon the voodoo religion, which the élite had conspired to suppress or deny.

Price-Mars had been looking at the bases of popular and folklore tradition since before the occupation, and this event gave his work an added impetus. When *Ainsi parla l'oncle* was published in 1928, it burst upon the Haitian scene and forced the literate population to take note of the voodoo tradition.

Through the 1930s, the quest for an authentic identity that did not deny this tradition gained ground, and led to the formation of an avant-garde group, Les Griots, by Carl Brouard, Lorimer Denis and François Duvalier, whose particular aim was to probe and recover the African values that had been denied in the dominant Haitian culture. This cult of Africanism was already a forerunner of negritude and indeed it was Brouard who coined the word 'nigritie' as early as 1929.

It was also during the 1930s that contact between surrealism and Haiti became important and had an impact on the way issues of cultural identity were considered there. For the writers of the Africanist movement, surrealism was one of the modernist ideas coming from Europe that gave some legitimation – in its reclamation of the 'primitive' and its assault on rationalism – to Haitian aims of developing a specifically black consciousness. To be sure, this influence was superficial, as was the surrealists' own interest in voodoo, in which they perceived confirmation of their own ideas of the value of dream, trance and automatic writing. However, over the next decade this mutual interest was to be deepened substantially by personal contacts and some extraordinary events.

It is, in fact, remarkable how many correspondences there were between the surrealists and Haiti during these years: several surrealists visited Haiti, taking a deep interest in the mythology of voodoo. But it was not only at the level of the 'exotic' that the surrealists found Haiti fascinating. They also had a serious political and anthropological interest in the unfolding of Haitian history, perceiving in it the germ of a society that had the potential to challenge the ethics of international capitalism. In his preface to *The Black Jacobins* by C.L.R. James (which he translated into French), the surrealist writer Pierre Naville noted the important issues that were raised by the Haitian Revolution, issues that France still found too uncomfortable to confront, but which were among the most vital of the age. Yet in French historiography, the Haitian Revolution had been relegated to a footnote of the French Revolution, hardly ever considered in itself, as though consideration of it was still too threatening.

Among the visitors to Haiti was the Dutch surrealist Hendrik Cramer who had stayed there several times during the twenties and thirties. A traveller somewhat in the mould of Lafcadio Hearn, Cramer similarly immersed himself in the legends and folklore of the Francophone Caribbean. More significantly, in 1940 Pierre Mabille was appointed head surgeon at the general hospital in Port-au-Prince. Whilst there he studied voodoo practices and helped to establish, alongside Haitian intellectuals like Price-Mars and Jacques Roumain, the Haitian Bureau d'Ethnologie, a political event of some significance in Haitian history.[33] In 1944, Aimé Césaire was there during September and gave a series of lectures which had a considerable impact, both on the audience and on Césaire himself. At the end of 1945 Mabille, who had been appointed French cultural attaché, invited André Breton to visit Haiti to give a series of lectures to coincide with an exhibition of paintings by Wifredo Lam to be held at the Centre d'Art in Port-au-Prince.

Breton's talks had a dramatic effect, as is detailed in essays by Paul Laraque and René Depestre, and were partially responsible for the fall of the government, with far-reaching consequences.[34] The government's fall led to the election as president of Dumarsais Estimé, a popular, progressively inclined and relatively honest politician. Estimé was a black, the first non-mulatto president since the US occupation and also the first not to be a pawn of US interests (the United States retained control of the Haitian treasury until 1947). His attempt to assert the independence of Haiti, breaking dependence on the United States and the power of the mulatto élite, failed, and he was overthrown in a *coup d'état* in 1948 which restored mulatto power. The terrible tragedy of Haitian history that has followed from this failure is well known.

Nevertheless, the political and social history of Haiti should not blind us to the significance of its cultural history. For Europeans, the effect of Breton's lectures in Haiti may come as a surprise.[35] We do not expect literary figures to make an intervention in the political arena; or if we do it is because they have cast aside their cultural robes and become politicians, if only temporarily. What Breton said was hardly incendiary. In our eyes at least. Or even in Breton's (one has the impression that he was somewhat bewildered by what happened, and not a little embarrassed, since he was a guest of the Haitian government and his trip was supported by a grant from the United States and sponsored by the Institut Français in Port-au-Prince). In interviews he was keen to play down the part he played in the revolution, pointing out that the social forces that caused it were all in place and would doubtless have become manifest if he had not visited the island. And yet, the revolution could not have taken the course it did without Breton's intervention. The importance of this should not be minimized, because it bears on our understanding of the nature of a Haitian society in which cultural values have a political impact they lack in the West. The Haitian people as a whole have never renounced the clarion call of the French Revolution; 'Liberty, Equality, Fraternity' remain living realities no matter how much a European perspective on Haitian political history may blind us to the fact. 'In Haiti,' according to René Depestre, 'even the political history is marked by surrealism. . . . The whole of Haitian culture is imbued with a popular surrealism, manifested in the voodoo religion, in the plastic arts and in the different forms of being among the people of Haiti.'[36] Breton's speeches were so important because they articulated this latent surrealist quality. As Aimé Césaire found in a personal way, the Haitians who heard Breton discovered an affinity with the aims of surrealism and experienced a collective recognition that confirmed their own sense of being. This recognition should be differentiated from the resentful and ungenerous response to surrealism of Alejo Carpentier: it does not posit an essential American or Haitian identity embedded in its Paideuma, but represents a facet of the particular qualities of

Haitian culture and its refusal to be overwhelmed by the values of the capitalist world economy.

Despite their affinity, none of the European surrealists claimed Haiti for their own purposes as Sartre did in respect of negritude; most of their writings are marked by a circumspection in which difference is always respected. This dimension is especially present in the texts by Pierre Mabille and Michel Leiris in the present collection. In particular in Mabille's complex 'Memories of Haiti', the uncertainties of assuming a knowledge of the Other are explored with an exemplary sensitivity.

This sensitivity on the part of the surrealists is no doubt due in great part to the Hegelian dimension of their work. Certainly one feels that the problematic raised by Hegelian anthropology (especially the master/slave discussion) had penetrated too deeply into surrealist thinking for them not to be alert to the acute difficulties that issues of identity and difference raise, especially in respect of the dangers of seeking identification with the Other for, as Hegel's anthropology makes clear, the 'Other' can conceptually only be a projection of oneself.

But another factor is also crucial. The exile of so many surrealists in the Americas during the Second World War undoubtedly led them to question their relation to their own culture in a fresh way and underlined in their minds sensitivity to issues of otherness, displacement and inter-cultural relations. It should not be forgotten that this was a singular occurrence. The Second World War was perhaps the only time that Western intellectuals were forced to take refuge outside Europe for political reasons and were therefore confronted with the experience of exile at first hand. This is something that was especially acute in the case of Breton himself, forced to live in New York, a city for which he had no affinity and which seemed to him to embody all the worst aspects of European culture, with few of its redeeming ones. On the other hand, he was enchanted by his various stays on the Canadian coast and in Martinique, Arizona, and Haiti. But all the surrealists in exile were affected profoundly by the experience and those who returned to Europe after the war went back with a changed relation to European culture.

In his interview with René Bélance while he was in Haiti, Breton gave a very clear reply when asked what he felt 'peoples of colour' could gain from surrealism:

> ... in considering race and other barriers that must before all else be corrected by other means, I think that surrealism aims and *is alone in*

*aiming systematically* at the abolition of these barriers [of the difference between people]. You know that in surrealism the accent has always been on displacing the ego, always more or less despotic, by the id, held in common by all. . . . Surrealism is allied with peoples of colour, first because it has always taken their side against all forms of imperialism and white banditry [. . .] and secondly because of the profound affinities that exist between surrealism and so-called 'primitive' thought, both of which seek the abolition of the conscious and the everyday, leading to the conquest of revelatory emotion.[37]

In suggesting that 'peoples of colour' are more responsive to the supposed aims of this 'primitive thought', Breton may appear to be making the same sort of reification as Sartre in respect of negritude. However, unlike Sartre he is careful not to assume the position of the other, nor is he suggesting that whatever 'primitive thought' may be (and it is an expression he is clearly ill at ease with) it is an exclusive or even particular preserve of specific peoples. Rather it is an intellectual category designating a way of thinking that is appropriate to all people but has been denigrated in the West. His caution here reflects the dislike he had for Lévy-Bruhl. In discussing 'primitive thought', he is trying less to reify particular thought patterns than to establish a quality of value: it defines a poetic and affective way of perceiving the world rather than a utilitarian one based upon causation. This distinction had been raised by Jules Monnerot in his 1932 article, 'The Consequences of Some Features Specific to Civilized Mentality', which had been published in *Le Surréalisme au service de la Révolution*.[38] Monnerot argued that Lévy-Bruhl's notion of the 'primitive mind' was a mystification, but a revealing one since it showed less the existence of such a mind than a 'civilized mentality' that limits or excludes anything not reducible to its pre-established categories and is thus an impoverishment of thought.

It is in this sense that Breton's statement must be read. In his first speech in Haiti, he suggested that the affinity surrealism feels for peoples of colour is due to the fact that

. . . they had remained closest to the sources, and that in the essential development of surrealism, which has consisted in *making heard* the interior voice within each human being, we have found ourselves linked from the beginning with 'primitive' thought, which remains less alien to you than to us and demonstrates a remarkable strength in Haitian voodoo. In periods of great social and moral crisis, I

believe it is indispensable that we enquire into primitive thought, to
rediscover the fundamental aspirations, the incontestably authentic
aspirations, of mankind.[39]

What is at issue here is not a one-way process of objectification of the
other, but the basis for a genuine recognition of the other's own subjectivity, albeit always framed by the aims of surrealist aspirations:
mankind's liberty in its most general form and the resolution of contradictions. Certainly, there is an unusual concern in post-Second
World War surrealism with themes taken from the surrealists' encounters with non-Western cultures, a concern that is quite different from
the pre-war encounter with the 'primitive'. Even prior to the war, the
impact of the Chilean Roberto Matta on the evolution of surrealist
painting hardly needs to be emphasized. And, as Breton and Mabille in
their essays in this collection make clear, the work of Césaire and Lam
fed back into European surrealism in ways that substantially affected
its evolution. The work of the Mexican Octavio Paz, too, had considerable impact in the movement of surrealism away from the critique of
Western culture towards a concern with locating new values, going
beyond the West whilst seeking out the essential qualities of human
becoming in the experience of the West itself. This movement is marked
by Breton's *Arcane 17*, and by his short essay 'Océanie' in which he
asserts with regret the impossibility of really understanding 'primitive'
cultures and the need to explore the 'Other' elements within European
culture itself.

For the European surrealists, fleeing a Europe that disgusted them,
the revelation that their American experience brought them was never
forgotten. If one may perceive a certain perturbed exoticism in the
'Creole Dialogue' of Masson and Breton, written at the start of their
exile (although even here there is much disquiet in the way the authors
approach their relation to American realities), by the end of the war
there is noticeable in surrealist work in exile generally a concern with
confronting the appearance of the exotic as related to other cultures
that is quite striking.[40] And this concern brought with it a clear need
for a rootedness that paralleled the concern of the Martiniquan surrealists with the roots of their own identity. Breton's purchase of a
modest cottage at St-Cirq-la-Popie in the South of France after the
Second World War offered the French Surrealist Group the possibility
to meet far from Paris for part of the year and explore the rural experience of their own land. Something more was at stake in this than an
escape from the urban experience; it also represented a yearning for

roots that is most profoundly witnessed perhaps in the poetry of René Char (even if he may have renounced collective surrealism by then) or Guy Cabanel, and by the profound interest in alchemy and configurations of the land to be found in the work of many surrealist artists and in the researches of the architects Bernard Roger and René-Guy Doumayrou. This perceived need for rootedness also connects with René Depestre's assertion:

> I had the revelation that to live in society inevitably implied a sort of cosmic liaison with human beings, animals, plants, stars, with all the light of the living phenomenon. I'm not talking about the romantic liaison of old, but of a sensual, vital, joyously erotic accord with existence, a harmonic value which came to me straightaway from my first childhood perceptions in Jacmal.[41]

It is in this context that the surrealist encounter with the Caribbean, and especially with Haiti, also needs to be considered. What Breton perceived in Haiti was not an exotic land of Utopian distance and promise but a place where the essential values of mankind had not been sacrificed to the immediate concerns of existing in a world devoted exclusively to material well-being. As he said in his speech to the Haitian students:

> . . . the beautiful name of Haiti immediately evokes, if not the most important chapters of your history, at least a will to freedom that has never been quixotic. The beautiful name of Haiti assumes such poignant overtones that it is etched forever in the minds of all who are *worthy of thinking*. It is a dynamic word, among the small number *moving forward*.

To speak of dynamism in relation to Haiti is already a provocation: dynamism is what the West likes to take exclusively for itself. The statement that Haiti is a dynamic society contradicts almost everything that has been written about it by European and North American writers. Yet Breton was not mistaken: a close reading of Haitian culture will reveal that it begins the process of elucidating the hidden paths through the forest of human becoming that the ideology of Western civilization would deny exist at all. Again, to quote Breton:

> I know that no nation as much as Haiti has the foundation to establish a more overwhelming indictment against practical indifference

and more or less disguised exploitation. The grandeur of its past and its struggles, which must make it something for the rest of the world to *strive towards*, is a long way from having acquired the indispensable co-operation its exceptional energy and vitality authorise it to claim.[42]

Clearly Breton's perception was one of the reasons for the reception he received in Haiti and the dramatic impact of his lectures. In the Caribbean context, too, Breton's insight accords with Edouard Glissant's view that, 'Haiti retains a strength derived from *historical memory*, which all Caribbean people will one day need.'[43]

In Haitian folklore, the key myth is that of the zombi. This is a specifically, one might even say archetypal, New World myth which, though having its roots in Africa, addressed American realities in its particularity. Most specifically, it has obviously been created out of the experience of slavery. Alfred Métraux emphasizes this element:

> He moves, eats, even speaks, but has no memory, and is not aware of his condition. The zombi is a beast of burden exploited mercilessly by his master who forces him to toil in the fields, crushes him with work, and whips him at the slightest pretext, whilst feeding him on the blandest of diets. . . . Zombis can be recognized by their vague look, their dull, almost glazed, eyes, and above all by the nasality of their voice, a trail also characteristic of the 'Guedé' spirits of the dead. Their docility is absolute so long as they are given no salt. If they inadvertently eat any food containing even a single grain of salt, the fog enveloping their minds is immediately dispelled and they become suddenly aware of their environment. This discovery arouses in them an immense anger and an uncontrollable desire for revenge. They hurl themselves on their master, kill him, ravage his goods, then go off in search of their graves.[44]

What is this but the collective memory of slavery and the certainty that it must, one day, be avenged? It is not simply a reflection of the slave's helplessness: it is also a myth of regeneration. Voodoo belief does not acknowledge death in the sense that it is understood in the West: there is no death only transformation. The zombi is a being denied this transformation and trapped in a world it ought to have left. The zombi is not at all a soul in purgatory, as Christian belief would see it, because it does not by definition have a soul and also because it is not actually dead. It is rather a being trapped in a state without identity and denied the right to a means of life that is rightfully its own.

But it also represents the image of death ensnaring life (which the being is unable to leave) so that the zombi haunts the world of the living and acts upon it as an unspoken condemnation. Zombification thereby implicates the world of the living: unable to die (that is, to be transformed), we are condemned not to be able to live. The Haitian writer Clément Magloire-Saint-Aude brings this element out in a passage from his story 'Vigil':

> But as I examined her face (I only had to stretch out my arm to touch her body) something caused me to shiver: the eyes were not completely closed and, from beneath the eyelids the dead girl seemed to be looking at me . . . and looking at me, in fact, with such fixity that filled me with a sense of panic . . . I tried to move but an intolerable cramp paralysed my movements. I wanted to speak but was voiceless.

> And Teresa was still looking at me.

> At me alone.
> And my own eyes felt magnetised and were unable to detach themselves from those eyes from the other world.[45]

The implication is that the gaze of the slave transfixes the master. By enslaving another we become enslaved to the slave and have perverted the real relations of life. Real life slips elsewhere and we find ourselves alienated from ourselves. The continuity of life asserts itself through death, but it is a death that is not death, a 'death' that straddles the borders of life and death, denying the authenticity of both and preventing their natural flow.

The zombi lacks salt, which would restore its creative and imaginative gifts. As René Depestre wrote: 'The history of colonialism is that of a process of generalized "zombification" of mankind. It is also the story of the quest for a revitalizing salt that is capable of restoring to man the use of his imagination and culture.'[46] However, this quest is also an interrupted one, one that can only be resumed through the restoration of reciprocity: the master who no longer withholds the salt from the zombi's diet also liberates himself. Such recognition is rarely, of course, in the nature of things and tends to emerge only through events that compel recognition of our mutual dependence.

Here we need to consider the contribution of Magloire-Saint-Aude, the only major poet of the Caribbean, with the exception of Césaire, to embrace surrealism wholeheartedly. Magloire-Saint-Aude's work could hardly be further from the aggressive political and lyrical poetry of Césaire. He is the poet of silence and refusal – even of indifference – in the face of the vagaries of life. Where Césaire is a magnificent poet of engagement, Magloire-Saint-Aude is as magnificently – even militantly – disengaged. His poems have simple titles: 'Peace', 'Nothingness', 'Emptiness', 'Poison'. Here is one, entitled 'Silence':

> *Le tuf aux dents aux chances aux chocs auburn*
> *Sur neuf villes.*
>
> *Magdeleines en dentelles de gaude.*
>
> *Rien le poète, lent dolent*
> *Pour mourir à Guadalajara.*[47]

What Magloire-Saint-Aude is effecting here is the contamination of the French language by the introduction of a Creole sensibility. His intent is as clearly political as Césaire's but in a different way. This is not hermetic poetry in the style of Mallarmé (even if Magloire-Saint-Aude was undoubtedly influenced by him), but an attempt to inscribe an 'other' voice into the French language. Meaning vanishes, language as representation is demolished, to be replaced with an essential language that is both rooted and reaching out towards an open universe. One of the greatest poets of both surrealism and the Caribbean, Magloire-Saint-Aude can no more be subsumed within a negritude or black sensibility than he can within a European one. With his work, surrealism places in evidence one of its most impressive claims to embody universal aspirations.

Finally we need to consider the contemporary value of these texts. Do they simply serve to document a moment in French colonialism that has been surpassed and thus primarily have an academic interest for the English-speaking world? Certainly the struggles against French imperialism followed quite a different course to those against British colonialism, and for the most part the issues raised by these texts stand apart from the specific context of our own post-colonial situation, whether we belong to the class of ex-colonists or of ex-colonized. Yet, as discussed through this Introduction, they raise wide and complex issues about the nature of identity and otherness. They also speak to us in a much wider sense. For the French policy of assimilation has much in common with the contemporary globalization that, emerging from US-based multinationalism, is the dominant ideology forming our world. This promotes a cosmopolitanism of culture resulting in an all-pervasive and totalizing ideology that homogenizes all particularity (even the indigenous culture of the United States itself). In the radical version of this ideology, 'multiculturalism' and 'post-modernity' are the watchwords, and not infrequently it even claims to respect cultural diversity. This new imperialism is not easy to resist. And the inevitable consequences of this homogenizing process are equally totalizing assertions of identity that have taken shape in recent years as various forms of fundamentalism, whose terrible consequences have already been felt and will doubtless continue to gain currency in coming years. Negritude may perhaps be seen as a forerunner of the fundamentalist impulse, arising from similar pressures and born too of a denial of the reality of difference, from the need to assert an identity *apart*, so separating itself from the insidious effects of ideologies that enforce a coeval identity based upon an unspoken dominance by a particular perspective of the world. The alarming rise of fundamentalism in the United States reveals the extent to which the ideology of cosmopolitanism is today even colonizing the culture of the nation that spawned it. By looking at the basis of the struggle against French colonialism and its assimilationist policies, we can see how the fundamentalist perspective starts to take root in the fertile soil such policies provide. But we can also see in this soil the roots of a different plant, one that is more difficult to cultivate. This plant acknowledges the differences between cultures and, while refusing to elide them, strives to establish routes of communication between them.

Identity is not a given but is always a complex matter, correlatively formed in the interplay between the universal and the particular, the individual and the collective, and the relation of self to other that never has constant qualities but is always subject to the shifting sands upon which existence is founded. Ideological assumptions have changed enormously in the past sixty years. At the time *Légitime défense* was formed, colonialism was at its very apex and the colonial attitude was all-pervasive. The defining feature of a colonial mentality – beyond the often vast differences between British and French attitudes to colonialism – was a strict distinction of self and other and a refusal of all communication between them. Non-Western cultures were denied all legitimacy in and of themselves; reduced to a cultural stage of evolution that had been surpassed by the West, they had value only as the remnant of what had once been.

Today colonial attitudes remain prevalent, but they have displaced their ideological thrust away from such crude determinism. What Edouard Glissant has called the 'West's striving for a single goal, that of imposing the whole of its own values on the world, as if they were universal', has gained an even greater subtlety. The self–other relation has even become unacceptable, and otherness has thereby been rejected, seen as an evil presence. The determinism of current colonial attitudes is assumed by a multinational culture that will doubtless in time go beyond its origins in European culture to embrace features from other cultures – especially in the East – that reinforce its values of high capitalism. But the relationship between oneself and the other is a given of human existence. If we are not to collapse into solipsism or a feeble moral relativism, we need to recognize, first, the self–other relation in its dynamic state. Second, we need to understand that 'it is the degree to which I go beyond my own immediate being that I apprehend the existence of the other as a natural and more than natural reality. If I close the circuit, if I prevent the accomplishment of movement in two directions, I keep the other within himself. Ultimately, I deprive him even of this being-for-itself.'[48] This circuit needs to be broken. We need, in other words, to recognize otherness without being seduced by it and without using it to define power relationships, but as the starting point for genuine communication. In surrealist terms, life must always be something to be reinvented, and human relationships must lie at the heart of such a transformation. What is needed, too, is research into what really constitutes the universal, once divested of ideological encumbrances. It is in this light that a consideration of surrealism in the context of the Caribbean is of especial significance.

*Michael Richardson*
*November 1995*

### Notes

1. Fanon, *Black Skins, White Masks*, p. 136.

2. They had come together in 1931 and collaborated on *Le Journal des deux mondes*, devoted to issues of concern to Caribbean students, but in a fairly conventional way.

3. See *Légitime défense*, this volume, p. 43.

4. René Ménil recalled that Breton directly engaged with them and encouraged them to concentrate their discussions on the links between politics, aesthetics and anti-colonialism, though without emphasizing the Caribbean context. (Response to questionnaire in Régis Antoine, *Les Écrivains noirs et les antilles: des premières pères blancs aux surréalistes noirs*.)

5. Jacqueline Leiner, 'Les Chevaliers du Graal au service de Marx', preface to the re-edition of *Le Surréalisme au service de la révolution*, p. xix (reprinted in her *Imaginaire, langage, identité culturelle, négritude*).

6. This legend was established by Lilyan Kesteloot in *Les Écrivains noirs: Naissance d'une littérature* in 1963. It was based upon suppositions about the content of *L'Étudiant noir*, culled from various sources (especially from what Damas, Senghor and Césaire had told her), since not a single copy of the journal appeared to have survived. Her contentions were elaborated on and amplified for more than a decade before a copy of the journal actually surfaced and revealed that its contents were not at all as described and it certainly did not engage with the issues raised by *Légitime défense*. Damas, in fact, was not included in it; it was focused entirely on issues for black West Indians (with little about Africa); and issues of black identity were addressed in a way that was less audacious than *Légitime défense*. There is no indication whether the authors had read or been aware of *Légitime défense*, and they certainly did not engage critically with it. Nevertheless the legend does give a focus to issues around the development of black consciousness. See the article by Edward O. Ako, '*L'Étudiant noir* and the Genesis of the Negritude Movement' in *Research in African Literatures*, 15 (3), 1984, for an excellent discussion of the way this legend was constructed.

7. See his introduction to the re-edition of *Légitime défense* included in this volume, p. 39.

8. However, had he lived longer, Etienne Léro might well have produced poetry to rival that of Césaire, Damas or Senghor.

9. The *Notebook* has a complex publishing history. A first version was published in 1939 in the Parisian journal *Volontés* followed by a Spanish version in 1943 (in a translation by Lydia Cabrera and with an introduction by Benjamin Péret), but Césaire continued to work on it throughout the next decade. The first integral edition appeared in New York in both English and French with an introduction by André Breton ('A Great Black Poet' included in the current volume). The poem was further revised for a 1947 version and then again for the definitive edition published by Présence Africaine in 1956. A new edition in 1983 contained further minor revisions.

10. There are several English translations of the *Notebook*. This quotation is taken from what in my opinion is the best version, that by John Berger and Anna Bostock (*Return to My Native Land* (1969) Harmondsworth: Penguin), pp. 76 and 62.

11. C.L.R. James, *The Black Jacobins*, p. 402.

12. See '1943: Surrealism and Us', this volume, p. 126.

13. Interview with Jacqueline Leiner, published in the reissue of *Tropiques* (1978) Paris: Jean-Michel Place, p. vi.

14. Unfortunately I have not felt able to include any of Ménil's essays on negritude in this collection, since they are not directly related to the theme of this book and publication here would unbalance the central issues documenting the relationship between surrealism and the Caribbean and make the book unwieldy. Nevertheless these are extremely important essays which it is to be hoped will one day be made available in an English translation, perhaps in a collection dealing in

a more general way with issues of surrealism and otherness. His most important essays on the theme are to be found under the sub-heading 'De la négritude' in *Tracées*, pp. 61–96.

15. Ménil, *Tracées*, p. 65.

16. Quoted in Jahn, *A History of Neo-African Literature*, pp. 265–6.

17. Compare these words by Le Brun: 'Each woman today finds herself virtually dispossessed of this individual renewal when she does not take care that each of her indiscretions risks being misappropriated to serve in the construction of an ideology as contradictory in its propositions as it is totalitarian in its intentions' (*Lachez tout* (1974) Paris: Sagittaire, p. 8).

18. Published in *Nouvelle revue français*, new series, 24–25 (1954–55).

19. See Césaire, *Discourse On Colonialism*, pp. 49–55.

20. To be sure, Caillois is arguing for the superiority of a notion of 'civilization', but this is not equated with the West specifically: it is a universal aspiration to which all societies respond. His target is relativist ideas that give universality to what in fact is the diversity of the particular. In so doing they deny any conception of a universal idea of civilization, something that Caillois sees as being nefarious. He is making a philosophical point: that ideas are always inter-dependent, they never stand on their own.

21. 'A propos d'une étude sur la poésie noire' in *Tracées*, pp. 169–77.

22. Kesteloot, *Les Écrivains noirs de langue française: Naissance d'une litterature*.

23. Ménil, *Tracées*, p. 174.

24. Quoted in Paul Laraque, 'André Breton in Haiti', this volume, p. 227.

25. Carpentier's critique is contained in 'Prologue', published as a preface to the English translation of his novel *The Kingdom of This World*.

26. Jacques Gourgue, 'Du surréalisme au réalisme merveilleux', *Conjonction*, no. 194, April–June 1992, p. 7. Consideration of the general reception of surrealism in Cuba is itself an interesting topic, but it is too tangential to be considered here.

27. René Ménil, 'For a Critical Reading of *Tropiques*', this volume, p. 71.

28. Note in Ménil, *Tracées*, p. 232.

29. Césaire's role in the history of Martinique has come under increasing scrutiny in recent years, especially his attitude towards Martiniquan independence and the importance of the Creole language. See especially Jean Bernabé, Patrick Chamoiseau and Raphaël Confiant, *Eloge de la créolité* (Paris: Gallimard, 1989) and the collective volume *Ecrire la 'parole de nuit': la nouvelle littérature antillaise* (Paris: Gallimard, 1994). For an account in English of these issues see Mireille Rosello's excellent introduction to the new translation of Césaire's *Notebook of a Return to my Native Land* by Rosello herself and Annie Pritchard (London: Bloodaxe, 1995).

30. Césaire, 'Presence', in *Corps perdu*.

31. See Francis Affergan, *L'Anthropologie à la Martinique*.

32. The pressures against Haiti in the nineteenth century are analogous to those used against Cuba since the 1959 Revolution, having a similar aim and effect.

33. The Bureau d'Ethnologie has played an important role in bringing attention to folklore and voodoo traditions, something that was of especial importance at the time. In 1941, the Catholic Church instituted a notorious 'anti-superstition'

campaign, designed to intimidate voodoo practitioners. Accompanied by violence and vandalism, it was tied to a United States agricultural development project that required the appropriation of peasant land. Details of this can be found in J. Michael Dash, *Haiti and the United States.* The Bureau d'Ethnologie was a thorn in the sides both of the government and the Church since, by providing evidence of the intellectual complexity of voodoo belief, it gave it legitimacy as a religion. The importance of the Bureau d'Ethnologie in the development of a very rich tradition of anthropological and ethnographic enquiry in Haiti remains to be researched.

34. See this volume, pp. 217–28 and pp. 229–33.

35. Unfortunately it has not been possible to include any of Breton's lectures in the current volume for copyright reasons; they will appear integrally for the first time in the third volume of his *Oeuvres complètes*, which is currently being prepared for publication in the Pléiade series. His speech to the Haitian students, though, has been published in English in André Breton, *What Is Surrealism?*, edited by Franklin Rosemont (1978) London: Pluto Press, pp. 258–61.

36. Personal letter to the editor, 19 July 1987.

37. Breton, p. 256

38. See this volume, pp. 61–5.

39. Breton, p. 256.

40. This is apparent in the work of Mabille and Breton in Haiti, but also of Wolfgang Paalen, Leonora Carrington, Remedios Varo, Benjamin Péret in Mexico and André Masson and Max Ernst in Arizona.

41. Depestre 'Parler de Jacmal', in *Conjonction*, 184–6 (1990), p. 368.

42. Breton, 'Le Surréalisme', lecture given at the Rex theatre, published in *Conjonction*, 1 (1946), reprinted in *Conjonction*, 194 (1992).

43. Glissant, *Caribbean Discourse*, p. 266.

44. Métraux, *Le Vaudou haitien*, p. 250–51.

45. This story is translated in *The Dedalus Book of Surrealism: the Identity of Things* (1993) Sawtry: Dedalus, pp. 210–11.

46. Quoted in Maximilien Laroche, *L'Image comme écho*, p. 185.

47. It is almost impossible to do justice to this in translation. Here is a rough approximation:

> *The tuff in teeth in risks in shocks auburn*
> *Above nine cities.*
>
> *Magdeleines in laces of weld.*
>
> *Untraced the poet, indolently plaintive*
> *To die in Guadalajara.*

48. Frantz Fanon, *Black Skins, White Masks*, p. 217.

PART I

# AN ENCOUNTER

# IN PARIS

RENÉ MÉNIL

# 1978 Introduction to
# Légitime défense

PUBLISHED IN PARIS in 1932 by a group of Martiniquan students, this first and sole issue of the journal *Légitime défense* was to remain practically unrecognized by Martiniquan society – a few intellectuals curious about our historical past excepted – for more than four decades.

It is a strange thing, this refusal of a society to acknowledge texts nevertheless written for it and by its own intellectuals.

Doubtless we must blame the ban it received from the colonial power when it was published. But beyond this, the reason for what has to be considered a rejection lies within Martiniquan social consciousness itself, which was distorted by the colonial regime to such an extent that it is blind to the truths of its own development as revealed in the mirror.

In the meantime, literary criticism in the different countries of Europe and Africa has underlined the historical role played by *Légitime défense* in the birth of modern black literature of French expression.

The reader who wishes to consider the criticism and evaluation of *Légitime défense* is referred to the studies by Lilyan Kesteloot, Jack Corzani, Régis Antoine, Janheinz Jahn, Iay Kimoni, and so on, who have come to different conclusions, as is only to be expected.[1]

I would point out, in passing, that it would be anachronistic to expect *Légitime défense* to have raised questions or to have proposed solutions that have arisen only after it appeared and disappeared, through the evolution of contemporary history. A journal dated June 1932 could not identify and express problems that would result from the upheavals that shook the colonial empires and the consciousness of colonized blacks in the aftermath of the Second World War.

Senghor's recent reading of *Légitime défense* which he reproaches with, among other things and in an unexpected way, failing, in 1932, to 'advocate the independence of Africa, still less that of the Caribbean' is undoubtedly anachronistic. The reason for this unpardonable error, in his view, was that those who signed *Légitime défense* were misled into Marxism. Is there any need to point out that, although Senghor did not commit the sin of being a Marxist, nevertheless he did not, any more than did the signatories of *Légitime défense*, dream in the thirties of demanding the independence of Africa – and even less that of Senegal, we would add.

If the main problems expressly raised in these texts – the political and social liberation of colonial peoples; the problem of a Caribbean culture taking account of race and history; the problem of an aesthetic to be worked out on the basis of what is particular about life in our islands – remain hanging in the air, subsequent unexpected events have still brought new content to the troubled problems and fresh ways of considering them. Some of the problems that seemed vital for us at the time these texts were published have become obsolete and the charge they had for us has become displaced elsewhere.

The sensual joy of writing shines through in *Légitime défense*. A cruel aggressive pleasure, a settling of accounts with colonial ugliness (sadism) and also a pleasure of experiencing the wounds received in order to be better able to proclaim the legitimacy of the cause (masochism).

Some critics have wondered, not without reason, whether *Légitime défense* did not, unknown to itself, contribute to some extent to negritude's entry onto the scene.

Certainly, considered in its unity and structure, the discourse of *Légitime défense* is not a discourse of negritude. Where negritude affirms the priority of the cultural struggle over the political struggle and the priority of 'black values' over social contradictions, *Légitime défense* was, on the contrary, principally alert to the anti-imperialist struggle which roused colonial peoples against both the Western and its own bourgeoisie, situating political action in the Marxist framework of social transformation without conceiving the development of 'black values' other than within such political conflict.

This project was more Fanonist before its time than Senghorian or even Césairist – although at that date Césaire had still not declared himself about this.

But it must be admitted that *Légitime défense*, making use of a naïve and spontaneous – thus false – psychology, had already begun (without knowing it) to sketch the features of a general black mentality which, amplified and pushed to an extreme, is found anew in the fantastic caricature of the 'African black' of which Senghor became the humourless theorist. Already in *Légitime défense* one can see the emergence of that black who is 'endowed with a sensual and colourful imagination', that black who 'refuses power and accepts life', that black who 'has a more generally elevated potential for revolt and joy in as much as he has a materially determined ethnic personality', the black who has 'a love of inspired dances', and so on.

In *Légitime défense* these psychological features had a polemical value, and were determined by a historically concrete and temporary situation – a situation imposed on colonized Caribbean blacks by imperialism – and not as eternal and universal features of a black mentality. The fact is that the signatories of the journal did not express this with enough prudence to preclude its use in the constitution of an alienating mythology.

It is perhaps this insufficiently critical approach to the black question that reveals most clearly the limits of *Légitime défense*. Nevertheless, the editors of the journal must be credited with having been aware of that insufficiency and giving a warning to their readers: 'We apologize,' they say, 'for the necessity to make a start, something that has not allowed a certain maturity.'

No doubt there are also limits in the way Marxism as it was conceived and practised in the thirties was applied – a Marxism still inflexible and incapable of adapting to life's complexities in order to grasp and illuminate them.

Because of this, it was unable to appreciate the unity between the world of material life (economy, social questions and politics) and the world of the imagination (poetic reverie). In *Légitime défense* we accommodated ourselves to a disjunction that was to be shocking for us after the event. On the one hand we took account of Caribbean colonial society and offered a realist critique and description of it. But on the other hand we produced poems with no roots in that society, poems from nowhere, and by no one.

In cries and in fury, *Légitime défense* announces and promises.

We did not have to wait long for *Pigments* by Damas (1937) and *Notebook of a Return to My Native Land* by Césaire (1939), both of which responded to this hunger for the kind of literature of which the journal was the impassioned expression.

*July 1978*

## Editor's Note

1. See, for example, Lilyan Kesteloot, *Les Écrivains noirs de langue française: Naissance d'une littérature*; Jack Corzani, *La Littérature des Antilles-Guyane français* (1978) Fort de France: Editions Désormeaux; Régis Antoine, *La Littérature franco-antillaise: Haïti, Guadeloupe, Martinique*; Janheinz Jahn, *A History of Neo-African Literature*; and Iay Kimoni, *Destin de la littérature négro-africaine* (1976) Kinshasa: Presses Universitaires du Zaïre.

# Légitime défense: *Declaration*

THIS IS JUST a foreword. We consider ourselves totally committed. We are sure that other young people like us exist prepared to add their signatures to ours and who – to the extent that it remains compatible with continuing to live – refuse to become part of the surrounding ignominy. And we've had it with those who try, consciously or not, with smiles, work, exactitude, propriety, speeches, writings, actions, and with their very being, to make us believe that things can continue as they are. We rise up against all those who don't feel suffocated by this capitalist, Christian, bourgeois world, to which our protesting bodies reluctantly belong. All around the world the Communist Party (Third International) is about to play the decisive card of the 'Spirit' – in the Hegelian sense of the word. Its defeat, however impossible it might be to imagine that, would be the definitive end of the road for us. We believe unreservedly in its triumph because we accept Marx's dialectical materialism freed of all misleading interpretation and victoriously put to the test of events by Lenin. In this respect, we are ready to accept the discipline such conviction demands. In the concrete realm of means of human expression, we equally unreservedly accept surrealism with which our destiny in 1932 is linked. We refer our readers to André Breton's two manifestos and to all the works of Aragon, André Breton, René Crevel, Salvador Dalí, Paul Eluard, Benjamin Péret and Tristan Tzara. We consider it to be one of the disgraces of our age that these works are not better known wherever French is read. And in Sade, Hegel, Lautréamont and Rimbaud – to mention just a few – we seek everything surrealism has taught us to find. We are ready to use the vast machinery that Freud has set in motion to dissolve the bourgeois family. We are hell-bent on sincerity.

We want to see clearly into our dreams and we are listening to what they have to tell us. And our dreams allow us to clearly perceive the life they claim to be able to impose on us for such a long time. Of all the filthy bourgeois conventions, we despise more than anything humanitarian hypocrisy, that stinking emanation of Christian decay. We despise pity. We don't give a damn about sentiments. We intend to shed a light on human psychic concretions similar to that which illuminates Salvador Dalí's splendid convulsive paintings, in which it sometimes seems that lovebirds, taking wing from assassinated conventions, could suddenly become inkwells or shoes or small morsels of bread.

This little journal is a provisional tool, and if it collapses we shall find others. We are indifferent to the conditions of time and space which, defining us in 1932 as people of the French Caribbean, have consequently established our initial boundaries without in the least limiting our field of action. This first collection of texts is devoted particularly to the Caribbean question as it appears to us. (The following issues, without abandoning this question, will take up many others.) And if, by its content, this collection is primarily addressed to young French Caribbeans, it is because we think it opportune to aim our first effort at people whose capacity for revolt we certainly do not underestimate. If it is especially aimed at young blacks, it is because we consider that they in particular suffer from the effects of capitalism (apart from Africa, witness Scottsboro) and that they seem to offer – in having a materially determined ethnic personality – a generally higher potential for revolt and joy. For want of a black proletariat, from which international capitalism has withheld the means of understanding us, we are addressing the children of the black bourgeoisie. We are speaking to those who are not already branded as killed established fucked-up academic successful decorated decayed provided for decorative prudish opportunists. We are speaking to those who can still accept life with some appearance of truthfulness.

Determined to be as objective as possible, we know nothing of anyone's personal life. We want to go a long way and, if we expect a lot from psychoanalytical investigation, we do not underestimate (among those initiated into psychoanalytic theory) pure and simple psychological confessions which, provided that the obstacles of everyday conventions are removed, can tell us much. We do not accept that we should be ashamed of what we suffer. The Useful is that convention constituting the very backbone of the bourgeois 'reality' we want to dissect. In the realm of intellectual investigation, we oppose this 'reality' with the sincerity that allows man, through his love, to disclose the ambivalence that tolerates the elimination of that contradiction decreed by logic by which we are forced to respond to a given affective object *either* with the feeling defined as love *or else* with the feeling defined as hate. Contradiction is one of the tasks of the Useful. It does not exist in love. It does not exist in dream. And it is only by gritting our teeth horribly that we are able to endure the abominable system of constraints and restrictions, the extermination of love and the confinement of dream, generally known under the name of Western civilization.

Emerging from the French mulatto bourgeoisie, one of the most depressing things on earth, we declare (and we shall not retract this declaration) that, faced with all the administrative, governmental, parliamentary, industrial, commercial corpses and so on, we intend – as traitors to this class – to take the path of treason so far as possible. We spit on everything they love and venerate, on everything that gives them sustenance and joy.

And all those who adopt the same attitude, no matter where they come from, will find a welcome among us.[1]

*Etienne Léro, Thélus Léro, René Ménil, Jules-Marcel Monnerot,*
*Michel Pilotin, Maurice-Sabas Quitman,*
*Auguste Thésée, Pierre Yoyotte*
*1 June 1932*

### Note

1. If our critique is purely negative here, if we put forward no positive proposals against what we irrevocably condemn, we apologize for the necessity to make a start, something that has not allowed a certain maturity. From the next issue, we hope to develop our ideology of revolt.

JULES-MARCEL MONNEROT

# Note Bearing on the Coloured
# French Bourgeoisie

A DOCUMENTARY FILM about the formation of the French mulatto
bourgeoisie, if speeded up to a sufficiently frantic pace, would
reveal the bent backs of black slaves *becoming* the grovelling spine of a
refined coloured bourgeoisie bowing to anyone able, in the imperceptible space between the two images, to sprout a lounge suit and a
bowler hat. But the bourgeoisie is one and indivisible, and in their conformism these grandsons of slaves – like those in Dijon, Boston and
Bremen – would be unable to conceive of themselves without that individualism which is both that conformism's cause and its effect. In order
to exist as such, to 'make their way', as they say, the lawyer, the doctor,
the university lecturer, etcetera, as newcomers, must be careful never to
offend their employers and must offer the class that receives them into
its bosom whatever image of itself it craves (something 'intellectuals'
are most especially entrusted with); must adopt its ideals (make a million, fervently admire all officials, diplomas and decorations, my friend
the governor, my friend the *minister*, etcetera), its morals (lucrative
marriage, catholicism – madame does so many good works; the little
girls take first communion; sir is a freemason but knows how to live),
its 'consciousness' of what is 'his' (My villa, My car, My daughter),
its discriminations (my wife's cousin is a worker, these people aren't
like us; of course, I have family feelings, but in the end business
comes first, you understand), its hypocrisy (thank God we're not
slaves of convention, but there are some things, etcetera . . .), its taste
for 'discussions' where all ideas are admitted so long as they touch on
nothing important, vaguely artistic events.

Etcetera.

I hasten to go beyond these extremely general features. It was in

Martinique that the coloured bourgeoisie's hideous face leaned over my cradle and that the ideal defined above was offered to me from the day I learned to read and write. In this land a white hereditary plutocracy, which no revolution has ever been able to dispossess, holds four-fifths of the land and uses the black proletariat as its human resource to cut the cane and turn it into sugar and rum. Every important post in the factories as well as in the management of many firms is occupied by members of this plutocracy. The white creoles who profited from slavery and whose profit still principally derives from forms of wage labour (the lot of the cane cutters in 1932 is no better than that of the cane cutters of 1832) constitute a closed society, unyielding in the face of the worldly ambitions of the most dashing coloured bourgeois. Nevertheless, the white creole male, for the success of his business, does not hesitate to go so far as to socialize with – to a certain extent and not at his own or their homes – coloured people. For the women there is nothing to do. This landed aristocracy, as it is a numerical minority, does not provide members of parliament. It buys them ready-made. These representatives are especially chosen from among the coloured bourgeoisie and their political ideas generally defy analysis. At the elections (which are always fraudulent) the colonial governors, police, magistrates, marines and so on take an active part. Sometimes people get killed.

The children of the coloured bourgeoisie are raised in the cult of fraud. There are those who, having finished school, go to France – generally successfully – to 'earn' the title of 'Doctor', 'Teacher' and so on. They reveal how avid they are to conform to the morality and character of the majority of their fellow European students. Those of the Law and Medicine faculties adopt the tastes and distastes (as well as the bowler hats) of the French bourgeoisie. Their desire 'not to be noticed' and to 'assimilate' can, given that they bear the incontestable marks of their race everywhere, confer a tragic character to their slightest move. They worship authority in all its forms. Some learn to accommodate the natives with the prospect of 'making' a career in Africa as Europeans. They go as administrators to plunder from their kindred, as magistrates to judge them; and as policemen to kill them. Others want to stay in France, to settle down and 'take root' thanks to that national institution 'connections'. Some 'succeed'. The whites, being born white, have no merit through their whiteness. Yet these blacks, through their conformism, procure whiteness. Those who return 'home' have learned how things are. They have the guarantee of a French university behind them. Moderate, tolerant and conciliating, they can now set the tone. They know that what is important is 'position': everything – from their women to their ideas by way of their car – is a logical consequence of that knowledge. So they unobtrusively set themselves up – thanking people, visiting them, being really refined. It intoxicates them: official rostrums, civic honours, from honours to mayor, from mayor to deputy, who knows? Some of them are seized with the vertigo of a boundless exhibitionism: inaugurating events, making introductions, giving speeches and holding conferences. No ceremony is complete without them giving vent to their super-correctness. Red ribbons streak their dreams. We're all well in with the Governor, our deputy is well in with the government, the director is so kind . . . Meanwhile, in the fields, the blacks continue to cut cane and it still hasn't occurred to them to cut off the heads of those who continually betray them.

NB: I am speaking about those of the coloured bourgeoisie who either are or are about to become successful. Those of my kindred who don't recognize themselves in the preceding lines will be all the better placed to recognize their truth.

MAURICE-SABAS QUITMAN

# *Heaven on Earth*

IT WOULD BE difficult to depict the panic that seized people in Martinique upon reading the army statement published recently by the journal *La Paix*: 'Of about 700 recruits enlisted, 11 have degrees or higher diplomas, 6 have ordinary diplomas, about fifty have passed their secondary exams, another 80 know how to read, write and count. The rest, in other words, more than five hundred, are illiterate: a hundred of them can only sign their names while nearly four hundred can neither read, write nor count.'

Clearly this little sketch serves to dim the lustre of that 'pearl' which is the pride and joy of our compatriots. In order to try to revive their thoroughly shaken prestige, there were those who wanted an investigation into whether these figures weren't in some way exaggerated. Will it reveal anything to amaze anyone interested in the country's affairs? We shall see. For the moment, let's pass over the investigation and the statistical data it may contain. There is one glaring fact: *illiterates exist and there are many of them*. How do we explain this?

It is not difficult to find the solution to such a problem if we consider the economic facts. Who, in fact, is privileged with education? Analysis of the army report makes it abundantly clear. Education being proportional to wealth, we can divide society into classes which exist in fact:

1. Degrees and Higher diplomas: *lower-middle class*;
2. Ordinary diplomas and secondary exams: *children of smallholders*;
3. Illiterates: *from poor families*.

Yet there is another category of individuals whose existence you would never suspect if you were only to consult the Army Report:

these are the children of millionaires, who only very rarely do military service.

The illiterate is the forgotten one, but also the principal – even the sole – agent of the social economy. The one that everyone unites to exploit: the worker in the fields.

What then does he do with his salary, some ask? I tell you that this salary does not exist, and I'm not exaggerating because the disproportion between the labour done and the few francs' payment made is such that the word 'salary' is inappropriate. For the sceptics, I will add that a worker earns on average 7 to 12 francs – and that for a day sometimes lasting thirteen hours. This is especially so for cattle drovers (with due respect to the deputy who called a vote for an eight-hour day!).

Those interested in current affairs will agree with me that it is no less difficult to organize 7 or 12 francs than billions. Obviously the burden is not heavy enough: the 'negro' doesn't kill himself. Such is Langston Hughes's 'Beggar Boy':

> *And yet he plays upon his flute a wild free tune*
> *As if fate had not bled him with her knife!*

What are the consequences of this situation? The worker in the fields, that 'wretched lump of black clay with a breath of life', barely manages to feed himself on his salary. Nevertheless he doesn't walk around naked. Clothing? Certainly, it doesn't come from the shops. Despite their European style, clothes are always cut from guano sacks, most often stolen, whose hemp bears the name 'Aubery khaki' on some parts of the island . . .

Without losing sight of this economic situation, let's consider the case of the worker who forms a family. Life becomes more difficult: the parents multiply their sacrifices until the day the children reach six or eight years old and can start to struggle for existence. They are then hired, without sexual distinction, into the profession known on the registers as 'little workers' and collectively as 'little gang'. Five francs more for the household kitty.

Here's the reason. The negro works while the white man gets rich at his expense, to the extent of being able to deposit a million in the town bank on the birth of 'mademoiselle his daughter'. Who is to blame?

'The Governor!'

'No,' as one of them, a passenger from the *Lamotte-Picquet*, author of *Civilian Among Sailors*, said to his hosts: 'Their certainty of not staying in the colony means that they are not inclined to govern.'

The blame lies with those who, not wanting to consider these outcasts as compatriots, should at least consider them human beings. The blame lies with those who place their intelligence at the service of the factory owners, skilful exploiters of their false pride which consists in denying their origins and disdaining 'niggers' who, despite them, remain their compatriots.

How can this state of things, which in my view constitutes a real plague for Martinique, be remedied? I believe that France, despite the views of those in metropolitan France who would like it 'not to over-civilize', would not hesitate for a moment – if 'our' deputies should ask – to send a commission to Martinique. (They certainly sent one to limit the quota!)

This commission would recognize that teaching is very well provided: six hundred primary schools, business schools, arts and crafts schools, professional schools and high schools, a preparatory law school. As Mr Gerbinis, the governor of Martinique, declared: 'The colony is fully equipped to encourage an intellectual culture.'

Therefore the remedy does not lie in creating primary schools in the countryside. They already exist. It is necessary to make it possible for the poor to attend them and this means improving their situation. Three-quarters of the island belongs to five or six families of factory owners whose cupidity is equalled only by their workers' patience. However, this patience shouldn't be relied on. A people cannot remain oppressed for ever. No government, even of the 'left', has ever limited feudal power through laws concerning the relations between owners and workers or has had the capacity even to *supervise the application of those laws.*

Failing such an intervention a day will come when the workers will revolt . . . And the doctors whom Chance has not placed among the ranks of the 'lazy and uncultivated' will perhaps try, in imitation of those French doctors examining a niggling problem, to explain this revolt through the triumph of some 'medullary automatism' over the will.

René Ménil

# General Observations about the
# Coloured 'Writer' in the Caribbean

IN COLONIZED LANDS, ideas for the natives to adopt that are suited to the effective exploitation of the conquered territory arrive along with the soldiers, administrators, tools and police. Among the colonists' ideas, Christianity generally appears, preaching resignation and suppressing anything among the natives that could prevent the smooth running of the operation. If accidentally the coloured West Indian – who is used for economic means even when he makes a profession of thinking – turns his mind towards literature, his work manifests a tiresome effort to be like the white colonizer. In fact, he generally expresses the sentiments that the best authors ceased expressing a long time ago and that have become part of the heritage of the average French person.

What is the coincidence of feelings whereby the grandchildren of Africans have become the same as those of the French petty bourgeoisie? We object that the French Lesser Antilles have, through the centuries, assimilated the lessons of French civilization to such an extent that now Caribbean blacks can think only as European whites. The evil appears to me even greater. For I am afraid that this is not a conscious, machiavellian hypocrisy, but an objective and unconscious one.

From an economic point of view, it is very useful for a European if the colonized person's thought exactly harmonizes with colonialist views or, more exactly, serves them. On the other hand, the genuine genius of the Caribbean black is being mechanically denied in school and at home, where European good taste has long reigned. It cannot be denied that the books upon which the Caribbean is nourished have been written in countries with other readers in mind. Progressively, the black Caribbean denies his race, his body, his fundamental and specific passions, his particular understanding of love and death, and finally exists in an unreal realm determined by another people's abstract and ideal forms. It is a tragic story when someone cannot be himself, when he is afraid and ashamed of himself. Besides, the colonialist reproaches him with giving way to the genius of his joy, his dancing, his music and his imagination. Public opinion is watchful and brings anyone who is inspired back to European conformism. But he is incapable of becoming other than himself, in other words white, and he will eternally read on the white man's face that this is a road that leads nowhere. Which is true. To be other does not mean to be inferior. What sometimes makes the black West Indian ridiculous in the eyes of the average French person is that he encounters his own deformed and darkened image in the former. From this point of view, they never laugh about Indochinese people who retain their Indochinese identity. With his deepest tendencies suppressed, the Caribbean writer lacks that burden that each being attaches to himself, and that gives organic unity to his expression.

There are black intellectuals who are adroit, lively, wise to society's games and have a personal enmity to what they call the 'heavy Germanic spirit' by which we risk feeling passions and especially recognizing passions that are genuinely experienced but injurious to the smooth running of social affairs. Amid the storm, the black West Indian takes the grand tour of ideas (very broadmindedly, he says)[1] and finds himself among the latest to recognize the artificial character of the crazes for Greco-Roman bric-à-brac, the Parthenon, Attic metre and wit, etcetera . . . *This abstract and objectively hypocritical literature doesn't interest anyone: not the white because it is only a pale imitation of French literature of the recent past;[2] not the black for the same reason.* It's not surprising that the Caribbean writer, in poetry for instance, offers only 'descriptions' and 'portraits' or expresses and inspires only a vague boredom. All that reveals is that he is held or holds himself a long way from his true being, and is hostile to the strength of his passions. He creates a fictive literature, therefore, where one claims to experience someone else's feelings and where plot complexities in the style of Mauriac replace the pagan and violent love of black people for the realities of the world (see the novel or novels that René Maran has published since *Batouala*), *in which expression is given neither to strange leaps from afar, nor millenarian revolts, nor fundamental needs; these are condemned merely because they are not encountered in European literature.* The feelings of the cane cutter as he faces the implacable factory, his feeling of the solitude of blacks throughout the world, the revolt against the injustices he often suffers, especially in his own country, the love of love, the love of alcoholic dreams, the love of inspired dances, the refusal of power and an acceptance of life, etcetera: here are the things our distinguished writers never speak about and which would affect black, yellow and white people as the poems of American blacks affect the feelings of the whole world. It is a literature that lacks energy and stirs vaguely, without attachment to the flesh. In fact it takes for masters all those (Hérédia, Banville, Samain, de Régnier, etcetera) who resolved neither to embark into the movement of life, nor to live in a complete dream world. Boredom. Boredom, condemnation of the self by the self, weighs on the shoulders of the black Caribbean writer. His works are bored and boring; they are depressed and depressing.

The black West Indian has always refused to take the two essential directions that literature can take. One of these directions goes towards the world and its estate, expresses fundamental needs, seeks to change existence, and addresses itself to those who endure the same passions (hunger, love, servitude, etcetera). This is useful literature.[3] The Caribbean writer is afraid of being suspected of not having the same passions and thoughts as Europeans, and of hiding within him the disturbed and dynamic reserves that come from his own originality. The other direction departs from the world to explore the purest parts of each being. It is the position of the sleeper who doesn't care about the perils of the world. The Caribbean black is chained to logical and utilitarian thought. In the Caribbean the masses are soon overtaken by the long and difficult work necessary to provide Europe with the rum it needs.

Here a disequilibrium is established that serves abstraction, since the black West Indian expresses the feelings of another, and the powers of passion and imagination are unrecognized. The black West Indian ought first to recognize his own passions and express only himself by taking the opposite direction to the useful, the route of dream and poetry. In the trajectory of his effort he would encounter the fantastic images of which African and Oceanic statuettes are one of the means of expression, the poems, tales and jazz of American blacks and the work of the French[4] which, beyond industry and by means of the power of passion and dream, have captured the brilliance of Africa.

### Notes

1. I am considering the privileged position of coloured intellectuals aged between thirty and forty.

2. If I open *Poems in False Verse* by G. Gratiant I see an objective anachronism of several centuries in the content (see the minor lyric poets of the seventeenth and eighteenth centuries) and of at least two centuries in the form. In fact, so far as free verse is concerned, La Fontaine was considerably bolder.

3. Proletarian writers in the USSR, the surrealists and a few others in France.

4. Lautréamont, Rimbaud, Apollinaire, Jarry, Réverdy, the Dadaists and the surrealists.

# ETIENNE LÉRO

## *Civilization*

THE MOST ADVANCED of all supposedly civilized countries, the United States, is preparing to murder eight young blacks who stand accused, against all evidence, of raping two white prostitutes. The French press – *Humanité* excepted – has remained unanimously and significantly silent. The coloured press in America, in the pay of whites and prisoner of its class interests and political deals, has hushed up the incident. The Association for the Advancement of Colored People, having to tiptoe around the criminal justice system of American capitalism, acknowledges that it is incapable of assuming the victims' defence. The local branch of the International Red Cross has had to take up the accused's cause and has struggled effectively to rouse world opinion against the sadism of the executioner-judges of Alabama.

Will the voice of the adolescents they want to roast on the other side of the Atlantic, in spite of everything, penetrate the cocoon of selfishness and prejudice of the European nations? Until now only the working class has howled out its indignation in its meetings. The blacks of the entire world owe it to themselves to be the first to militate in favour of their brothers who have been unjustly threatened with the electric chair by Yankee sexual neurosis.

When will American blacks realize in an effective way that the only possible escape from the American hell lies in communism?

# Etienne Léro

# *Poverty of a Poetry*

IT IS PROFOUNDLY inaccurate to speak of a Caribbean poetry. The broad mass of the population of the Caribbean does not read, write or speak French. Some of the members of the mulatto society, intellectually and physically corrupt and nourished by literature on white decadence, have developed, in complicity with the French bourgeoisie that uses them, as the ambassadors of a mass they choke and, moreover, reject for being too dark.

There, the poet (or the 'bard' as they say) is recruited exclusively from within the class that has the privilege of comfort and education. (And if it were necessary to seek poetry where it is forced to take refuge, one would have to look to Creole, which is not a written language, to the songs of love, sadness and revolt of the black workers.)

The exceptionally mediocre character of Caribbean poetry is thus clearly connected to the existing social order.

In the Caribbean, one is a poet as one is a verger or a gravedigger, as a job on the side. Any doctor, lecturer, lawyer, president of the Republic, can earn a little renown among the mulatto bourgeoisie as he serves its image and tastes by penning alexandrines.

The Caribbean poet, stuffed full to bursting with white morality, white culture, white education and white prejudices, displays his own puffed-up image in slim volumes. To imitate a white man properly, social as well as poetic sensibilities must be brought into play. He can never be as modest or correct as he'd like. 'You're acting like a nigger,' is inevitably his indignant cry if, in his presence, you give way to natural exuberance. Equally, he does not want 'to act like a nigger' in his verses. He considers it a point of honour that a white should be able to read the whole of his book without guessing the colour of his skin. In the same way, ashamed of what remains within him of African polygamy, he furtively sleeps with his maids; likewise, he is careful to purge himself before 'singing' (*sic*), careful indeed to put on the skin of a white man, and leave nothing to betray him. He invariably describes landscapes for you or recounts stories in which hypocrisy makes him veer between rambling on and playing at being Louis Napoleon. (Perhaps France owed its tiresome Parnassus merely to the fact that Leconte de Lisle and Dierx were from Réunion, and Herédia from Cuba.)

There is, as you see, some quite good humour in the bourgeois mulatto but this humour escapes him, just as all his poetic gifts as a mimic do. He maintains that it is his right to reveal only what he believes it good to show, because, raised among priests, or indirectly imbued with their imported religion, he is a frightful casuist.

The outsider would seek in vain for an original or profound tone in this literature, the sensual and colourful imagination of the black, the echo of the aversions and the aspirations of an oppressed people. Daniel Thaly, one of the pontiffs of this class poetry, has commemorated the death of the Caribs (something of indifference to us, since they were exterminated to the last man), but has suppressed the revolt of the slave (who was torn away from his land and his family).

Sad subjects, but no less sad poetic means.

The Caribbean bourgeois is more suspicious here than ever. His inferiority complex leads him along the well-beaten tracks. 'I'm a nigger,' he'll tell you. 'Extravagance doesn't suit me.'[1]

In the same way as he refuses to see in France today anything other than the France of '89, the Caribbean bourgeois refuses to adopt any poetic rule not sanctioned by a century of white experiment. The bold neutrality of Gilbert Gratiant is quite characteristic in this respect when he says: 'Many of the rules, whether traditional or revolutionary, are known: they are all fertile. But why submit only to one rule? The more tyrants there are and the more alternatives, it might be said, the less tyranny.'

As I said before, the Caribbean bourgeoisie always has its reasons.

Not content with using a prosody, and an antiquated prosody at that, the Caribbean poet will adorn it with a hint of archaism: it gives a touch of 'old France'.

Over-indulgence in *l'esprit français* and the classical humanities has earned us these chatterboxes and their sedative poetry. I shall cite just a few of these caricatural poets: Vieux and Moravia in Haiti; Lara in Guadeloupe; Salavina, Duquesnay, Thaly and Marcel Achard in Martinique.

It would be equally unpardonable not to mention, as they approach thirty, two Caribbean poets whose respectability, impenitent conformism, Greco-Roman university education, attachment to the past and affectedness indicate for us that they are worthy successors of their pretentious elders.

Everyone knows that the poem recently published by Henri Flavia-Léopold, 'The Vagabond', is a gratuitous composition in alexandrine verse.

Gilbert Gratiant offers us more substantial fare in his book entitled *Poems in False Verse*.

As regards the title Mr Gratiant is being dishonest. Sadly, his verses are not false, and we insist on giving him credit for his *tour de force* of 240 pages of honest versification. Mr Gratiant's verses express neither the social iniquities of his country, nor the passions of his race, nor its own values of disorder and dream. Each of his pieces appears to be a self-indulgent commentary on a poem still to be written. There is not a gleam of innocence or a moment of courage; no attempt is made to express, fleeting and indirect, the human violence that is poetry.

Mr Gratiant serves us up with all the bric-à-brac of the past century and a half: 'wings of gold', 'diaphanous' swans, moons and zigzags. The best verse in the book is certainly the phrase from 'Yves, Aged Five': 'Garden paths are like a well-roasted steak' which Mr Gratiant felt obliged to burden with a dull explanatory text.

The author has preceded his verses with what he calls 'A Hundred and Seven "Sub-verities" about the Poet's art'. Mr Gratiant's prose disagreeably recalls the style of Alain, the theoretician of inner liberty, the grand master of buffoonery. A preliminary reading of these 'sub-verities' offers the disadvantage (or the advantage, if you like) of putting us off his verses. The author tells us, among other things, that a poem must be understood, tasted, inhaled, etcetera. But no. It either communicates or it doesn't; it is a ribbon of dynamite which will – sooner or later – explode within a given individual. Mr Gratiant gives us the ribbon without the powder. This isn't a game.

I admire the highly academic detachment of the author concerning schools or 'isms'. He is probably afraid that, if he rubs up against them, he will lose his dowager's affectation, his kindness and his impulsiveness. It is the honour and strength of surrealism to have fundamentally integrated the poetic function and laid poetry bare.

A little girl, before seeing her father naked, always identified him with the clothes he wore. Naked, he immediately became mysterious and incomprehensible. That's the way it is when the prudish come face to face with surrealist poetry.

In Messrs Flavia-Léopold and Gratiant, we choose to see the two last Caribbean representatives of a lyricism of the condemned class.

Let's hope the wind rising from black America will quickly cleanse our Caribbean of the aborted fruits of a decrepit culture. Two black revolutionary poets, Langston Hughes and Claude MacKay, bring us, soaked in red alcohol, the African love of life, the African joy of love, the African dream of death. And already young Haitian poets offer us verse pregnant with future dynamism.

From that day, the black proletariat – sucked dry in the Caribbean by a parasitic hybrid caste in the pocket of degenerate whites – will manage, by breaking this double yoke, to establish that one has a right both to eat and have a life of the mind, from that day forth alone will a Caribbean poetry exist.

### Note

1. Has not a teacher belonging to this bourgeoisie declared that Blanche, being black, should not have left university just because he felt like it and 'found that the beans eaten by Taine and Renan were bad'? (Do I have to teach this physics professor that the unfrocked priest Renan never touched the university's beans?)

JULES-MARCEL MONNEROT

# *On Certain Common Characteristics of the Civilized Mentality*[1]

WHAT GETS MY back up are things that are sick but still living, muddy everyday ideas, the backbone of everyone's thought – of a whole detested world – things I will only consider in the course of a wandering, abstract stroll among them, flimsy castles, fields of rust, the hopeless vegetation of a 'collective consciousness' (we don't worry about the end, the far door really does open onto THE OUTSIDE). Few moments in our waking lives allow us to grasp as an abstraction the fact that capitalism presupposes as its necessary complement certain ways of thinking or not thinking which by definition tend to assure its effective continuity. Conventions that slowly eat even into the purest; concepts, circulating like blood, thanks to which the virulence of these conventions is permanent and concrete: this is the paralysing environment in which the minds of those concerned with the spirit wallow. These specialists – like all specialists – invariably display a fundamental disparity between their official and their true existence. Understandably enough, a mortal vertigo would grip them if they succeeded in picturing themselves outside the conventions – principally of a professional, familial and military order – that are the shaky clothes hooks on which they hang their person every night BEFORE GOING TO SLEEP. It certainly isn't through kindness that the person will be taken away from a good many of these people. What is more, their 'reality' is a mask, like their person. Their positivism – a submission to what was there before they existed – is one of the ideological tricks the bourgeoisie uses to perpetuate its existence. It considers 'facts' as *taken for granted*, neglecting the dialectic law of their becoming by which alone they can assume a meaning. To deny 'reality' is to refuse the social organization that is its necessary infrastructure (conversely, actively to refuse society is also to deny the reality it claims to impose). It is by means of a vicious circle that civilized mentality, applying its own categories to itself, finds itself in the notorious 'facts'. Moreover, positivism endlessly suckles a newborn babe covered in scabs which it is always necessary to beat to death: realist art consisting of 'observations' which can in no circumstances ever contribute to real investigation, *because the only true research is that which is against THIS world.*

So that this world can constitute itself – at a rate that corresponds *directly* to the rising ambitions of the great exploiters – we have seen work in modern times elevated to the level of a moral absolute. I won't linger on the evident interest which the small number of people whom all work ends up primarily benefiting in a capitalist regime had in this; no one is unaware that we only speak of work to designate an accord (coincidence and agreement) of the most externally visible aspect of man's activity and of certain social requirements. Usefulness and uselessness are never substantive properties of human activity, but are only relative. Work whose course allows the continuation and extension of the society it animates is detestable in exact proportion to how detestable that society is. Then only counter-work – itself a form of work – appears desirable to *those who will never have anything to lose.* Up to the point when there might be a correspondence between their activity and the needs of social form.

The professional work that is offered to the child they intend to brutalize through the well-known claims of family and school – that work is the small personal contribution everyone must make to the monumental contemporary enterprise to reduce the spirit, where the person contributing is both agent and victim of the aforesaid reduction – this very type of concrete *duty* is not even indicated in the chapter on duties in Victor Cousin's philosophy course published in 1836.

The moral character of the aforesaid work is scarcely even incidentally mentioned in Paul Janet's 'ethics' (1874). By contrast, in current manuals used in philosophy classes, 'it is through his occupation that the individual fully realizes (*sic*) himself . . . this is what testifies to his intelligence and capacities . . . the more intense professional life is, the stricter the personal morality' (A. Cuvillier, *Manuel de Philosophie,* 1928). Between Paul Janet and Cuvillier comes capitalism's apogee, its entry into the imperialist period of perfection culminating in its own negation. Merely by casting a glance at the stalls set out by the two pedlars of morality we have just mentioned we can, as we compare them, grasp the extent to which the exploitation of man by man has advanced.

But that's just the beginning. Shake the principal notions of bourgeois morality and you hear the jangle of money. I would argue that all the words expressing these notions ALSO have – or have had – a mercantile and financial sense. If one pays even the slightest attention to the meaning of these words, the 'moral' swindle can be seen at once. DUTY means DEBT, a perfectly Christian notion of a debt man has never finished repaying. This duty, which primarily profits the holders of obligations, is itself called OBLIGATION. Its fulfilment, the ethical manuals tell us, confers a VALUE on the subject. (The word value is the one that most often appears in this kind of work, more often than the word GOOD.) Put obligation, value and good in the plural and you immediately see what is going on. You can also add merit (from a Greek word signifying share) and incidentally verify that the words ENRICHMENT and TO ACHIEVE, taken of course in their 'spiritual' sense, are the favourite expressions of professors of official morality. Certain other directly military terms (hierarchy, sanction, etcetera) also figure in a modest attitude of earnest obedience to the foul language of finance. If the theory in the manuals is justly opposed to bourgeois practice (thought is here the reversed real image of being), this powerful Christian duplicity is reflected vengefully in those words which have two very precise meanings, each of which illustrates the other. The slipperiest 'philosophers' make a poor job of dressing up notions which are quite evidently 'IN THE SERVICE OF THE MOST MONSTROUS INDUSTRIAL AND MILITARY EXPLOITATION'.

In the civilized mentality, the essential category of value or of goods, in other words of the thing possessed, correlatively supposes that of the person possessing the value or goods. In France, for example, there is *nothing* about which one cannot ask the indispensable, ignoble, sacramental question 'Who owns it?' Consciousness itself is only ever conceived there as the property of a subject. Books and other publications invariably speak of the thought of Mr So-and-so, of the mind or spirit of a particular individual, nation, corporation, family or landscape. I will take it upon myself, because this is the place to do so, to churn out the following propositions: The person who writes does not express *his* thought, but *thought, in other words what is thought* and of which he can consider himself only the most temporary *location*. The thought passing through me cannot to any extent be considered as mine. It comes *to me* from what is *not me*, it is a use-value for the world. The ultimate untroubled expression of individualism comes in the renowned *cogito* (born of Christian parents) where Descartes, founding the philosophy of the French bourgeoisie, puts the *I* before thought and thought before being. In this respect I can transcribe Arthur Rimbaud's declaration: 'It is false to say I think, one should say I am thought.' (The mind enclosed in such miserable limits decays; this decay, in one form or another, is god.) For the civilized individual it is only ever a question of HAVING. What the *ego* has must be taken away *from others*. Thus he must be the strongest, in other words he secures for his person – arbitrarily abstracted from everyone else – a *superiority* over them. The goal of the civilized person – the sign of his success in the world (an incomprehensible expression, furthermore) – is objectively to impose externally his own limits on other beings. Individualism, nationalism, imperialism, colonialism, etcetera. 'Our civilization,' says Mr René Hubert (*Manuel de Sociologie*, p. 397), 'can be defined as the sum of values susceptible of being thought of in an abstract manner and IN CONSEQUENCE APPLIED TO THE WHOLE HUMAN RACE.' The emphasis in this tenet of imperialist catechism is mine. The books by Mr Lévy-Bruhl with pretty well-known titles in which he sets down on the chart of the bourgeoisie's scientific hunt the mental inferiority of 'primitives' (a concept to make ethnologists scream) began to appear in 1910, the date when, as everyone knows, the Third Republic had taken its colonial fill. For this scholar, non-logic is almost exclusively the prerogative of the 'primitive'; logic (simultaneously cause and consequence of material force) belongs by all rights to the civilized. Strictly speaking, the strongest and most active forms of non-rational thought in civilized and capitalist societies (religion, the mystique of the homeland, the celebrated female-principle which stems from a word signifying father, etcetera), *with the sole exception of poetry*, seem to me to be inferior on all counts (as Lévy-Bruhl or Gobineau would say) to the whole of the non-rational manifestations they tell us are the reality of various 'tribes'. Society, individualism, imperialism, industry and so on, which have worked to obtain this separation of two normal modes of the real functioning of the mind – oneiric and logical activity – have believed in it, correlative with an increasing – principally religious – degradation of oneiric activity. The inferiority[2] of primitives forced to contribute their lives and deaths to the colonists' material power is the same as that of the insane, poets and children. *They have no defence, they can always be OVERCOME.* They do not have force to support their conception of the world. This means nothing to them. They are in the world, of the world. Thus they mark themselves out for 'repression', a more specifically civilized concept. (One of those who best sounded out his contemporaries, Freud, noted (*Totem and Taboo*) 'the identity of the repressed desires among criminals and those charged with avenging outraged society', which is not saying much.) The madman *who can no longer command respect*, who no longer adjusts to reality, is the victim amongst the civilized of taboos that have certainly not been studied by sociologists as have those protecting him among certain savages, and which are the filthiest and most revolting imaginable.[3] As for the poets,[4] the civilized begin by making their lives very difficult, by expressing the severest reservations about the significance of their work; then when it is certain that they are dead, they study them.

Poetry[5] does not mean language. Instead it combines in a fairly rigorous way with non-directed thought, especially in its oneiric form, thought by which the pleasure principle tends to govern the world. This non-directed thinking – not thought but rather seen, heard, smelled and tasted – is currently, in its waking state, by definition incompatible with the present concrete content of the reality principle which amounts to adaptation to the infamous civilized society. From childhood onwards, education discourages everything that is not activity useful to society, and the desires expressing pure being that tend to make dream outside sleep mix familiarly with things are repressed (one could compose an ethical treatise on the basis of the integral acceptance of being by the self which, using the psychoanalytic method of the interpretation of dreams, would manage rigorously to define the pure human being and explain the reduction of this purity by the surroundings). Around the adult who they have not entirely succeeded in cutting off from his childhood, the doors grate on their hinges and restrictions multiply. If he has what Freud calls 'the precious faculty' of finding substitute satisfactions for his repressed powers by any conventional means of expression (language, painting, music, and so on), the individual damage done is noticeably diminished. The precise modes of conventional expression limit poetry in the interest of civilized society. But they have let certain accents slip through which portend nothing good since they help us to live. As Tzara has remarked,[6] poetry in France from the eighteenth century to the present day has shown a constant effort both to liberate itself from utility as expressed by logic, the subject, expressionism or clarity and, by returning to its own sources, to become less and less limited by language and other conventions. The poetry one writes, paints, sculpts and so on bears witness among some people (among the least subordinated) to a subordinate oneiric activity that tends to break the heavy carapace that crushes them. The poetry closest to dream[7] that Breton has magnificently inaugurated under the name of automatic writing is nevertheless still distanced from dream by all that brings it close to discourse (syntax, words bullied by education, memory). The slightest dream is more perfect than the best poem because it is by definition concretely adequate to the dreamer for whom it is an individually historical fact. Words are the immediate matter of poetry. Actions, perceptions, a truly experienced living state in which the living being is ENGAGED, this is the dream's matter. Poetry, even in the privileged instance when specific concrete irrationality systematically characterizes its content (as above all in Raymond Roussel, Benjamin Péret and Salvador Dalí) is only ever a conventional symbolic *figuration* of oneiric realities. Poetry is a reflection of dream.[8] Surrealism, as the dialectical continuation of Dada, has led poetry to shores where already it ceases to belong to literature. Standing at the very tip of the poem, poetry merely has to leap. Its continuing existence as a literary form is explained by antipoetic social conditions, which will only be completely checked soon after the victory of the communist revolution on a world scale. The surrealists are clearing the way for that 'pathway from quality to quantity' Tzara speaks of,[9] whose necessary condition is a classless society. A pathway along which poetry will cease to be form in order to become matter. A group of people foretell the formidable return of poetry to its sources, from being an expression of the world to being participation in the world. The poetry denied by capitalist civilization will benefit from every means of communication between people created by this civilization. Directed-thought, science and industry will be able to serve as vehicles for dream. 'Distribution,' Engels says (*Anti-Dühring*, Volume 2), 'to the extent that it will be ruled by purely economic perspectives, will be regulated in the interests of production, and what will best support this production is a mode of distribution allowing every member of society to develop, maintain and exercise their faculties as much as possible in every sense.' And Lautréamont adds: 'Poetry must be made by all, not by one.' The means by which we will lay hands on the levers controlling the *changes of state* are not known. We can only affirm the dialectical necessity of their production. The dialectical progress of surrealism must consist in forcing the distance separating the word from the very substance of representation. It is a question of using the results of an age that has denied sorcery to reinvent sorcery dialectically. Then the poet will be able to picture himself as the engineer of the passage of the word into the world. These considerations on poetry should not reassure anyone: the surrealists are devoting an increasingly large proportion of their time to the most directed thought – revolutionary theory and propaganda; that's for the present. But what the poet was will subsequently be the sorcerer liberator of dream, the sorcerer of a world where bad conscience – moral conscience (which, Freud reservedly says (*Totem and Taboo*), 'presents a great affinity with anxiety') – is reabsorbed, where the pleasure principle is identified with the reality principle and the rational with the real in an absolute marriage. Morality devours psychology, poetry devours verses, acts devour individuals, man devours the ego, the world devours things. The lucid roads bear their continuous diamond away.

## Notes

1. The notion of a solely descriptive, functional and static civilized mentality is here just the LOCATION for various observations. Capitalism has definitively compromised the word civilization.

2. When the 'primitives' rid themselves of the whites there will be no one left to defend the theses of Mr Lévy-Bruhl.

3. Cf. the admirable protests of André Breton and the entire surrealist attitude in this regard. Here, as elsewhere, it is founded as the start of something.

4. Warning. I am talking only about poets. May anyone called that, now, for example Paul Valéry, stop here. This article is not for him but against him.

5. Anyone not understanding why I am speaking about poetry here should consider themselves henceforth dangerously illiterate.

6. Tristan Tzara, 'Essai sur la situation de la poésie', *Le Surréalisme au service de la révolution*, no. 4 (1931).

7. Dream projected onto diurnal life (Tristan Tzara), a veritable spoken dream as analytically interpretable as the nocturnal dream.

8. Certain poems by Paul Eluard have caused on first reading a veritable, immediate and precise *nostalgia for dream* within me.

9. Tzara, 'Essai sur la situation de la poésie'.

[published in *Le Surréalisme au service de la révolution*, 5 (1933)]

PART II

# *TROPIQUES*: UNDERMINING VICHY IN MARTINIQUE

RENÉ MÉNIL

# For a Critical Reading of

# Tropiques

[*TROPIQUES*] WAS PUBLISHED in Fort-de-France from 1941 to 1945. Its publication was subject to censorship by Vichy until May 1943 when the editors were informed that its production was forbidden and thus they had to suspend publication until the collapse of the Pétain regime in the Caribbean.

The reading we have in mind for readers today is a critical one – mindful, consequently, of identifying the implications of these texts in such a way as to establish their objective significance, something that includes a need to locate whatever may have escaped the review's editors for one reason or another.

Such a reading would not only try to resolve some of the problems but also pose new problems of a different nature.

First, the initial censorship had an impact, hardly surprisingly, on the style and thought in these texts in a way that a well-informed reading must be able to identify.[1]

The students and high school students, who were virtually the only readers of *Tropiques* during the forties (some contributed to it), knew that it was necessary to 'read between the lines', fill in the blanks and silences, and interpret the symbols, ellipses and antiphrasis.

These different rhetorical figures, in specific places in the texts, were intended, in the political context of the moment and with the Caribbean reader in mind, to express the writers' thought whilst masking it from the eyes of the Vichy authorities.

There is, therefore, while the Pétain regime remained in power in the Caribbean, an absence haunting these texts: Pétain and his regime are denounced but not named. They are thus present, but through an act of writing that systematically expels them from the texts, leaving their place empty.

In the same way, Marxism being outlawed, an obituary notice dedicated to Jules Monnerot, the founder of the communist movement in the Caribbean, was made in the form of an address whose function was both to express and to conceal a profession of Marxist faith by means of a diversion through lyricism, metaphor and dramatic emphasis (*Tropiques*, nos 6–7, February 1943).[2]

Assuming the mantle of poetry, even insults directly addressed to the regime managed (one must suppose) to deceive the censor, who gave approval for the publication of poems whose political intent cannot be doubted.

> Ah, you can't prevent me from speaking – me who makes a point of displeasing you.
> The wind will overturn the gentle sails to the rustling of my nostrils your fine honourable corruption of cops well and truly shot in the stifling heat of the mornes. (Césaire)

But the reader will not forget that there was naturally added to the circumstantial state censorship an internal auto-censorship (in the Freudian sense) in the writing of the contributors to *Tropiques*, a constant preventive censorship on the part of the community and the individual (morals and prejudices, desires and fears) acting unknown to the writers and affecting the writing with all the weight of the unconscious.

Thus the reader must question these texts.

In the final analysis, it is necessary to place oneself in a resolutely up-to-the-minute position to be able to judge everything correctly whilst not confusing the problems of the past with those of the present.

For the limits of the past are only revealed in the present. It is with today's (philosophical and scientific) tools that reflection must be enlightened. It is thanks to the progress accomplished by modern thought in the decades separating us from the 1940s that some of the gaps may come to light in places where, for the writers of *Tropiques*, there was no void but on the contrary the fullness of their thought and faith.

Only by subjecting these texts to different readings will the reader gain entrance with some rigour to the different meanings not spontaneously offered up by the texts themselves.

These readings might among other things be, in turn, literary to examine poetic productions, scientific to appreciate research of a positive and experimental character, philosophical and political to discern and gauge the doctrines of knowledge and the social conceptions at work in these writings.

For a literary reading, the reader should establish himself within the framework of the relative autonomy of literature.

This reading would only consider the aesthetic character of these texts in so far as they derive from rhetoric (what Roman Jakobson calls literariness).

Then there is the issue of why a particular style of poetic writing was manifested in Martinique in the forties.

The exact determination of this style's characteristics remains to be made.

Thus, while recognizing the debt to surrealism (something explicitly announced in various places in the texts), this recognition must not allow the analysis to be paralysed nor prompt lazy, mechanistic interpretations.

To picture the appropriation of what are called 'surrealist processes' or the 'surrealist image' as coins slipped from one hand (French) to another (Caribbean) is really and truly an admission of analytical incomprehension and impotence.

Certainly, the 'surrealist image' (like any other rhetorical figure) is not something ready-made but a functional operation redefined by the operator in terms of his own inspiration.

Moreover, cultural appropriation, which is a fact of universal civilization, could not in the present case be reduced – prematurely and in a simplistic way – to being no more than a negative, colonial phenomenon of political assimilationism, as some Caribbean critics have claimed.

It is a question here of an active operation of a literary character. And of an overestimated operation, since we are dealing with the inscription of one writing within another, in other words a (Caribbean) writing that will develop against the background of another (French) literature.

Obviously the analysis must become complex and refined, especially to reveal the extent to which the poetic texts in *Tropiques* distort French surrealist form in order to establish another form in a new literary structure imposed by Caribbean socio-historical circumstances at a particular date.

Contrary to an analytical method which would explain Césaire's poetry by using as point of departure the images and linguistic constructions of Breton or Rimbaud, etcetera, it is more satisfactory to find first the dominant factor in Césaire's poetic texts in order to determine the mythological themes his poetry contains (of the man–plant, the rebel, the end of the world, the avenging fire, etcetera). In fact this is the focal element of writing which gives meaning to the linguistic details – not the other way around.

In the same attitude of investigation, the analysis needs to determine, within the poetic vision expressed in the poems, which Caribbean realities are revealed and placed full in the literary light and which were not seen and remained unsaid. And what does this poet's insight – clairvoyant here, blind there – signify?

Thus the light of poetry does not seem to illuminate the man at work, the tools of the trade, or the results of the labour. Rather, the landscape (in deflagration), the vegetation (in tumult), animality (enraged), the human heart and society (in torment) burst forth – in gestures and colours – in heart-rending realization.

In the same way, the critical reader cannot fail to be struck by what could be called the *excess of literature* (as when one keeps talking endlessly in order to forget), by a complacent taste for abstraction and hermeticism that both conceals and proclaims the overwhelming power of mystery.

But what mystery? Who is knocking on the door without announcing himself, without revealing who he is, as mystery requires?

The romanticism in action in *Tropiques* assumes that it is a question of the appearance of beauty onto the scene (the veiled beauty of André Breton). But (this is just a hypothesis) is this romanticism not the aesthetic mask of the trivial contemporary and political demands of a nationalism that was then only foretold in poetic sensibility?

A misunderstanding awaits the reader if we speak of an agricultural or peasant or Third World civilization, something that will be encouraged by certain aesthetic formulas in play in these texts: this misunderstanding consists in taking the literature in the journal for a spontaneous and naïve literature, as though it belonged to a kind of primitive art considered *a priori* to be characteristic of underdeveloped countries.

On the contrary, we are concerned with a complex and constructed literature (as all art is) – a literature at one remove recorded and developed (as we have already suggested) on the foundations of French literature from which it contradictorily keeps its distance in a constant engagement.

Especially significant in this respect is the example of the great Cuban painter Wifredo Lam who, during his visit to Martinique in

1941, showed his solidarity with Césaire's poetry and the aesthetic of *Tropiques* and who today defines his painting as 'a plastic expression of the Third World'. Certainly, the innovatory quality of his famous painting *The Jungle*, which dates from the same period, was not due to a 'naïve' or 'natural' or 'spontaneous' given of his sensibility, but was the result of reflections about cultures and civilizations, passionate enquiries about the 'cosa negra', a fertile experience of life (it must not be forgotten that he was a militiaman in the Spanish Civil War) and, perhaps most especially, his successive experiments with different styles of expression which both reflected and yet contradicted that of the greatest painters of the West.

It is the complexity of the writing in *Tropiques* that explains its exoticism for those French people inquisitive about new horizons, but also for any reader able to feel the effect of the unfamiliarity caused by a continual telescoping of two cultural languages separated within the same tongue – French.

This also allows us to recognize a certain mannerist and precious tone which the alert reader will easily discern.

Obviously none of the terms we are using taken from current literary vocabulary is meant in a pejorative sense.

Rather, they should really be introduced and rethought in a positive way within the framework of a Caribbean aesthetic elaborated beyond the usual concepts. This would seek, at the level of the relative autonomy of experimental research, to account for poetic processes in our particular conditions of existence.

As for claiming, as certain critics have done, that Caribbean literature is unable to define itself as Caribbean if the French language is its vehicle, this is as outrageous an absurdity as it would be to refuse all authenticity to South American and Caribbean (Chilean, Guatemalan, Mexican, Cuban) literatures on the pretext that they use the Spanish language.

This error results from a confused idea about the nature of languages and their relation to the mentality of peoples, cultures and nationalities.

For its part, a scientific reading would need to resolve, in another direction, other problems: it would need to circumscribe and evaluate the extent to which the research presents an experimental character appropriate to the sciences.

It would need a study of the Caribbean environment (history, flora, fauna), an outline of a logical and phenomenological examination of the imaginary in various places, an ethnographic approach to Creole tales and an attempted inventory of the folklore elements, a cross-checking of forms of civilization common to Africa and the Caribbean, an attempt at objective analysis of literary texts, and so on.

This scientific element (especially applied to Caribbean subjectivity) does not immediately leap to the reader's mind and does not draw attention to its scientific quality, adorned as it generally is in forms of literary language and situated at the borders where scientific research and poetic activity often tend to mingle.

It was from a reading of Bachelard (whose most original works had not yet been published in 1940) that we appreciated, retroactively, the real meaning of the stumblings and unresolved contradictions in a study of the imagination that we had wanted to be logical, materialist and dialectical.

Thus, the insistent theme in *Tropiques* – the conjugation (where and how?) of sorcerer and scholar, poetry and science, imagination and reasoned judgement – is illustrated through the concept of 'true magic', as Bachelard describes it in *Le Matérialisme rationnel*, published in 1953 and showing the close involvement of poetic intuition in scientific intuition and the path that leads from the former to the latter by critical operations of correction and purification.

Concerning the explanation of Creole tales, our reading today perceives the absence, in our analysis, of structuralist and formalist methods that were themselves absent from the intellectual horizon of the forties. The methods used in our texts are historical, psychoanalytical and functionalist in the style of Malinowski.

Perhaps the critical reader will consider the main interest of the texts to lie on the philosophical (and political in the widest sense) level.

Equally it is on this level that the issue of knowing how and under what conditions the texts that follow can aid in situating and resolving the current problems of the Caribbean can be posed with the greatest clarity – all readings in the past being governed, in the final analysis, by the practical and theoretical needs of their time.

The present publication undoubtedly responds to a general social need, even if the request for it came from the ranks of university lecturers, students and high school pupils (conversely, one should also consider why this long-awaited re-edition has been so much delayed).

In reading André Breton's text 'A Great Black Poet', from the first glance the reader will see the socio-historical conditions (food rationing, suppression of liberties, institutional racism) that were encountered in a colonial situation aggravated by military blockade and by the rise of Hitlerism in Europe and how this led to the journal being born on Césaire's initiative as our response, engaging with Caribbean problems and sketching out solutions and in an appropriate (essentially literary) language. In the manner of a research laboratory, each writer in *Tropiques* was absolutely free in the work they undertook for the production of texts.

This latter feature is characteristic enough for its bearing in mind to be useful when thinking about the perspective, the content, and, in each issue of *Tropiques*, the fortuitous encounter of texts.

Breton notes, on reading the first issue of *Tropiques*, that the texts collected are clearly oriented in the same direction and towards the same end – towards mankind in its generality and Caribbean man in particular. As we read the eleven issues of *Tropiques* today, in a more critical way because we are more distant and armed with better scientific and philosophical tools, we will certainly perceive dissonances and contradictions not only between different writers in the review, but sometimes within texts by the same writer. The texts in *Tropiques* do not reflect a single unified philosophy, but diverse philosophies – some of them allied and closely related; others opposed and frankly contradictory.

And if, at the end of the day, philosophies of *élan vital*, sensitive intuition and instinctive forces (references that were tacit in the case of Bergson or explicit in the cases of Novalis, Nietzsche, Freud, etcetera) predominate, this must be seen against the contradictory background of opposed rationalist philosophies. Bergsonian irrationalism went hand in hand with scientific rationalism; Nietzschean voluntarism and revelation with historical materialism and belief in the essential laws of social evolution; Mallarméan occultism with an insistent effort to rationalize the irrational and give a focus to political action through the exact sciences.

The fact remains that, faced with a regime that had to be combated as quickly as possible with a total refusal, the writers in *Tropiques*, running as fast as they could and inspired to varying degrees by an idealism that was both pragmatic and romantic (with references to Baudelaire, Mallarmé, Rimbaud, Lautréamont, Breton, etcetera) considered the act of writing as a poetic operation of suggestion capable, through calculated use of a myth invented in a literary way, of provoking such a shock in Caribbean man that, submissive to the tumultuous forces of life, he would revolutionize both himself and society.

Let me point out that this method is justified in the first instance when poetry, outstripping the age, assumes responsibility for the political problem of expressing Caribbean nationalism without being able to name it. This method tends to continue, as I said – through weight of inertia – into the present, different stage, where it is a matter of confronting the struggle for liberation not in the imagination (by use of metaphor) but in reality, through the rational deployment of means adequate to the ends pursued.

Whatever the case, *Tropiques* accentuated the idealist (Hegelian) and irrational (surrealist) aspects of *Légitime défense* (1932) in the face of Marx's rationalism, which was to some extent diminished.

But we should be careful. As it addressed the historical past and the emotional roots of our community (notably the racial dimension) more concretely, the journal developed and revealed Caribbean reality as much as it could at the level of spiritual life. This had to be done. And it (the fusion of materiality and ideality in the idea of *social practice*) is something that Marxism, far from condemning, needs if it is to be complete.

A certain fresh romanticism, reinvigorated by May 1968 in France and by the new dynamic of world struggles of national liberation, throbs through the Caribbean today.

Three decades later, it very nearly – unknowingly – repeated the romanticism of *Tropiques* as it emerged from the socio-historical situation of 1940 and expressed, with feverish impatience, a new feeling of Caribbean life, an unknown future, the uneasy quest for a distinguished past, the uniqueness of island life and local colour.

If you think about it, you will notice that the style of this enterprise tends to express the intense, immeasurable and disparate quality of life that could only be *baroque* (see the analyses by Eugenio d'Ors). This style would be affirmed in the framework already established by surrealist aesthetics, according to a rule that was verified in other American countries such as Haiti, Cuba, Guatemala and so on.

The reader should not too hastily deplore the impossibility of reducing the multiplicity of philosophies in *Tropiques* to one alone.

In reality, the panoply of philosophies that will be discerned by analysis of these texts responds to a panoply of problems posed on different levels of Caribbean reality, requiring different means of reflection and study for their resolution.

A differential philosophy (according to another of Bachelard's terms) acts in *Tropiques* (considering the totality of texts) in such a way as to tackle the problems according to their nature, either, for instance, from the angle of subjective idealism (in the realm of aesthetics) or from the angle of historical materialism and necessity defined by Marxists (in the socio-political realm), and so on.

Thus, from the perspective of our philosophical consciousness today (this is the writer of *Tropiques* defending himself) what in fact can legitimately shock and really does shock our critical sense is neither the diversity nor the contradictions of the philosophies in evidence in the texts of *Tropiques*.

What shocks us today is that we did not perceive these oppositions, differences and contradictions in philosophical conceptions – as though they were 'self-evident'. With the result that they were neither identified, nor defined, nor named in order finally to be conquered and resolved. Thus, at the aesthetic level which remains essential in *Tropiques*, an insufficiently developed idealism, too often congealed in metaphysics, encounters a materialism that claims to be dialectical but hesitates to assume the full extent of the ideological world of the imaginary. This opposition was not noticed by our critical considerations as a problem to be resolved philosophically at the heart of our aesthetic.

*Tropiques* was the expression of the perspectives, the hopes, and the will of the revolutionary Caribbean left in the forties.

But here is today's drama.

The texts of *Tropiques* were not reprinted immediately after the Second World War when they had already become unfindable in bookshops. This resulted in the following paradox: *ever since then the Caribbean intellectual left has engaged with the concepts it presented in a confused way and without having read the originals,* if one considers the isolated quotations one comes across here and there to be negligible.

Thus there are numerous Caribbean intellectuals who have received a heritage of philosophical concepts, ideological themes, and working methods without knowing their actual source, internal meaning and precise limits. And it is in an obscure and confused way that they revive for their own purposes particular mythological themes, cultural problems and research practices that functioned in *Tropiques* and that act upon current Caribbean mentality as a sort of *repressed of thought,* as Althusser put it.

These conceptions, like all unconscious thought, bear heavily on reflection without really illuminating it.

There has thus been a rupture between our present intellectual Caribbean history and a particular stage of its prehistory.

This rupture involves drawbacks, the most immediate of which are those of a thought that, instead of going back to its hidden principles to ascertain their legitimacy, contents itself with an approximation and, when it comes to it, with declaiming poetry at the very moment when it claims to establish the theorems of which our political action has a pressing need.

Such ideological tools do not allow us to engage the problems of current relevance with the necessary theoretical rigour: problems of language and its nature and function are badly defined; folklore is not differentiated from literature and is introduced at random into political action; the relative independence of the reciprocal limits and interactions of literature and politics are sometimes forgotten; nationalism is not defined except in terms of dead abstractions, and so on.

With the re-publication of these texts, a gap in the logic of our intellectual history will be filled.

There is no doubt that the ensuing confrontation of today's Caribbean thought with its past realizations will result in welcome readjustments in aesthetic, political and cultural conceptions that have been in circulation for a considerable time but whose shortcomings are flagrant.

Such are the demands that these exhumed texts make upon the reader's attention.

*October 1973*

### Notes

1. See Engels: 'From the outset, censorship forces every element, even if they don't like it, to choose as abstract a means of expression as possible.' He is referring to Prussian censorship in 1830.

2. Editor's note: Not included in the present collection. Jules Monnerot was the father of Jules-Marcel Monnerot.

[published as an introduction to the reissue of *Tropiques* (1978) Paris: Jean-Michel Place]

AIMÉ CÉSAIRE

# *Panorama*

T HIS LAND IS suffering from a repressed revolution.
Our revolution has been stolen from us.

[T]he worst mistake would be to believe that the West Indies devoid of
strong political parties are devoid of powerful will. We know very well
what we want.

Liberty, dignity, justice, Christmas torched.

[T]he condition for a rebirth or a birth cannot be stressed enough: an
overthrow of the economy and of society. The *Fourth Republic* must come.

[O]ne day history will severely judge those men who in three centuries
of unprecedented ease, on the world's most beautiful island, could
construct nothing but this monument of obscurantism, sloth and
jesuitism that is Martiniquan capitalism.

[O]ne of the elements, the principal element of the Caribbean malaise,
is the existence on these islands of a homogeneous group, of a *people*
which for three centuries has sought to *express itself* and to *create*.

[S]lavery weighs heavily upon us, we know. But to attribute our present
*poverty* to this alone is to forget that under the slave regime the nigger
was magnificent. The better to treat him as a beast, they had to make
him a beast. They broke his body. They tormented his soul. And the
nigger resisted. Resisted the whip, professors in their mortarboards,
theologians, sadists. Contempt was met with humour – that force that

the dour Indian never knew. The gloom of false science was combated with ringing laughter. Cruelty was sometimes combated with *patience*, sometimes with revolt, never with resignation.

Only those who don't know what Africa was would be surprised at this.

Vast empires. Monarchies full of splendour. Strange and beautiful ceremonies. Unusual and pure relations. An unsurpassed dignity and sincerity. And the nigger overflowed with life and strength. And with riches. Rich with sensuality and spirituality: rich . . . And he braced himself, struck out, bit . . . Tamed he never was.

A powerful page from Michelet:
'What delayed the Renaissance and rendered it almost impossible from the thirteenth to the sixteenth centuries was not that every vigorous drive to become manifest was destroyed by iron and fire; others would have sprung up from the same base. But an artificial world of ponderous mediocrity was created over this productive base, a leaden world, which kept all nobility of life and thought, all grandeur and *ingegno*, submerged.'

What makes our Renaissance impossible is that, for three centuries, all thought here has been profaned, all independence broken, all boldness defied, all pride debased. And at the same time all cowardice and baseness is honoured, extolled, promoted, encouraged and rewarded.

You tremble when you think of the quality of souls brought up here over nearly a century. A century of underhand slavery, resignation and individual and collective cowardice.

A ferocious egoism.

A repulsive conformism.

A century after the abolition of slavery you could not imagine the degree of indifference and scorn that the bourgeoisie of this land professes for the black proletariat.

It may be conceded that 90 per cent of the young people *turned out* here by school (alas!), family – yes family – and EVERYTHING ELSE (EVERYTHING ELSE especially) are in a state of moral torpor bordering on imbecility.

What has the youth been offered during these last fifty years? Positions. Trades. Words. Not one *feeling*. Not one *idea*.

If the great and healthy anger of the people does not (as it did a century ago) stand in its way, we will march straight ahead to the logical conclusion of three centuries of Caribbean history: the triumph of total *flunkeyism*.

When the essential problems (the weight of facts) discourage the mind's *elation*, a society is at a pre-revolutionary stage.

The Martiniquan revolution will be made in the name of bread, of course; but also in the name of fresh air and poetry (which comes to the same thing).

I tell you we are choking.

The principle of a healthy Caribbean politics: open the windows. More air. More air.

Thus I condemn any idea of *Caribbean independence*.

. . . But this is not in order to bark with the dogs.

. . . But this is not so as to cast my pearls before swine. Martiniquan *dependency* – willed, calculated, reasoned as much as sentimental – will be neither dis-grace nor sub-grace.

I only know one France. That of the Revolution. That of Toussaint L'Ouverture. Too bad for the gothic cathedral.

We want to be able to live passionately.

And in the last resort the resolution will come from the blood of this land. And this blood has its tolerances and its intolerances, its patiences and its impatiences, its resignations and its brutalities, its whims and its forbearances, its stillnesses and its tempests, its calms and its whirlwinds.
And this is what, in the end, will act.
This kind of blood doesn't cast votes.
This kind of blood reinvigorates or strangles.

[published in *Tropiques*, no. 1 (April 1941)]

SUZANNE CÉSAIRE

# Leo Frobenius and the
# Problem of Civilizations

THE CRUCIAL PROBLEM is that of civilization. We live as part of it.
We celebrate its progress or deplore its decadence. But what is its
essence?

First the traditional responses. The humanist one: it is the work of
man made for man; the agnostic one: it is 'a giant organism whose limits and grandeur we can no more perceive than one of our cells could
perceive (given the power of reasoning) the structure and organization
of our body'.

Traditional responses, and there is someone who knows it – a historian, archaeologist, anthropologist; this is inadequate: a poet. What is
his response? The most extraordinary of all, the most revolutionary,
the most laden with consequences. No, man does not create civilization; no, civilization is not man's work. On the contrary, man is the
instrument of civilization, simply a means of expression of an organic
power that is infinitely superior to him. Man does not act, he is acted
upon, moved by a force that is prior to humanity, a force comparable
to the vital force itself, the fundamental Paideuma.

And is this Paideuma – as creator of civilizations – inaccessible to
mankind? No, someone really conscious of his outstanding dignity is
capable of grasping it, not directly (for its secret is as impenetrable as
the vital force itself) but indirectly, in its diverse manifestations,
through humanity. It is a superior presence, perceptible only to one
who knows how to 'see into the depths'.

Let's listen to Frobenius: 'The Paideuma reveals its own laws
everywhere. Cultures live and die, they are reborn and supplant one
another according to particular laws as though man was not there,

man who is but an instrument which the Paideuma uses to manifest itself.'

Study of manifestations of the Paideuma constitutes a new science that Frobenius calls the 'morphology of cultures'. A morphology of cultures is neither primitive history, nor prehistory, nor modern history: it does not accumulate facts and dates. Nor is it archaeology – any more than it is ethnology or ethnography. No. What it aims to study is the 'organic being' of civilization. That is, civilization itself conceived as a 'metaphysical entity'. It aims at grasping, beyond the established framework of civilizations, this secret and terrible force that Frobenius calls the Paideuma.

A grandiose conception, embracing human development as a whole; an admirable exigence which requires man to heed all other men in all times. It is a science that no longer offers a luminous order and a spiritual domination of facts, but a quest for intimate knowledge, for the secret reality revealed in the life force itself.

This gigantic project is doubly interesting, both because it illuminates the human problem and because, for its realization, Leo Frobenius has devoted himself to the study of African civilizations and, as he affirms, established an African soul and genuinely African ways of thinking and feeling.

This profound study of African civilizations, and numerous voyages of discovery and detailed observations of rock drawings across the African continent and in Europe – comparative observations on religions, morals, customs, habitats, tools and objects currently in use among the majority of the earth's people – is the rich material that serves the elaboration of a methodology and a science allying cold scientific precision with the mind's most beautiful audacity.

Leo Frobenius's analytic method is applied in two directions.

1.  *Study of 'forms and places'*: the external aspects of civilizations and their spatial distribution. Charts can then be produced (charts about houses on stilts, for example, during a particular period). Diagrams can be prepared and statistics obtained.
2.  *Study of 'substances'*: this is what especially interests Frobenius. He also calls it: 'Study of the meaning of life'. He explains: 'a civilization, in the sense we give this word, is not merely the external appearance of a people, but the *internal substance* of a community around which all of its members participate.

The first result of this method is the finding that the Paideuma, through a phenomenon found in all manifestations of the vital force (the phenomenon of bi-polarity) is manifested under two literally opposed forms: (1) Ethiopian civilization; (2) Hamitic civilization.

Ethiopian civilization is connected to plant life and the vegetal cycle. It is dreamy, completely enfolded within itself, and mystical. The Ethiopian personality does not try to understand phenomena, or to seize and dominate external facts. The Ethiopian is content to live a life identical to that of the plant that is confident in the continuity of life: it germinates, shoots up, blossoms, yields fruit and the cycle begins anew. A lived and deeply felt poetry that the Ethiopian is almost never capable of expressing and externalizing. In addition, the notion of the father, of patriarchal kinship, is fundamental. To sum up: 'the Ethiopian sentiment of life is defined as a sense of the real and primitive mystical faith'. Hamitic civilization, on the other hand, is linked with the animal, with conquest of the right to live through struggle. The Hamite is active, conscious of the external facts that stand against him and that he must overcome to survive. He never abandons himself to things but strives to dominate them through force or through magical practice. He has a sense not of the continuity of generations, but of individual life. His concept of the clan is matriarchal. The mother is not expected to remain faithful to her husband if he is defeated. She becomes the wife of the conqueror. In short, 'Hamitic civilization is characterized by the meaning of the act and by primitive magic.'

Today, these two fundamental expressions of the Paideuma are only found buried deep in the depths of the consciousness of the European, Asian and American peoples who supposedly comprise 'high civilizations'. In Africa, by contrast, these forms of civilization can be studied in an almost pure state among so-called 'primitive' tribes. There are people in whom the plant-man and the animal-man subsist in their primal grandiose simplicity.

It is enough, for example, to interpret the strange rituals of forest tribes, where harvesting becomes a religious act, or else to recover the original meaning of the cruelties of adolescent initiation rituals among most Hamites. The geographical position and sheer size of the African continent has allowed it to retain – so to speak, in isolation – forms of civilization as they sprang spontaneously from the earth, since here the deterioration, or rather the inevitable evolution, has taken place more slowly than elsewhere – one should say, 'in more depth', giving birth in some parts of African territory to civilizations as brilliant as that of the

Gao Empire, at a time when Europe was covered with impenetrable forests and swamps.

From his first journey to Africa in 1904, Leo Frobenius was amazed by what remained of a very ancient splendour. He admired the 'gestures, manners and morals . . . of an entirely natural meticulousness, dignity and grace'. And he adds: 'I do not know of any Northern people who can compare with these primitives for the unity of their civilization.'

His *History of African Civilization* is a vast effort of synthesis whose aim is to understand all these very ancient forms of civilization, which today appear primitive and petrified when in fact they are often symbols of grandiose cultures, the astonishing complexity and richness of which we remain unaware.

As such, Africa's value to someone considering the tormenting question of human becoming seems inestimable: 'For us, Africa does not merely signify an enlargement towards the beyond but also a deepening within ourselves.'

This is why Leo Frobenius and his disciples consider the comparative study of civilization to be not only an illumination of the human, but a vision of the future, for thanks to the results of the new science, they believe they are empowered to offer solutions to questions as serious as 'mankind's role' and 'the drama of the earth'.

In fact Frobenius has discovered that the idea of continual progress, dear to the nineteenth century, which showed civilization as progressing in a single line from primitive barbarism to the highest modern culture, is a false idea. Humanity does not possess a will to perfection. To emphasize this, it does not create civilization and then try to take it ever higher. On the contrary, it develops in multiple directions transformed by the inner Paideuma, from one sudden 'shock' to another, in the same way as the vital force passes from one mutation to another through the diversity of living species. But before defining this new idea of 'shock' it is indispensable to show how the vital force expresses itself in the Paideuma, the creator of civilizations. First we find the fundamental polarity – the sign of life itself, and which we have already seen manifested in the great Ethiopian–Hamite opposition – in the details of the life of cultures.

For example, the astral bodies (the Moon, the Sun, Venus, etcetera) are attributed a sex. The determination of this sex is not arbitrary. It responds to a precise spatial order. Stars are coupled – twins, brothers and sisters, lovers – command particular regions and propagate according to laws defined by the charts. In the same way, numbers participate in feminine or masculine nature. The number 4 is linked to space, with its 4 cardinal points; the sun, which discloses space; movement; and the masculine. The number 3 is linked to time past, present and future; to the phases of the moon and its birth, its waxing and waning; to peace; and to the feminine.

An encounter charged with meaning, the symbolism of numbers is the very reflection of astral symbolism, being the profound expression both of the primitive polarity of time and space and of the reality of life.

Let's now consider the psychological processes of the 'shocks': how have numbers, astral bodies and seasons delivered up to man what Leo Frobenius calls their 'essence'? How have numbers, astral bodies and seasons determined a 'revolution of the spirit' in the plant-man and animal-man, a veritable modification of his nature characterized by the 'shock'?

The phases of the moon, the course of the sun and the changing of the seasons have not been subject to methodological observations by man, who has not sought enlightenment from them.

No. He has suddenly been 'shocked' by the essence of these phenomena, by their secret and intimate reality. He has been overcome by a sudden, imperious and irresistible emotion. Thus the rhythmic appearances and disappearances of the moon have given rise to the shocks of time and death. This is the shock that is expressed by all rituals connected to the theme of the predetermination of the death of the god in most civilizations. In the same way, the sun's light shining on the world gives rise to the shocks of space, spatial confinement and a delimited order.

When the changing of the seasons provoked the shock of the rhythm of the periodic life and death of nature, a new 'sentiment of life' was born. Man became aware of his individual existence and the problem of his destiny. We can say that this is the shock of man himself as an isolated reality in the external world.

It does not necessarily follow that all these 'shocks' have been successive stages: plants, animals, astral bodies and seasons have created and altered the nature of the sentiment of life in different times and places, have genuinely created and transformed civilizations, making them more profound in some places, causing them to deteriorate in others, intermingling in yet others as they are linked together in an ever-increasing complexity.

And this is how Leo Frobenius establishes his vision of the future, for he is now able to write: 'The history of human civilization is the history of the transformations of the sentiments of life.' Today he can consider whether a fresh shock is not being manifested; whether our unhappy age is not the eruption of a new sentiment of life.

It seems that in the nineteenth century Euro-American humanity was seized with a real craze for science, technology and machines, the result of which has been an imperialist philosophy that has generated the world economy and the encircling of the globe. This veritable mania for power and domination, which has brought humanity to catastrophes as terrible as the wars of 1914 and 1939, is symptomatic of a fresh surging of the Paideuma. We do not yet fully understand the significance of this upsurge whose real meaning is still hidden from us. This is the earth's drama. Mankind's role is to prepare to live this other future, to let itself be carried along by the Real, without losing the sense of piety, conquest and destiny which is its unique and precious heritage.

This is the magnificent message Leo Frobenius offers modern man. His philosophy goes beyond the scholarly arguments of his predecessors and contemporaries. He has given sociology life and strength. He has recovered the meaning of cosmologies and myths that have been lost since the time of Anaxagoras and Plato.

And this philosophy is Poetry, the world re-created, man as master of a new destiny, fortified with a new experience of life.

And the fertility of this admirable doctrine is such that it immediately asks each of us questions we cannot avoid without cowardice. It is now imperative to dare to know ourselves, to dare to admit our nature, to dare to consider what we want to be. Here, too, men are born, live and die. Here, too, the entire drama is played out.

'The time has come to gird our loins like valiant men.'

[published in *Tropiques*, no. 1 (April 1941)]

# AIMÉ CÉSAIRE

# Presentation

A SILENT AND sterile land. I am speaking about ours. And my hearing measures by the Caribbean Sea the terrifying silence of man. Europe. Africa. Asia. I hear screaming steel, drumbeats in the bush, temples praying amidst banyan trees. And I know it is man speaking: now as always, and I am listening. But here is the monstrous atrophy of the voice, the age-old exhaustion, the incredible mutism. No city. No art. No poetry. No civilization, at least in its true sense, meaning that projection of man onto the world; that modelling of the world by man; that stamp of man's effigy on the universe.

A death more frightful than death, where the living drift. And it is elsewhere that sciences progress, elsewhere that philosophies are renewed, elsewhere that aesthetics succeed each other. And in vain that on this our land the hand sows seeds.

No city. No art. No poetry. Not one seed. Not one shoot. Or else the hideous leprosy of imitations. In truth, a sterile and silent land . . .

But it is no longer the time to feed off the world. Rather it is a question of saving it. The time has come to gird our loins like valiant men.

Wherever we look, the shadow is encroaching. One after the other the home fires are extinguished. The circle of shadow closes in, amid the cries of men and the howls of beasts. Yet we are the kind who refuse the shadow. We know that the world's salvation depends on us too. That the land needs its sons, no matter who they be. The humblest.

The shadow encroaches . . .

'Ah! All the hope in the world would not be enough to look the century in the face!'

Strong-willed men will make a new light for this world.

[published in *Tropiques*, no. 1 (April 1941)]

RENÉ MÉNIL

# Introduction to the

# Marvellous

HISTORY INEVITABLY TURNS an era that is drawing to a close into a mockery of history. Every event becomes parody, all action farce, all words a joke. Life withdraws from the living, and characters who have already ceased to be anything but phantoms linger on the disused stage. And legend, which is a living people's greatest truth, can no longer be distinguished from news items.

Having made practical reason its chief quality, this century will not have been afraid to demand that we admire traders as heroes, soldiers of the temporal as saints, and simple commentators of established facts as philosophers. But if we depart too much from the forces of nature in order to domesticate them, we risk eluding reality and, in short, passing our destiny by.

The great eras of history do not result from the exercise of understanding, which is the instrument of human solitude because it is an instrument of appropriation. They are the rewards for mankind's temporary abandon to life's powerful shocks. Individuals and peoples, as they integrate with history through their docility to life, thereby cease to restrain their destiny but, on the contrary, advance into their loves and epics with the secret complicity of the world. Man experiences new fertility. He conceives himself in the true light of his possibilities, creates himself, transcends himself and asserts himself with the blood coursing through his temples beating the harsh song of Odysseys, Renaissances and Revolutions.

When moralists put forward ridiculous images of man, the fault is not theirs but lies with the age. But their propositions may produce within us impatience with the everyday banality of life rather than the marvellous Act that they insistently try to pass off as our reason to exist. A being is not defined by its uncertainties but by its plenitude. An individual or a people can secure this plenitude, which is their greatness, only by deliberately cleansing their history of its insipid moments, only by refusing to recognize the image they proffer when they are lazy, absent or weak, in order to carve only exceptional images of themselves whose value arises only when they crystallize a certain spark of exultation. History, so restored to its substance by those who live it, becomes embellished with the tension and gravity of tragedy. According to the age and the individual, it reveals to us a greater or lesser number of instants whose existence really matters and can genuinely be considered the price of existence.

The history of humanity's electrifying acts is the very history of human sensibility. That is why the best lessons about human behaviour must be sought in aesthetics. It alone gives mankind the images it deserves. It alone conceives of worlds in which man, if he lived in them, would cease to feel himself a stranger. This results from the fact that different aesthetic expressions constitute, in symbolic form, a solemn declaration of the most imperious desires inherent in individuals and peoples. Among these expressions, poems and stories hold a privileged place. If, in fact, through sounds and colours, music and painting reveal to us a fragment of the world we would like to have lived in or the kind of person we would like to have been, it is stories and poems that alone generally allow us with sufficient clarity 'consciousness of our greatness within, of which we are unaware' and represent, in a very coherent and spectacular way, the world we have dreamed of inhabiting.

Through a sort of magical incantation, stories and poems transport us into an extraordinary world: the land of the marvellous.[1] It is the land which (unlike this world of real life) finally responds to our fundamental desires and has been constructed accordingly. There are innumerable human desires that ordinarily do not dare to be confessed, let alone realized, because they come up against severe prohibitions in social reality and difficult or insuperable obstacles in the physical world. Yet if these aspirations resulting from the very exercise of life are discouraged, they are by no means annihilated. They course indistinctly through peoples and individuals, animating them with an ordinarily invisible flame which still manages, even if only through symbols, to gleam mysteriously in stories and poems.

The dramas given form in these works find their place in the conflict that pits our living desires against that real world that is unable to assure their satisfaction.

The land of the marvellous is the most stunning revenge we have – at the level of subjective reality – against a life that, however little we are inclined to joke about it, depresses us to the extent that it is in thrall to practical reason. In the world of stories where such revenge is especially striking, it is with joy that we see the reality principle vanish.

Here *everything is possible* and man, at once enlightened, moved and guided by desire alone, travels into a docile world where everything hastens to respond to his wishes. It is the golden age. The child, our master of marvels, knows more than anyone the magical power of moving into the real world, bearing around him like a king his personal land of joy and power.

Here is a world governed only by the pleasure principle. Man sees the intolerable limits of everyday life fall from him like so much tawdry finery. Everything really becomes possible for him. He can transgress his spatial boundaries: he transforms himself into a tree, an animal, a peaceful lake, so discovering precious secrets as in a game. He overcomes space by instantly crossing infinite distances. He overcomes time: if, in the exaltation of a madly captivating life, he dies apparently inadvertently, it is to be reborn into a more beautiful life. He holds past and future, space and time, life and death in his hands and the genies open every avenue before him. He also holds, amongst his fabulous riches, the most valuable of all, the cause and effect of all desires, love: he appears and the princess comes towards him, the one she has always known and always loved and always expected.

His trials, which are many, merely serve to exercise his heroism, express his eternal dissonance and justify the joy which, in the end, will unfailingly engulf his heart.

But if man thereby achieves happiness, it is because he holds the Great Secret. He knows the hearts of men and things. Through the talisman and the magical word, the universe becomes a house of glass. He knows that by rubbing the lamp or ring, impassable doors will open before him. He knows the words he must say for obedient genies to appear. He utters the sovereign formula, makes the magic sign, and bewitched things and men yield: the rock opens, the palace constructs itself, the flame vanishes, the waters are calmed, the sleeping beauty awakens . . .

If we cease to consider the land of the marvellous as an idyllic but silent painting and examine its living genesis, we are led, as we pass from the imagined to the imagining, to wonderstruck mankind. It is man (that aspect of nature that gains access to the Spirit through consciousness of the self) that creates the marvels which, in the indivisible unity of nature, are found no more within us than outside us. But what immediately accounts within us for the marvellous is the exaltation of sensibility. As soon as the life within man, individuals and peoples, reaches a sufficiently hectic rhythm and sufficiently violent intensity, the inflamed senses will gain access to regions of the universe that usually elude them. It even propels us, you might say, 'by secret demand, through the senses'.

The clairvoyance displayed by the heroes of tales is exactly the same, in transposed form, as that of exalted man.

Therefore it is not by means of ruses of the intelligence that we can gain entrance to the world of marvels. As magic traditions imply, only a man armed with the powers of the heart is admitted, through a higher grace, to contemplate the revelations of the forbidden world. Marvels appear only at the moment when life, in the emotion felt, truly grasps man so as to throw him unwillingly outside the habitual and common conditions of life into unknown and more profound conditions of life, into unknown and more profound regions of reality. In this *rapture,* one is lost to the self and saved from its restrictive circumstances. Lost to the self but found to the world.

The fundamental properties of the marvellous are the very ones that analytic psychology determines as being characteristic of the feelings. If the tale ignores contradictions, it is because the feelings from which it has sprung in the irreducible unity of this intuition, no more contain contradictions than the life whose every moment contains affirmation or denial. In the land of marvels, contraries can intimately rub shoulders or, more accurately, are able to communicate, to be mutually compelling, as confirmation of the hero's power. Life and death, the communicable and the incommunicable, past and future, the possible and the impossible, are interdependent and cease to be perceived as contradictory. At last man is no longer forced to choose. Amazement and joy: the living hero is immortal; passing through rock, he sees the future in the magic mirror, becomes a tree, summons flame and tempest and, in the midst of this royal game, in the midst of the heart of the world, is his heart. The universe, converted to unity, may now be experienced . . .

The marvellous is the image of our absolute liberty.

But a symbolic image. Stories are a compromise, on the one hand between our deepest tendencies and external (especially social) necessities, and on the other between these tendencies themselves. The dramas resulting from this composition of forces are expressed in a veiled way by means of symbols. We do not exhaust the story by following the vicissitudes of the tale and admiring the lands through which the hero has travelled. The passage through waters and grottoes, the life-giving blood, the gate of fire, the princess sleeping as if dead: so many symbolic themes that analytical psychology and ethnography have sought to explain.

If stories (by stories I mean those cultural expressions that are determined by the life of a people and not tales deliberately composed by an individual) express the collective marvellous, poems represent the individual marvellous. The story is crystallized in myth; the poem takes shape through metaphor. These two kinds of the marvellous interact (we find the same symbols in each) but are qualitatively different. Everyone within a given society can relate to the world created by the story. Poets create worlds that, while identical in essence, differ in their imagery and perspectives: the spell effected in society through the poem is generally less stable and of a less general scope. None the less, both stories and poems satisfy human desires but in the different spheres of social and individual dynamics.

In a divided society, the social marvellous is as oppressive as physical reality is, for instance, for some individuals. In a harmonized society the individual marvellous and the social marvellous, although not interchangeable, are reconciled in the effervescence of an exalted social life.

Those people who lag behind their history 'admire' (so they claim, but can they admire anything at all?) the marvellous of bygone ages. Those who are in tune with their times are moved (and it could hardly be otherwise) only by a certain marvellous of the present, by which I mean an active one, which constitutes the keynote of the age. There is a false as well as a true marvellous. The first is the *ready-made* or, more accurately, depleted marvellous, a sort of cultural waste product that societies and people expel by the very process of evolution.

The second is the *lived marvellous*, a moment that is unique and cannot be detached from an inspiring becoming. In the final analysis, the production of marvels is one with pure duration and the pure activity of the mind. (This definition is also valid for poetry, all poetry being marvellous.)

The conception of the marvellous, a simple abstract idea, should not be confused with the imagined marvellous which lives in the mind with the full force of its emotion and which is consequently inseparable from the human body which *actualizes* it in time and space. The gravest misunderstandings arise here from an abuse of language: don't tell me that you only admire the old Graeco-Roman trappings. I don't believe you: you don't know what it means to speak.

It goes without saying, given the psycho-physiology of this apparition, that the very fact of the marvellous appearing is crucial to the being to whom it appears, in other words to whom it is specific and, consequently, to whom only it has a value as a sign. The liberty it represents is the liberty of this being.

For the same reason it is clear that the marvellous appears only when it has to. In other words, it is always historically situated. The marvellous of the age of knights in armour is not the marvellous of the age of merchants. Indeed, the time of the former has passed and it no longer appears in *life* but only in the intellect as a stylized representation: it no longer has an impact on us. When it *exists*, the marvellous has to do with the future not the past and bears, through its very existence, the proof of its validity.

Dream is a natural function within man that ensures the advent of marvels. The marvellous is thereby part of the conditions of mankind's existence.

This explains why our wonderment contains the whole of our past life and its surge presents us with an ideal projection of a world of heroic and happy characters. This world could never take shape in order to offer its landscapes as a theatre for so many dramas. These dramas themselves and their characters could not emerge from their state of nonexistence if the exigencies of our becoming did not act within us. When we properly consider works of the imagination dynamically and dramatically, they signify at once (being sustained by desire) what we lack and what is needed to satisfy this lack. They announce our hopeful future. The marvellous, adequate to its creator, projects a light onto the instant of becoming that pierces the darkness to reveal the future path of deliverance. The story is a prophecy.

If the story at once satisfies and disappoints, it is because the deliverance it announces is not realized, and the plenitude it projects is not experienced. The land of marvels, like all imaginary things, is situated vertiginously between nothingness and being. Any encouragement can only be in the direction of reality. Mankind's task can only consist in trying to integrate the marvellous into real life in such a way as to reach some grandeur. So long as myth is unable to inscribe itself into every banality, human life will be nothing but a boring expedient, good for nothing, as they say, but killing time. No man worthy of the name can accept such a complacency.

### Note

1. Pierre Mabille's book *Le Miroir du merveilleux* makes a vital contribution to the scientific study of this question.

[published in *Tropiques*, no. 3 (October 1941)]

# SUZANNE CÉSAIRE

# *A Civilization's Discontent*

I F WE SEE a suffering and sensitive – at times mocking – being, which can be recognized as our collective self, appearing in our legends and stories, we would seek in vain the expression of this self in Martinique's ordinary literary products.

Why in the past have we been so little interested in speaking in a direct way about our ancestral anxiety?

The urgency of this cultural problem eludes only those who have decided to close their eyes in order to avoid having their artificial tranquillity upset: at any price, be it stupidity and death.

We sense that this disturbing age will see a ripened fruit burst forth, irresistibly invoked by solar ardour to scatter its creative energy to the winds. We sense the formidable and ineluctable pressure of destiny on this tranquil and sunlit earth as it stains the world red with blood in order to endow it with a fresh face tomorrow.

Let's question life on this island that is ours.

What do we find?

First, the geographical position of this plot of earth: it is tropical. These are the Tropics.

This is why an African population could adapt here. The imported blacks had to struggle against the terrible mortality rates at the start of slavery, against the hardest working conditions imaginable, against chronic undernourishment (something that remains a current reality). And yet it can hardly be denied that on Martiniquan soil the coloured race produces strong, resistant, supple men and women of natural elegance and great beauty.

But isn't it amazing that though this people, this authentically

Martiniquan people, has adapted to the earth in the course of centuries, it has only just started to produce authentic works of art? Why has a viable survival of original styles – which have blossomed so magnificently on African soil – not been revealed during the centuries? Where are the sculptures, the decorated fabrics, the paintings and the poetry? Let's leave it to imbeciles to blame race and the people's supposed instincts for laziness, theft and malice.

Let's speak seriously.

If this lack among blacks is not explained by the severity of the tropical climate that we have adapted to, and even less by some kind of inferiority, it is explained, believe me, by:

1. the appalling conditions of brutal transportation to a foreign land; – we have been too quick to forget the slave traders and the sufferings of our enslaved fathers. Here forgetting amounts to cowardice.

2. an obligatory submission, upon pain of flogging or death, to a system of 'civilization' and a 'style' that was even more alien to the new arrivals than the tropical earth;

3. finally, after the liberation of coloured people, a collective error about our true nature, an error born of an idea rooted in the depths of popular consciousness through centuries of suffering: 'Since the colonizers' superiority arises from a particular way of living, we will gain this strength only by mastering the technique of this "style" in our turn.'

Let's pause and gauge the significance of this massive mistake.

What, at root, intimately, immutably, is the Martiniquan, and how does he live?

In response to these questions we see an astonishing contradiction appear between his deepest being, desires, impulses and unconscious powers and the life he lives, with its necessities, urgent demands and heavy burdens. This is a phenomenon of decisive importance for the future of this land.

What is the Martiniquan?

He is the plant-man.

Like the plant, he abandons himself to the rhythm of universal life. He makes no effort to dominate nature. He is a poor farmer. Perhaps. I'm not saying that he makes the plants grow; I'm saying that he grows, that he lives like a plant. His indolence has a vegetal form. If you were to say not 'he's lazy', but, 'he vegetates', you would be doubly right. His favourite phrase is 'go with the flow'. Recognize that he allows himself to be carried along by life: docile, light, without insistence or revolt, but amicably and tenderly. Stubborn as only the plant knows how to be. Independent (an independence that is the autonomy of the plant). Abandoned to himself, to the seasons, to the moon, to the length or brevity of the day. Harvesting. And always and everywhere, in everything he does, the primacy of the plant, the trampled but tenacious plant lives, dead and yet reborn, the free plant, silent and proud.

Open your eyes – a child is born. To which god should it be entrusted? To the tree god, either the coconut or the banana, among whose roots the placenta will be interred.

Open your ears. A story from Martiniquan folklore: the grass growing on the grave is the living hair of the dead woman protesting against death. Always the same symbol: the plant. A vibrant sentiment of a living-dead community. In short, an *Ethiopian sentiment of life*.[1]

The Martiniquan is thus typically Ethiopian.[2] In the depths of his consciousness he is the plant-man and, in identifying himself with the plant, he desires to abandon himself to the rhythm of life.

Does this attitude explain his failure in the world?

No. The Martiniquan has failed because, not recognizing his true nature, he tries to live a life that is not his own. This is a massive phenomenon of collective self-deceit, of 'pseudomorphosis'. And the current state of civilization in the Caribbean shows us the consequences of this error.

Repression, suffering, sterility.

How and why is it that this people who yesterday were slaves should be subject to such a fatal misunderstanding? Through the most natural process of all: the play of the instinct of survival.

Let us remember that above all else the slave regime forbade *the assimilation of the black to the white*. Laws included one of 30 April 1764 forbidding blacks and mulattos from practising medicine, one of 9 May 1765 which banned them from becoming notary clerks, and the notorious law of 9 February 1779 which explicitly forbade blacks from wearing the same clothes as whites, while demanding respect and submission to 'all whites in general', and so on.

Again, let me cite the law of 3 January 1788, which forced free men of colour 'to obtain permits to work *other than on the land*'. We can see how the essential goal for coloured people became, from that moment, *assimilation*. And in consequence a disastrous confusion takes effect in their mind with extraordinary force: *liberation equals assimilation*.

The beginnings were auspicious. In 1848 the majority of free blacks, in a sudden explosion of the primitive self, rejected all regular work despite the threat of famine. But the blacks, tamed by economics, no longer slaves but salaried employees, submitted once more to the discipline of the hoe and the cutlass.

This was the period too in which the ancestral desire for abandon was definitively repressed.

It was replaced, especially among the mulatto middle class, by the alien desire for struggle.

This is where the drama lies that is apparent to all those who analyse the collective self of the Martiniquan people: its unconscious continues to be inhabited by the Ethiopian desire for abandon. But its conscious, and especially its preconscious, accepts the Hamitic desire for struggle. The rat race. Diplomas. Naked ambition. Struggle reduced to the bourgeoisie's level. Buffoon race. Vanity Fairs.

What is most serious is that the desire to imitate, which we have recently become vaguely conscious of (being a defence reaction against an oppressive society), has now passed into the ranks of the formidable secret forces of the unconscious.

No cultured Martiniquan would accept that he is only imitating, in so far as his contemporary situation appears to him natural, spontaneous and born from his rightful aspirations. And, in so doing, he would be sincere. He genuinely does not KNOW that he is imitating. *He is unaware* of his true nature, which no less does exist.

In the same way, the *hysteric* does not realize that he is *imitating* a sickness, but the doctor, who treats him and relieves his morbid symptoms, does know.

In the same way, analysis reveals to us that the effort of adaptation to an alien way of life that is required of the Martiniquan will not have been expended without creating a state of pseudo-civilization that can be described as *abnormal* and *teratical*.

The problem now is to determine whether the Ethiopian attitude we have uncovered as being the very essence of the perception of life among Martiniquans can be the point of departure for a viable (and so grandiose) cultural way of life.

It is inspiring to imagine these tropical lands being restored at last to their inner truth, the lasting and fertile accord of man and the land. Under the sign of the plant.

We are now called to recognize ourselves, and before us are splendours and hopes. Surrealism has given us back some of our possibilities. It is up to us to find the others. In its light.

Let it be clearly understood.

It is not at all a matter of a return to the past, of the resurrection of an African past that we have learned to understand and to respect. It is a matter, on the contrary, of the mobilization of all the combined vital forces on this land where race is the result of continual mingling. It is a matter of becoming conscious of the formidable mass of different energies that until now have been trapped within us. We must now use them in their plenitude, without deviation or falsification. Too bad for those who consider us dreamers.

The most disturbing reality is ours.

We will act.

This earth, our earth, can only be what we want it to be.

### Notes

1. See 'Leo Frobenius and the Problem of Civilizations' (pp. 82–7 of this volume).

2. Another argument could be drawn from architecture: the Martiniquan hut is the exact reproduction (in opposition to the conical roof in the form of a saddle) of the huts of Beni-Mai (domain of Congo Kassai) dominated by the 'Ethiopian' sentiment of life. See Frobenius, *History of Civilization*.

[published in *Tropiques*, no. 5 (April 1942)]

AIMÉ CÉSAIRE AND RENÉ MÉNIL

# An Introduction to
# Martiniquan Folklore

ONCE UPON A TIME . . .
Don't expect to find cosmogonies or metaphysics here. Nor even the expression of the great sentimental adventures that characterize mankind. Thought, like sentiment, is a luxury.

Once upon a time, a time of misfortune, a time of misery and shame, a black man was hitched to the black earth . . .

However you look at it, a whole population is hungry. There's not a tale in which – a vision of revelry and satiety – this obsession with empty bellies does not appear. Hearn pointed it out:

> Poor Yé! – you still live for me only too vividly outside of those strange folk-tales of eating and drinking which so cruelly reveal the long slave-hunger of your race. For I have seen you cutting cane on the mountain slopes above the clouds. I have seen you climbing from plantation to plantation with your cutlass in your hand . . . I have seen you ascending through serpent-swarming woods to some dead crater to find a cabbage-palm – and always hungry, always shiftless![1]

Whether we are talking about Yé, Nanie-Rosette, or the tale of Lady Kélément, the inspiration remains the same: poverty and hunger. There is always the same revenge of dream over reality. A magnificent revenge. A paradise of feastings is ours! And a Ti-Jean-l'oraison, or a St-Jean Bango owe their greatest glory to the victory of feasting. And even when the ideal (that ideal recognized by morality) is not eating, there remains at least the supreme and irresistible temptation, in its most engaging form, as the most perfidious of sins. You know it, Nanie-Rosette, prisoner of the rock watched over by the devil, well enough never to be able to resist the succulence of what is 'fierce'.

Eating and drinking, over and over the same dream is constantly repeated. Don't smile at such 'naïvety'. Under a form that initially seems childish, but in any case direct, it provides invaluable historical documentation. When we have finally logged all the archives, inspected all the records and unearthed all the abolitionists' papers, it will be to these tales that those who want to grasp the great misery of our slave fathers in all its eloquence and poignancy will turn.

And they also reveal the secret mechanism of the marvellous. When man is crushed by an iniquitous society and seeks vainly all around him for help then, discouraged and powerless, he projects his misery and revolt into a sky of promise and dynamite.[2]

After the cycle of hunger, the cycle of fear. The master and companion of slavery: the whip and denunciation. It is the age in which some adventurers, black as well as white, specialize in hunting down maroons, the age in which mastiffs prowl the ravines and mountains, in which denunciation assures freedom for the traitor. Which is to say the time of Fear, the great Fear and Universal Suspicion.

This is what accounts for the strange and characteristic mythology of the zombi. Everything is zombi. Be watchful, suspicious of everything. Their charming or reassuring forms? A snare! A trap! Beware the crab limping down the street, the rabbit making off in the night, the over-friendly and over-seductive woman: zombi, zombi, I tell you! Recognize that humanity and animality and the whole of nature is conspiring against you.

'Zombi,' writes Hearn, 'the word is perhaps full of mystery even for those who made it. . . . The *zombi* deludes under the appearance of a travelling companion, an old comrade – like the desert spirits of the Arabs, or even under the form of an animal.'[3]

Don't confuse it with the vulgar ghost that has become a zombi through an abuse of language. Equally, don't confuse it with the Haitian zombi, that docile and conscientious robot, that compliant living dead. The Martiniquan phenomenon is brutal in another way. You are afraid. You are suspicious. Of what? Of everything. Of evil affirming itself, like the evil that disguises itself. Beware of being; but at the same time beware of appearance . . .

*

A drum. Great voodoo laughter descends from the mornes. How many rebellions started like that over the centuries? What ephemeral victories! But also what defeats! What repressions! Hands cut off, bodies torn asunder, gibbets, that's what populates the byways of colonial history. And nothing of all that would have passed into folklore? You know the tale of Colibri. Colibri, against whom the Horse, the Ox, the Poisson-Armé and God himself unite. Colibri and his true friend, the drum!

> Pouesson-Armé charged on. After two thrusts it was all over.
> 'My last stand,' said Colibri, falling down dead.
> As quickly as he could, Pouesson-Armé seized a large cutlass that was lying there, cut off Colibri's head, and put it under the freestone in the courtyard of the house. Only then did he take the drum and carry it away. (L. Hearn, *Trois fois bel conte . . .*)

And now what remains? Hunger, fear, defeat. The great triangular itinerary and its monotonous ports of call. What remains? Colibri, brave Colibri is well and truly dead. His drum no longer beats the charge. He remains next to the mutilated Toad and the Tiger – a beast whose strength is forgotten – there remains. . . . Rabbit, the Rabbit who is weak, like Colibri, but also sly, cunning and knowing. . . . the unreliable one. The degeneracy of the race. And that's that. Individual solutions replace mass solutions. Crafty solutions replace enforced solutions.

What remains? Small-time rogues and con men who know how to get away with it. Henceforth humanity is divided into two groups: those who can and those who can't get by. An admirable result of two centuries of civilization!

Once upon a time a black man was hitched to the black earth.

### Notes

1. Editors' note: Lafcadio Hearn, *Two Years in the French Caribbean* (1890) New York: Harper & Brothers, p. 409.

2. a. 'The artful son of Yé reclaims abundance under the paternal roof. Cf. Hearn: 'Then the mother got ready a *calabou-crab*, a *tonton-banane*, a *matété cirique*, several calabashes of *couscayes*, two *régimes-figues* (bunches of small bananas), in short, a very fine dinner indeed, with a *chapione* of tafia to wash it all well down.'

b. Remember that it needed a law (of 18 March 1845), a regulation (of 5 June 1846), a ministerial circular (of 13 June 1846), a governor's decree (of October

1846) to ensure that the master owed his slave 6 pounds of cassava flour and $3\frac{1}{2}$ pounds of cod a week, an indication that generally they always received less than these modest proportions.

3. Editors' note: Hearn, p. 370.

[published in *Tropiques*, no. 4 (January 1942)]

# René Ménil

## Birth of Our Art

*The sphere of poetry is not outside the world, the impossible dream of a poet's mind; it aims to be precisely the opposite, the natural expression of the truth.*

Nietzsche

No matter how far mankind develops, the successive differences that constitute its evolution are always differences from itself, with itself, within itself. Whether it rises or falls its destiny can only ever be within itself. Every being is enclosed in its specificity. This is why human manifestations, acts, passions and dreams are inseparably attached to man. And so cultural expressions are the most durable and perfect of these manifestations. Mankind's culture is mankind itself in its social expressions: it is mankind that has reached a certain form through the natural path leading from power to action. At first it is social man's driving force that sustains it. When it has reached its completion, it does not fall from man like a fruit: it consists of mankind's very actions.

It is the role of the intellect, as creator of abstractions, to separate being from action and man from his expression. What these mirages of the fallacious realm of the Identical offer us are different cultural forms (technical, scientific, moral, artistic, etcetera) conceived as absolute entities separate from the human subject and requiring, for their fulfilment, that man emerges from himself. The worst misunderstandings are born from this illusion: convinced that cultural expression exists independently to himself, man spends most of the time pursuing the impossible task of discovery and realization outside of himself.

Sometimes he even seriously questions the choice of culture and the destiny that would best become him among the most attractive cultures and destinies stored in the warehouse of History and Ethnography.

We do not choose reality: it makes the choice. Culture (I do not mean the idea of culture, an innocent intellectual conception, but real culture, which is comprised of a living set of determined conditions – land, race, economic forms, etcetera – which is mitigated by all the contingencies of everyday life and concretely experienced by the human individual) is *necessary*, meaning that it eludes the extravagances of those people who actually live it. It is, for the same reason, *untransmissable*. It is not detachable, except in the form of an abstraction or an idea, being only a way of living in a given society. *It cannot even be imitated* because, compared to life, imitation is an absurdity. To imitate is to want to be other. Nature never allows this to occur. Any realization attributed to an imitation of the other is in fact the result of an imitation of the self. Every act presupposes power and a development of power. The imitating subject does not derive this indispensable power from what it imitates but from itself. You may think you are imitating, but what you are really doing is developing your own possibilities. Every society, at any given moment, only has one possible culture which is whatever can free it through realizing the promises comprised in its existence and development. Everything else is alien to it, as least within what concerns reality. It can attain the enchantment of the culture's Ideas, but this is merely a childish game. To adopt an idea does not, by that fact alone, bring possession of whatever the idea is about.

When we turn our backs on conceptual appearance, the inseparability of cultural expression and the human Person[1] appears as the effect of a necessity of nature. In the domain of art, this inseparability assumes a particular significance because art is personal in a total sense. Not only does it express the social Person, as do other cultural forms, but this social expression is only achieved within the artist through the cult of individual difference. In other words, social expression in the work of art is in direct proportion to the individual's expression within the work. The work becomes so much more powerful in proportion to how much of himself the artist has put into it. Science, being merely *conception*, aims directly at generalities and constructs itself in a way that is external to the vicissitudes of the scientist's life. Art tries to effect the penetration and apprehension of the real: its point of departure is in impressions and images formed in our sensory contact with the world and which constitute a life unique to us.

But man is merely the world in the sphere of self-consciousness and the artist, by cultivating his difference, does not isolate himself but on the contrary reaches out in a real way to people and things in order to express them validly. The tree has access to the world not through the external but through its inner being: through its roots. In man, the communicating paths to the world also necessarily pass through the internal: through the human body, the only bridge linking him to the world. 'Our only access to the world is through ourselves.' All other paths lead to abstract Appearance, to transcendental illusion or pretence. And we penetrate the reality of people and things in proportion to how profoundly we penetrate ourselves. The depths and complexities of the world are simply external projections of our own depths and complexities. The work of art cannot exist without sensory contact with the world – contact which is possible only as, through the passage of man into himself, *expression of the whole is indivisibly attached to expression of the self.*

There is a means of access to realities outside which everything is lacking. Whoever loses consciousness of the self knows nothing. When we take nature as guide, we are inevitably our own primal reality. Beyond the ego and through the ego, as we gradually approach the universe without losing ground – in fact whilst pushing our true roots ever deeper – we find those realities (men, monuments, trees, rocks) crowding in and moving ever closer to us – realities which we will call, as an extrinsic and convenient designation and according to their distance from us, village, regional, social, etc. The characteristics, no matter whether lowly or exalted, that form individual life are not obstacles to universal expression: they are moments leading to it. All progress, in life and in its expression, supposes a simultaneous surpassing and conservation of the moments that define existence previous to its becoming.

It is perhaps the advocates of classicism who have created the greatest confusion here: generally they have not realized that the art they envision can do no more than achieve 'the completely apt unity of content and form'.[2] Classical art is the art that attains its highest point of perfection no matter how much content and form are organically integrated. If we are to believe classical artists, artistic expression is achieved by the suppression of the particularities of individual existence, by constant distrust of the ego, its sensibility and imagination. But art is art for irresistible reasons. It is an expression of the universal through individual expression, rooted in his (let's say village) existence. And universality is attained not through suppression of the

artist's most individual internal characteristics, but through expression
of that individuality in a suitable language. Language is the form of the
universal. The artist does not require great exertion to express the
world: he merely has to come to terms with himself in order to express
everything, since he is, after all, coextensible with the world in his
poetic attitude.[3]

*The cult of difference and the cult of communion are equated in the work
of art to express the human person.*

Who is speaking here? The Martiniquan people, who live in the Tropics,
between the two Americas, and share the fortune of its imperial culture
with France, and who today are wondering about their destiny at a
time when Western civilization is revolutionizing itself in order to
retrieve the life that had surpassed it. A people with three centuries of
recitation lessons behind them and who have always arrived empty-
handed at the courts of culture, never having created anything. We
have READ the culture of others. The most dim-witted among us consider culture to be the texts they learned at school and believe that it is
something that occurs through memory. The mechanical recitation of
past times, the infantile craze for collecting images from Epinal, for
reciting words that others have invented, can only have made the best of
us political sorcerers, players to the gallery, prophesying with less conviction and beauty than Australian rain-makers. Culture is elsewhere.
So is life, moreover. The wind is turning . . .

And then there is the climate, the habitat and the extraordinary
internal commingling of our collectivity and the particular characteristics of our genesis and the singular life we lead and which sets us the
lead, everything that creates fears and hopes, desires and passions, acts
and dreams, sadnesses and joys within us that are unique in the world.
In the imperial concert of a common culture, we have our own special
tone to which we have not previously been able to give voice. We alone
can express the qualities that make us unique. If we do not want to be
mere spectators of the human adventure, if we believe that we must
offer ourselves if we are to participate in a genuine humanity, if we are
convinced that here understanding means nothing and that what matters is to create, we know what tasks fall to us and what path leads to
their realization.

All our cultural manifestations in the domain of art have until now
been nothing but pastiches. But imitation in this domain, as in anything else, can lead to nothing of value because 'in imitation quality

flees'. Consequently, our necessarily sterile imitation has resulted only in worthless 'works'. Worthless because they are not viable, being created against nature. They are forms without content, worthless because they are not historically valid: they are not integrated into the real evolution of art but are an adjunct to it; useless reflections of it. The first crucial task is to distinguish the sphere of real art from the sphere of erudite recitation. Erudition is abstract evocation. Living art or poetry is creation. To create, it is necessary to engage not with the haze of conceptual life, but with the course of the real life of the individual and the collectivity. You must play your hand and take risks in the *actual* course of events: this is the condition upon which nature operates within us and which gives the work its substance. When man creates, it is nature that is creating through him. Have we not reached a point when we should abandon books and close our eyes for a moment, to accept ourselves as we are (whether we be great or small – for reasons that are necessary – what does it matter!) and try to express ourselves by other means than the mute arts of naïve dance and street pantomime? If we express ourselves in our entirety and if we do so properly, we will have expressed, through natural necessity, more than ourselves.

Baudelaire announced: 'Absolute candour is a means of originality.'

The poet's candour is poetry. As Martiniquans we have not yet reached the golden age of Poetry. We are at the age of criticism and our candour today will take the form of a critique of our art. For the past decade some of us, as we considered the evolution of art in civilized countries, have categorically opposed everything that has been done in the French Caribbean founded in the desire for integration with the real art of the age. Can we honestly take our place in art with nothing in our hands but the borrowed graces of a borrowed poetry? Do we have to have the effrontery to put forward copies whose models denounce us? It's time for the shadows to return to the shadows so that finally what exists will be what is worthy of existing. We can already conceive the means that will allow us, without shame, to take our place with others at the rendezvous of culture, raising us to the very peak of our development. We can foresee the future works that will owe their validity to a unique originality. We can glimpse what our poems will be like once we have cast aside the shackles of our repressed imagination. We are already studying the means for their realization. But this does not yet constitute art; it is only reflection on art. The form of our art has taken shape, not yet its content. Our task is to prepare for the Poet's arrival: the one who will fulfil our conception. We are taking the path that leads from the critique of art to art itself.

The present moment comprises a duality which exists not simply in the minds of those who can have a clear vision of our historical development but in this development itself. It is the resolution of this duality that will give birth to the art we anticipate. The first condition of this duality is the existence in the Caribbean of that condemned art that may be called the *abstract art of pastiche*. Abstraction is the most impoverished phase of reality. In the order of things, the seed is both the plant's most abstract and most impoverished phase. The seed contains the plant but in a state of mere virtuality. Our abstract art contains promises which, given our cultural evolution, have not been kept and cannot be kept. In this art, *expression is an expression without content*, at least without any valid content; it is devoid of the genuine images, genuine desires, and genuine aspirations of the person who is supposed to be expressing himself. It is word play. Our 'poets' are still innocently playing with language.[4] None of the phases of an evolution is wasted: their scholastic exercises in prosody prepare the way for a more flexible language for future poets. The docility of the language will allow the immediate integration of a genuine content into this prepared form. Then we might achieve 'the completely apt unity of content and form' that constitutes true art. The abstract quality of 'Martiniquan art' betrays its inadequacy. The dynamics of evolution literally carry this form without substance towards its future content. This isolated content is the second condition of the present duality. It is there, in the lives of each of us, as the perceptible and emotive vision of the world. No being of flesh and blood can elude the vision that is absolute poetry. Absolute poetry means poetry *for itself* and not *for us*. This is why our expression has until now been alienated in some way: as abstract, vain, fleeting or mad words; and with content separated: this is speechlessness. Until now this has been so marked that those who have spoken have not expressed themselves, and those who had something to say were unable to say it.

A total conversion of our aesthetic attitude is required to enable us to pass from the formal conception of our art to art itself. It is not a question of improving a doomed art: to improve a fault is to make it worse. It is otherness that is needed, not a modification of the same. It must effect a qualitative change within us: this is what we announce.

Real human problems are not resolved through intellectual operations but through those of life. We fully understand the direction of our future evolution and yet nothing has happened. We expect a future art to emerge from real life. It is not the idea of the seed, but the seed itself that creates the young plant; and the plant germinates not through logic but through its sap. Our ideas emerge from this world, which is the only one: the very existence within us of the idea of a future art signifies that this art has already been sown within us. But we must wait for the idea to acquire flesh or rather, for this descent is against nature, life itself must flourish into the art that this idea imagines. The Martiniquan poet will make his entrance when his life has been transformed into a vital practice and when, consequently, as he dances in natural step with the world, he attains by himself the greatest possible Expression, which means the greatest liberty.

'One is an artist on condition that one feels as content, as the "thing itself", what non-artists call the form. This fact means that one belongs to an *overturned* world; because now all content appears to us as purely formal, including our lives.'[5]

The existence of the poet will coincide with our existence for ourselves as approximate people.

### Notes

1. The reader himself will have understood that it is only the question of the social person or society that can here be considered specific. It is not a matter of an individual creating a culture.

2. Baudelaire, *Fusées*, in *Oeuvres complètes* (1961) Paris: Gallimard.

3. We are the cosmos to the extent to which we have understood or dreamed it (Nietzsche).

4. Those who strive to animate the corpse of an obviously dead poetry can be recognized without being named, since this note is not intended to be polemical. The only exception I would make to this is L. Damas (see his collection of poems *Pigments*).

5. Nietzsche.

[published in *Tropiques*, no. 1 (April 1941); reprinted in *Tracées*]

# René Ménil

## Orientation of Poetry

*All poetry must be legendary and enchanted*

Novalis

T HE POINT AT which reality might seem pure to us, without needing recourse to illusion merely in order to *exist*, is, when all is said and done, just theoretical: it cannot be humanly experienced. Already, when the dreadful nudity of nature ventures to make itself known to us (perhaps in a lightning flash), we tragically feel the lassitude and precariousness of life's instincts. It is a time of despondency and the desire for death. Man cannot and does not survive in this cruel zone. This means that all lived reality is already so destitute that it reveals itself transfigured, veiled or enriched in proportion to the strength of our capacity for passion and dream. As we live we no less burden the world with the weight of our illusions. We question our dreams, listen to their voices and walk in their light. For us it is never anything but a matter of comprehending what our dreams whisper to us about journeys and rest, about conquests and games, about pursuing what their radiance illuminates in us of roads, castles and landscapes. The most clearly defined human task is to construct of ourselves the desired statue, to shape the world in the likeness of images of waking and sleeping, and to carve out our future as far ahead of us as the distant place from which our dreams return to us.

Nevertheless, let's conceive, theoretically, of the vision of reality derived from itself and itself alone and, intensely calling upon the affection of illusion to veil it, making it possible for us to grasp, against reality, the infinity of an *other* world in its full extent and necessity. In fact it is here that, faced with the emptiness and misery that become the essential features of things when brought down to themselves, a vertigo seizes holds of us that causes us to fall slowly into ourselves with wings outstretched, into a human domain created for our joy, our consolation and our audacity. Here there are other skies, other trees, other lives which make real skies, real trees and real lives bearable and sometimes even exciting. An imaginary voyage; a happy voyage.

The mind is so made that, fundamentally propelled by infinite movement, it opens within itself innumerable sights, courses and gulfs and that these sights, courses and gulfs, and their continual sublation, are not accidental but intrinsic to it. And this inherent hunger of the mind, without which the mind would revert to the humility of things, is something that brings man face to face with the reality already moulded – remotely, it's true – in the image of his dreams, and that always makes him think *beyond* and even conceive of other dreams beyond his own dreams. To think what one thinks, to believe what one believes, to imagine what one imagines and nothing else is really neither to think, nor to believe, nor to imagine. It is a listless thought, an anaesthetized thought. All living thought dynamically conceals the infinite zone of gymnastic possibilities and limitless hopes within itself, and this is the price it pays for life. The needs of the mind are thus *total*, even though, through lack of courage, we do not normally dare to gauge their immensity, even though we normally take them as they come, at the point where, through laziness, we normally accept that they stupidly coincide with what exists, as we are unable to measure up to their stature. This is why, as impoverished, insufficient and beggarly as reality appears in the eyes of the mind, the latter is pathetically forced, in order to tolerate reality, to compensate for the poverty, insufficiency and mendacity of things by the compensatory cascade of a sumptuous reverie.

This is how poetry is born. Poetry that is necessary.

I imagine that you have, like me, encountered the inevitable labourer in a field of bones under a sky now aflame who, desperately solitary and poor, was playing, against all expectation, at being a labourer. With great care, you will recall, he moved his cracked feet desperate for water over a porous and ravenous earth. The poverty of man and nature was glaring. The ground pathetically begged for a tribute from the rivulet, the foliage or, at least, for some shade. As for the man's gestures, they pathetically underlined the immense emptiness of rural riches. The tragedy of his performance was that he could not claim to be a sower in whom the profound hope of the future harvest inevitably lay. And like me you will have felt irritation – already long-felt at the implacability of good weather – growing immeasurably in your heart. So ridiculous and precarious as the existence of this man was – like an insect over a nature extensively eroded with emptiness – so marvellous was the lack of man and nature within themselves that, like me, you could not for long have tolerated the overwhelming vision. The void you read in nature and that gave rhythm to the breath of your oppression promptly demanded a necessary compensation in your mind. Soon, before your very eyes, silent streams scaled the parched clods of earth, and the labourer's dejected and intolerably dry feet vanished under a glorious life-promising mud. The man's stony face was surrounded with an extraordinary freshness and even by aerial streams. On his brow, steaming with the sun's warmth, gathered drops of imminent rain . . .

Like me, you will have smiled at your divinity.

It is within the very heart of reality that the marvellous door opens, and it will open out onto what is beyond this reality. 'The realm of the poet is formed within the place where phenomena emerge.'[1] Turning his back on the world, without ever ceasing to be reliant upon it (since he lives), the poet tries to grasp it as he seizes its imaginary complement. This imaginary complement is reality itself. Illusion is within man, as man is within nature and illusion is within the nature of things. Everything that, from far and near, touches living man, things, ideas and images must, for the same reason, be stamped with reality. Real blood courses through the veins of our dreams, no matter how crazy they may seem. Nothing is more real than the imaginary considered as the imaginary.[2] Reality and the imaginary are opposed not in the same way as being and nothingness, but as being and becoming. The imaginary is what, still abstract, tends to become real or, rather, more real. And it becomes so when we have the strength of our desires. In fact, the path that opens up before man in poetic activity, no matter how far it leads (and it does lead a long way) cannot go beyond the limits of being. Have no fear, no matter how far you travel along this dazzling track, you will never fall into the other side of life. On the motionless and dreamlike voyage, we walk in the heart of the world and it is life that bears our imaginary steps.

If poetic activity is not an escape from reality, it can only be an unlimited enlargement of it, an attempt to grasp it in its totality, an attempt to attain a limitless vision of the universe.

And this is what makes poetic bearing so marvellous. Finally overcoming the narrow zone of being we call reality (a system of perception), the poet gains, within and beyond this fragment of the whole, possession and understanding of absolute reality (a system of perception and imagination).

Thereby we rediscover a realm that our laziness and lack of faith in the reality of the mind degrades and diminishes and which, driven by our desperate determination, we usually exert control over, when it seems that we can – in joy and truth – attain an essential simplicity and the fundamental truths of early youth, the first genesis, those wild hopes that are the only hopes, and to infinite confidence. What is called present-day life realizes that it is life, and man realizes that everything is promised, owed and given to him, if he responds to the needs of the mind.

When the poet belittles himself and, at the end of this belittling which contracts his vision, falls into prosaic reality, that cramped location of utilitarian action, he grasps the minimum of the reality of himself and the world that is humanly tolerable. When we let go of this impoverished reality from which an unaffected life is constructed, we plunge into death. The limitless margin of reality into which it is our duty to venture and which is revealed by poetry allows us to grasp both the stature of the poet and the meaning of his activity. The whole of infinity is to be reconciled. But all the poet's audacity, as he aims at the unlimited conquest of the real, can only be a leap into the imaginary. The other leap, at the scale of things and towards these things themselves, merely consists in banging your head against a brick wall or stepping off the tightrope to make a death leap to the ground.

Let there be no misunderstanding: reality perceived and experienced is here a point of departure not of arrival. For the poet everything is a springboard. The beach stupidly comprised of sand – a springboard; the forest and its obvious wood – a springboard; the inevitable sky – a springboard; the sky, the forest, the beach . . . The poet will depart and as he does so he pronounces words of peaceful conquest:

> *The coloured leaves in the nocturnal trees*
> *And the green and blue lianas join the sky to the trees*
> *The wind's broad face . . .*[3]

To rise to the world's scale in an immense vision and bring back the regions contacted, as the diver does pearls: this is the poet's task.

The poem maintains a toehold in daily reality (the poet lives, don't forget) but it glows suffused with a concealed fire, conquered against reality, in the imaginary, and delivers to man an absolute reality, a sur-reality if you like, in which in primitive unity, real and imaginary are animated with the same life's breath.[4]

Not only is the realist endeavour in art a mistake but, reassuringly, it reveals the impossibility of realist art. It represents an error of aes-thetic conception that inspires a research at the end of which, in the better examples, one finds the copy of exactly that reality from which we expect art to cure us. The fatal contradiction that undermines realist art is that the more it approaches perfection, the more exactly it represents reality, the more it approaches its own negation since the limit of its success would foolishly coincide with a reality that is anti-poetic. What results from this vain quest are hideous paintings which are aptly called 'still-lives' (guaranteed in true likeness, unfor-tunately); music that more than anything values the imitation of noises and natural sounds; novels that passionately aim to offer the illusion 'that it's true'; even poems that gravely teach us about reality and life; all those things once highly appreciated in the best circles of stupidity and 'good taste'.[5] Fortunately, when art sinks to such a level of degradation, it cannot survive as it is, but escapes its own nature by transforming itself into recipes: say for cookery, when the painter paints apples he wants to appear appetizing; for horticul-ture, when the 'poet' describes carnations; or by transforming itself into historical sketches or moral precepts in edifying poems, etcetera, in short into an uncertain technique or a debased science. All that remains to be done is to return the woodcutter–poet who describes the forest to the trees so that he can cut or prune them. All's well that ends well.

The satisfaction generated in a work through its resemblance to reality is not inherent to poetry. Its only concern is successful technique. If a poetic element slips in, it is determined by the minimal and involuntary transfiguration the artist has unknowingly performed on reality or by the weight of reverie with which the spectator, through his emotional involvement, entrusts the descriptive work.

The poem being 'ideal and prophetic',[6] its resemblance to the world is that of the tale of wonders.
    Such are the dramatic affinities and correspondences of contraries.

All the world's springs are to be found within the head of the traveller lost in the burning desert.

It must be understood that the description of things in poetry clouds vision and prevents the infinite transport and magnitude of the song. Mallarmé, the prince of poetry, made us aware that ideality, without which the poem does not exist, only erupts on condition that the materiality of facts is erased. Poetry is the art of suggestion and transposition, 'so that the pure notion emanates without being hampered by an immediate and concrete reminder'.

Poetry being a commentary on things and not their presentation, it follows that the poetic power of the mind is measured by the extension and nature of the margin formed at the edge of the world. The further the mind's activity advances towards conquest of the imagination (which I insist is not imaginary), the greater its poetic value.

But nothing can hold back the mind once it is embarked upon this course except its accidental and extrinsic characteristics of laziness, timidity, human respect or stupidity. Once they have been traced out by a momentary pause of the mind, the frontiers can be surpassed indefinitely by means of the 'intensification of the mind's irritability' (Max Ernst). A perceived or imagined object can, at will, be poetically involved (beyond its rigid and uniquely utilitarian significance or, in other words, beyond its usage) in a number of relations determined only by the mind's imaginative capacity. When Eluard affirms

*By way of wings the silence has frozen plains*

he reveals a relationship of striking identification (wings – frozen plains) which is nevertheless true (more than true, one could say) once discovered. The proliferation of these poetic discoveries or metaphors which are discoveries of the real (if the reality of the mind is taken seriously) depends only on the poet's daring. This daring can fortunately be borne along on the groundswell of psychic automatism which, allowed its natural movement, necessarily leads the mind to encounter its own virtualities which, once attained, are, by that very fact, realized.

These visions conquered despite the mind's laziness lead into the unknown to a greater or lesser extent. In fact, poetic images sometimes linger at the level of things and tyrannically bind the mind to them, while at other times on the contrary they blossom dazzlingly, like fabulous flowers, upon unsuspected horizons and illuminate a land never before seen. The value of images lies in their power of surprise, disorientation, and fresh learning. This fundamental truth has been established once and for all in modern aesthetics by Pierre Reverdy:

> The image is a creation of the Mind.
>
> It cannot be born of a comparison but from a bringing together of two more or less distant realities.
>
> The more the relationship between two conjoined realities remains both distant and pertinent, the stronger the image will be – and the greater its emotional and poetic power.

A special light streams from the poetic image[7] which man, coarse as he may be, finds it hard to resist. So long as it lasts, the drama of the mind enjoys confounding common sense which is, in fact, merely what the useful means. Released for a moment from the dictatorship of things, man can conceive of an ideal of life and truth that finally ceases to be ridiculous. Then is the time of the mind's liberty.

### Notes

1. Roland de Renéville in *L'Expérience poétique* (1938) Paris: Gallimard.

2. Hegel: 'Nothing is more true than appearance considered as appearance.'

3. Paul Eluard, *Capitale de la douleur* (1926) Paris: Gallimard.

4. On this subject see André Breton's 'Manifesto of Surrealism', in his *Oeuvres complètes*, vol. 1 (1988) Paris: Gallimard.

5. Photography, sound recordings and films that break all records for faithful imitation have fortunately made such works impossible by making their nonsense and uselessness blindingly obvious. Let's leave taking the trouble to imitate and play with things to things themselves.

6. Novalis.

7. Breton, 'Manifesto of Surrealism'.

[published in *Tropiques*, no. 2 (July 1941); reprinted in *Tracées*]

AIMÉ CÉSAIRE

# Calling the Magician:
# A Few Words for a Caribbean
# Civilization

### 1

FROM ALL OUR machines put together, from all our roads charted in miles, from all our accumulated tonnage, from all our arrayed aeroplanes, from our regulations, from our conditioning, not the slightest feeling could emerge. That is of another order, and real, and infinitely more exalted.

From all your manufactured thoughts, from all your graded concepts, from all your concerted measures, not the slightest *frisson* of genuine civilization could result. That is of another order, infinitely more exalted and sur-rational.

### 2

I cannot stop admiring the great Caribbean silence, our insolent wealth, our cynical poverty.

### 3

You have encircled the globe. You have yet to embrace it. Warmly.

### 4

True civilizations are poetic shocks: the shock of the stars, of the sun, the plant, the animal, the shock of the round globe, of the rain, of the light, of numbers, the shock of life, the shock of death.

Since the sun temple, since the mask, since the Indian, since the African man, too much distance has been calculated here, has been granted here, between things and ourselves.

## 5

The true manifestation of civilization is myth.

Social organization, religion, partnerships, philosophies, morals, architecture and sculpture are the representations and expressions of myth.

## 6

Civilization is dying all around the world because myths are dead or dying or being born.

We must wait for the powdery frost of outdated or emaciated myths to blow apart. We are awaiting the debacle.

## 7

. . . And we shall be fulfilled.

## 8

In the current state of things, the only avowed refuge of the mythic spirit is poetry.

And poetry is an insurrection against society because it is a devotion to abandoned or exiled or obliterated myth.

## 9

Civilization is not built by means of schools, clinics and statistical calculations.

Only the poetic spirit corrodes and builds, erases and invigorates.

## 10

The Caribbean has no civilization because the Caribbean shuns poetry. Scandalously.

We have lost the meaning of the symbol. The literal has devoured our world. Scandalously.

## 11

Civilization is a generalized participation in essence.
Civilization is a wondrous generalized communion.
We are at its mass stage. And the essence of facts, like that of the real, escapes us, initiated as we are to application alone: crude application.
Only the poetic spirit links and reunites.

## 12

The most vital thing is to re-establish a personal, fresh, compelling, magical contact with things.
The revolution will be social and poetic or will not be.

## 13

I don't hide the fact that I expect everything from a new barbarism.

## 14

True civilization is in the realm of obsession.
Civilization is an absurd idea which, felt and lived in its entirety, by that very fact and by that fact alone, becomes true.
I preach obsession.
The true ideal: the 'possessed' woman.

## 15

To resituate joy and pain, acceptance and creation in the cosmos.

## 16

Civilization is born of individual sincerity, individual daring, from that part of individual disorder that everyone carries within him and that he owes it to himself to expand and communicate and that gradually takes over like irresistible tall flames.

Keep your distance, wet blankets.
Give us back our power of wonderment.

## 17

I'm calling upon the magician.

## 18

Civilization is neither a policeman nor a mechanic. Its foundation is neither order as order, nor work as work.

I admire the perspicacity of poets: true poets. Baudelaire celebrating the useless and the dandy. Mallarmé pouring scorn on bread. Rimbaud spewing on the 'centuries of hands'.

And Breton announcing:

'Professions are withering away.'

The true poet does not preach work. He preaches availability.

To be better able to reach the heart of things.

I demand the right to indolence.

## 19

A new attitude towards the object. After the exploitative nonsense that is our bourgeois, comfortable attitude, it is healthy and profoundly important that André Breton restores liberating, catalysing and *dangerous* power to the object, that he gives back the profaned object its dignity of mystery and its radiant force, that, when all's said and done, he makes of it again what it should never have ceased to be: the *Great Intercessor*.

Once generalized, this attitude will lead us to the great mad sweep of renewal.

## 20

I'm calling upon the Enraged.

[published in *Haiti-Journal* (20 May 1944)]

# Suzanne Césaire

# *1943: Surrealism and Us*

*The river of grass snakes I call my veins*
*The river of battlements I call my blood*
*The river of assegais men call my face*
*The river on alert around the world*
*will strike the Artesian rock with a hundred monsoon stars*
*Liberty my only pirate water of the new year my only thirst*
*Love my only sampan*
*We shall run our fingers of calabash and laughter*
*Between the Sleeping Beauty's icy teeth.*

Aimé Césaire, 'Batouque'

M ANY BELIEVE SURREALISM dead. They have said as much. Pure infantilism: its activity today extends throughout the world and surrealism remains bolder and more tenacious than ever. André Breton can proudly look back over the inter-war period and affirm that the means of expression he created more than twenty years ago has revealed an increasingly vast and immense 'beyond'.

If the entire world is struck by the radiance of French poetry at the moment when the most terrible disaster in its history has descended upon France, it is partly because the great voice of André Breton has not been silenced; it is because voices that would not be what they are (in tone and resonance) without surrealism resound everywhere: in New York, in Brazil, in Mexico, in Argentina, in Cuba, in Canada, in Algiers. In reality, today as twenty years ago, surrealism can claim the glory of being at the cusp of life's bow, stretched to breaking point.

Let's speak, then, of surrealism's living presence: young, ardent and revolutionary. In 1943, surrealism certainly remains what it has always been: an activity whose aim is to explore and express systematically the forbidden zones of the human mind in order to neutralize them; it is an activity that seeks desperately to offer man the means to reduce those old antinomies that are the 'real alembics of suffering'; the only force which allows us to regain 'that unique, original faculty, of which the primitive and the child retain a trace, that lifts the curse of an impassable barrier between internal and external worlds'. But surrealism has evolved: the very sign of its vitality. It would be more accurate to say it has blossomed. When Breton created surrealism, the most urgent task was to liberate the mind from the shackles of absurd logic and so-called reason.

But in 1943, when liberty itself is threatened throughout the world, surrealism (which has not ceased for a moment to remain resolutely in the service of the greatest emancipation of mankind) can be summed up with a single magic word: liberty.

'The surrealist cause, in art as in life, is the cause of liberty itself. Today more than ever, abstractly to make claims of liberty, or to celebrate it in conventional terms, is to serve it badly. To illuminate the world, liberty must incarnate itself and to do so needs to reflect and re-create itself ceaselessly in the word.'

That's what Breton said. The demand for liberty. The need for complete purity: this is Breton's Saint-Just aspect, which explains his refusals that have been harshly condemned by those in league with compromise.

To those who periodically ask why splits have occurred in the heart of the surrealist movement, why sudden exclusions have been proclaimed, I believe I am able to reply in all honesty that those eliminating themselves from it on the way are those who had – in a more or less manifest way – forfeited the claim to liberty, liberty being revered in surrealism in its pure state, in other words extolled in all its forms. Of course there are many ways of forfeiting it – as far as I am concerned, one example is to return, as certain former surrealists have, to fixed forms of poetry when it has been shown, especially in the French language (and the exceptional radiance of French poetry since romanticism allows us to generalize in this way) that the quality of lyrical expression has benefited most of all from the will to be released from decrepit rules: Rimbaud, Lautréamont, the Mallarmé of 'Coup de dès', the more important symbolists (Maeterlinck, Saint-Pol-Roux), the Apollinaire of the 'conversation-poems'. The same thing is just as true for painting in the same period. Instead of the preceding names it would be enough to insert those of Van Gogh, Seurat, Rousseau, Matisse, Picasso and Duchamp. You also prove to have forfeited the right to liberty once and for all if you reject personal expression (always dangerous for that reason) outside the strict framework within which a 'party' (even a party that you consider to represent liberty) wants to confine you (a loss of a sense of uniqueness). You are also placed in the same position when you believe you are always so in control that you can compromise yourself with anyone you like with impunity (a loss of the feeling of dependence). What gives liberty the right to be jealous is both its wildly desirable and entirely fragile quality.

This is liberty's intransigence, which is moreover the very condition of its fertility. And we see Breton, at the end of his most moving research, unhesitatingly commit himself to the immense uncharted expanses that surrealism has revealed to human audacity. What does Breton demand of the most prescient minds of the age? Nothing less than the courage to embark on an adventure when one cannot yet know whether or not it will be fatal but in which one can hope (and this is the essential thing) for total conquest of the mind.

> In an age like the one in which we live there is justification, so long as their aim is to defy all conventional thinking (whose bankruptcy is only too evident), for all those departures on journeys in the manner of Bergerac or Gulliver. And, after certain detours, this journey upon which I am today inviting you to embark does not preclude the possibility of arriving somewhere more reasonable than what we are leaving behind.

Surrealism is living, intensely and magnificently, having found and perfected such an efficacious method of knowledge. There is a dynamism in surrealism. And this sense of movement has always kept it in the vanguard, ever aware of the agitation of the times of an age that is 'the curse of balance'.

'If the impatient gravediggers will allow me,' Breton writes, 'I think I have a greater claim than they to ponder the significance of surrealism's final hour: a more emancipatory movement would emerge from it. Moreover, the dynamic force to which I and my best friends continue to respond above everything would make it a point of honour for us immediately to rally to any such movement.'

Such is surrealist activity, a total activity, which alone is able to free man by revealing his unconscious and among those that will contribute to people's liberation by illuminating the blind myths that have brought humanity to this point.

And now a return to ourselves.

We know our situation here in Martinique. Our human task is dizzily revealed to us by the arrow of history: a society tarnished in its very origins by crime and maintained today through injustice and hypocrisy, made to fear its development by an uneasy conscience, must – morally, historically and necessarily – vanish. And from among the powerful machines of war, the bombs and explosives, the modern world places at our disposal, our audacity chooses surrealism which currently offers it the best chance of success.

One result is already secured. Not for a moment during the hard years of Vichy domination did the image of freedom completely fade here, and surrealism was responsible for that. We are glad to have maintained this image of freedom under the noses of those who believed they had erased it forever. Their blindness was the result of their ignorance and they didn't see its insolent and aggressive laughter in our pages. When they did realize it, they became faint-hearted, scared and ashamed.

And so, far from contradicting, reducing or diverting our revolutionary attitude to life, surrealism gives it a focus. It nourishes an impatient force within us, ceaselessly maintaining the vast army of negations.

And I'm also considering tomorrow.

Millions of black hands will thrust their terror into the raging skies of world war. Delivered from a long slumber, the most disadvantaged of all peoples will rise up across plains of ashes.

Our surrealism will then deliver it the bread of its depths. Finally those sordid contemporary antinomies of black/white, European/African, civilized/savage will be transcended. The magical power of the mahoulis will be recovered, drawn forth from living sources. Colonial stupidity will be purified in the blue welding flame. Our value as metal, our cutting edge of steel, our amazing communions will be rediscovered.

Surrealism – the tightrope of our hope.

[published in *Tropiques*, nos 8–9 (October 1943)]

RENÉ MÉNIL

# The Situation of Poetry
# in the Caribbean

EVERY RENAISSANCE PUTS the old quarrel of substance and form back on the agenda. Every renaissance results, on the one hand, from a renewal of the substance of human realities that have become outmoded: ideas, feelings and acts. But, on the other hand, life so re-created must tend towards a new form and expression. Most people in a society in which such a transformation takes effect, nostalgically attached (as they unfailingly are) to the old style of life, will bad-temperedly debate the problem of the validity of the new life as well as its new expression.

It was thus predictable that the crisis of consciousness that, at this very moment, is in the process of upsetting Caribbean mentality – a crisis determined by historical evolution but also in part by how much consciousness we have assumed of its necessity and meaning – it was, as I say, predictable that, at a certain stage of its development, this crisis would lead of itself to the traditional quarrel. The new conception of life that, through our efforts, currently haunts the Caribbean community with the authority and seduction of a myth, already constitutes the historic originality of our renaissance. But this internal renewal seeks its expression in the light and shade of a cultural creation in which, everything being put in question, the old models and styles have been disqualified precisely because of their age. It is at this juncture that the agitated critical mind, on the margins of cultural criticism, gets exhausted in useless discussions and proposes principles that, as a good philistine, it draws from 'eternal reason'. It is pertinent – even if only to confirm the poet in his peace and quiet, for he writes poems in an age when the critical mind wonders if poems are possible – to establish some evidence in such a controversial matter as the balance between substance and form in the cultural work.

Let's not waste time refuting the reactionary nonsense so often mumbled: 'It's too late, everything has already been said . . .' as well as another equally widespread misconception that, if human realities change, at least the language in which they are expressed must be immutable; these two misrepresentations are sufficiently well disproved by the sequence of heterogeneous transitions that form the history of peoples. For my part, I believe it is possible to determine the following points, which have the value for us of being both theoretical and practical.

1. Every renewal of mankind brings with it a corresponding renewal of cultural expression.

It follows from this principle that we need to create a new style to express the new sentiment of life. 'In spite of André Chénier's precept,

*Let us form ancient verses on new thinking*

I believe,' wrote André Gide, 'that no new thinking enters into the temple of art in borrowed robes.'

2. Besides, the idea of pouring new content into an old form arises from a 'false dialectical appearance', which makes the two *notions* of substance and form independent metaphysical entities. Yet for anything that has concrete reality, substance and form are inseparable. (Without its stripes the zebra does not exist.)

The idea of clothing new feelings in old forms would not occur to us, for we know that if the feeling is a reality qualified by the simple fact that we feel it at the moment, the old form, which is only a *notion*, is disqualified by the fact that it is, in comparison with the living feeling, only the emptiness of the conjurer.

3. It is within the new thing itself that, in a virtual state, the form of the newness lies. (The zebra doesn't need to chase after its stripes.) Form and substance are moreover one and the same thing. Form does not join substance on the outside; it is essentially inherent in it.

In the poetic process, we are therefore waiting for thought itself to find its form, in other words for it successfully to complete itself. This is what the idea of perfection really means once purged of the fetishistic prejudices of 'people of taste'.

4. And for this reason, finally, the *formless does not exist*. All that exists does so because of its form. The formless is the void. You cannot

have a thought with no form, which would be the thought of nothing.

Take care not to call something formless simply because you are unable to find a *fixed form* you are seeking.[1]

It would appear from these considerations that the cultural work will develop through life (a period indistinctly seeks its expression, like an adolescent undergoing a crisis of maturity; an idea leads organically towards its form) rather than by an artificial overlapping of new thoughts in a ready-made style. On the other hand, if we define culture as the ordinarily fetishized tradition of earlier cultural works and forms, it would not amaze us to find that all truly new art affects, perhaps especially in the eyes of 'cultivated people', the appearance of a barbaric style precisely because its newness negates the old formulas. In the end, it is easy to understand how a whole population (of idle onlookers) can hanker after perfection face to face with perfect works whose perfection is invisible because of its unwonted quality. The whole history of art lies in these misunderstandings.

For us, the important phenomenon of jazz notably allows us, more certainly than any critical reflection, to conceive of the *historical* character of substance and form within the work, while ultimately conceding it only a so to speak instantaneous value.

The essence of jazz is improvisation.

An aesthetic derived from jazz would be a *technique for creating beauty as you go along.* For jazz results from an approach constituted precisely by the jolts of life and its *style* is only an immediate investigation by music or any other means (I can see how such an aesthetic might interest poetry in general) of feelings and images as they appear in the mind. Any crystallization, any indolent self-imitation, any hardening of life threatens the validity of our fragile formulation.

No detailed rhythm is fixed in advance.

No concrete content is preconceived.

No rhythm, no content except in the form of a *hunger for life*, a life delineated by, let's say, a passion that demands satisfaction, substitutively, by the sublimation of song.

The 'player' does not know and must not know what he will play next, what his next word will be, what his next adventure will be; yet he goes on, like an acrobat, across the tightrope of circumstance.

A beautiful work is a work of circumstance.

But who will believe that, in Goethe's words, the only durable works are those of circumstance?

The age in which we live is poisoned with eternity. Jazz has been one of the best means to purge it and re-create within us the meaning of the instant and of transition. For our part, we do not hesitate to see in *actuality*, however poorly defined, the place of resolution of all human problems in this realm as well as others. In fact all human faults (aesthetic as well as moral or political) seem to us on analysis to stem from a certain oversight concerning the actuality of a particular age. But it is worth recalling, to avoid misunderstanding, that since Hegel it has been impossible to conceive of actuality except, in any becoming, as the ultimate outcome of this becoming that assumes the becoming. Otherwise, what would it be the actuality of? Consequently, all the previous moments of this becoming lie within the actuality, since in a life 'what is surpassed at the same time remains conserved, having merely lost its immediate existence, but for all that it is not destroyed'.[2]

The actuality of a being is its present, but this present is that very being marked by the extreme temporal sign of its duration. For a living being, there is thus no irreconcilable contradiction between its present and its past except in the minds of those who like splitting hairs. Equally, in a social sphere there is no antinomy between modernity and older works, between new (unconsecrated) works and culture. The latest work, however little qualified it is (I mean currently of value), supposes all the stages society has passed through in the realm under discussion.

Thus the poet is not modern through rejecting or ignoring the past, but by a dialectical sublation of its stages, which means at once a vibrant negation and a conservation of previous cultural forms. And his modernity will be so much more complete and valid to the extent that he is fully aware of the past.

Yet if the cultural tradition exists within the poet, it cannot be as a model (there is no model for what is not yet born), but as the past which is entrusted within him and inflexibly situates him in time, making him the modern man of a given age.

Such is poetic necessity: the whole past within you.

Such is poetic liberty: the indistinct future ahead of you.

These abstract considerations about form and substance are set down here only to serve as an introduction to these propositions which seem to us able to situate poetic activity in the Caribbean.

For poets the fundamental problem during the past century has rightly been not how they might refurbish poems endlessly reproduced from earlier times, but how to discover previously forbidden zones of the mind and of reality, in order to claim them for the poetic domain. The problem for them was not so much of style as of fresh territory. Baudelaire, Lautréamont, Rimbaud, Breton: the first two annexing the domains of evil and humour (which had previously been considered prosaic) to poetry; the latter two giving us access to human regions whose existence was unsuspected before them. It was discovered that the poetic problem is for this reason that of the conquest of man by himself. And this benefits us. For is not our task, if we want to reclassify our place within humanity, in all necessity to devote all our efforts to the discovery within us of a freshness able to bring forth a content worthy of being universally applicable in our lives? More than for anyone, the problem for us is not of form, but of a new element within us.

One of the most effective ways to bring about this renewal, without the slightest doubt, is surrealism as defined by Breton in his *Manifesto of Surrealism*. This method, founded on Freud's important discoveries, offers us the best means today in the psychological domain to bring to light the miraculous spoils of those tendencies, feelings and reactions that have been repressed in the Caribbean mentality by a particularly obnoxious psychological authority. A particularly obnoxious psychological authority, we say: in fact an analytical and historical examination of Caribbean mentality reveals that the present *superego* of the Caribbean people (formed, let's not forget, in the not-too-distant good old days of slavery) results from a triple process. First, a traumatic repression of the way of life (African totemism) of black slaves, which explains the pressure of secular anxiety which, in the face of this world, overwhelms the collective consciousness in the Caribbean. Second, *the establishment, in place of the repressed spirit, of the representative authority of the master in slave consciousness*, an authority instituted at the heart of the collectivity and keeping watch over it as a garrison does over a conquered city. This explains the inferiority complex of the Caribbean people. Third, a return towards blackness, even in its aggressiveness which, unable to be manifested even slightly in a society founded on an exceptional cruelty, returned to strangle its own consciousness. This explains the existence of a certain masochism among Caribbean people. This enables us to see that the critical mind of the Caribbean community could not present any evidence to confirm the role as persecutor and moralist that it plays in relation to our unconscious. It would therefore be incumbent on us to *listen*, within ourselves, scornful of that critical spirit, to grasp our physiologically most concealed voices. Bringing our gifts into the light could be effected thanks to the natural mechanism of *psychic automatism* granted its functional irresistibility.

Let's recall: 'Surrealism: *n.* pure psychic automatism, by which it is proposed to express (whether verbally, in writing or by any other means), *the real functioning of thought.* Dictation of thought in the absence of any control exercised by reason and beyond any aesthetic or moral preoccupation.'[3]

To give content to our lamentably formal life is the most urgent task. But the style of that life must guarantee it a certain beauty, already visible through the gap in the curtains. And we propose another principle: if the content of our life is merely the result of our black anatomy,[4] the style of this life can come only from the West, cast as we are into the current of French culture. But let us also add that a form encountering an alien content adapts itself, through the mysterious processes of life, to become one with that content and so itself necessarily changes.

If we try to be as precise as we can, we would say that, from the technical point of view, the present situation of poetry in the French Caribbean can only be that of France: I mean that in its expression it can only be the extreme moment of an evolution whose landmarks are (to mention arbitrarily only the most significant) Racine, Hugo, Baudelaire, Rimbaud, Lautréamont, Breton. Each of these examples represents the surpassing and conservation of earlier moments. The Caribbean poet will be qualified on condition that he contains organically within himself these significant and indispensable stages of French poetic necessity cast by life.[5]

This is where Caribbean romanticism and its new conception of Creole beauty is to be found.

To sum up:

*Caribbean Romanticism*: a cultural movement of the Caribbean people convulsively overwhelmed with consciousness of its own life. Conceived in 1932 with the publication of *Légitime défense*, this movement was effectively launched only in 1940, in an extraordinary way, through spontaneous poetic suggestion. It was constantly oriented on firm techniques arising from human sciences such as psychoanalysis, historical materialism and ethnography. The key figure in this revolution was Aimé Césaire.

## Notes

1. Gide: 'Any completely new appearance or thoroughly astounding form (of a poem, sonata or painting) is soon declared formless, even though form is required by the newness of the content.'

2. Hegel.

3. André Breton, 'Manifesto of Surrealism', in his *Oeuvres complètes*, no. 1 (1988) Paris: Gallimard (my emphasis).

4. I know! Caribbean people insist on being called mulattos in order to have the right to despise Africans. What would become of us, in this world made hierarchical in such a corrupt way, if there was no one to despise? How fortunate that Caribbean negroes have negroes who are more negro than they. So much the better!

5. We are not excluding any style, something which, let us be clear, is to be invented. Here I am defining a point of departure and not of arrival. As much should be self-evident.

[published in *Tropiques*, no. 11 (May 1944); reprinted in *Tracées*]

# AIMÉ CÉSAIRE

# *Poetry and Knowledge*

Poetic knowledge is born in the great silence of scientific knowledge.

Through reflection, observation and experience, man finally dominates the facts that bewilder him. Henceforth he knows how to find his way through the forest of phenomena. He knows how to use the world.

But that does not mean he is king of the world.

A perspective on the world, yes. Science offers him a perspective on the world. But a summary one. One that is superficial.

Physics classifies and explains, but the essence of things eludes it. The natural sciences classify, but the *quid proprium* of things eludes them.

As for mathematics, what eludes its abstract and logical activity is the real.

In short, scientific knowledge enumerates, measures, classifies and kills.

But it is not enough to say that scientific knowledge is summary. One must add that it is *impoverished and undernourished*.

Man has sacrificed everything to acquire it: desires, fears, feelings and psychological complexes.

To acquire this impersonal knowledge that is scientific knowledge, man has *depersonalized* and *deindividualized* himself.

I say an impoverished knowledge for, at its origin, whatever its richness in other ways, lies an impoverished man.

The essay 'One and Many' by Aldous Huxley contains a very amusing passage.

We all think we know what a lion is. A lion is a desert-coloured animal with a mane and claws and an expression like Garibaldi's. But it is also, in Africa, all the neighbouring antelopes and zebras, and therefore, indirectly, all the neighbouring grass . . . If there were no antelopes and zebras there would be no lion. When the supply of game runs low, the king of the beasts grows thin and mangy; it ceases altogether and he dies.[1]

The same goes for knowledge. Scientific knowledge is a lion without antelopes and zebras. It is gnawed away from within. Gnawed away by hunger, the hunger for feelings, the hunger for life.

And then, being unsatisfied, man has looked elsewhere for salvation, which here means plenitude.

And, little by little, man has become aware that beside this scientific and undernourished knowledge another form of knowledge exists. A satisfying knowledge.

This discovery contains Ariadne's thread: a few very simple remarks about the faculty that has allowed those who must really be called primitive scholars to discover, not by induction or deduction but as if by scent, the most solid truths.

And this is what takes us back to humanity's earliest times. The error is to believe that knowledge was waiting for the methodical exercise of thought or the meticulousness of experimentation to be born. I even believe that mankind has never been closer to certain truths than in the first days of the species. At the time mankind discovered with great emotion its first sunrise, its first rain, its first wind and its first moon. At the time when mankind, in fear and rapture, discovered the palpitating freshness of the world.

Fascination and terror. Trembling and wonder. Strangeness and intimacy. Only the sacred phenomenon of love can still give us an idea of what this solemn encounter could have been like . . .

It is in this state of dread and of love, in this climate of emotion and imagination, that mankind made its first, most fundamental and most decisive discoveries.

It was fateful and desirable that humanity should attain the greatest precision.

It was fateful and desirable that humanity should lament what was most keenly felt.

It is this nostalgia for a warm Brumaire that sent mankind back from the broad daylight of science to the nocturnal forces of poetry.

In every age, poets have known. All the ancient legends attest to this. But in modern times it was only in the nineteenth century, just as the Apollonian era drew to a close, that poets dared to claim that they knew.

1850 – the revenge of Dionysus over Apollo
1850 – the great leap into the poetic void.

An extraordinary phenomenon . . . Until then the French attitude was made up of prudence, circumspection and distrust. France was dying of prose. And then came the great nervous trembling in the face of adventure. The most prosaic of nations – through its most eminent members, taking the steepest and most difficult paths, those that were the highest and had the thinnest air, the only ones I allow to be called sacred and royal – passed over to the enemy lock, stock and barrel. I mean to that army under the death's-head banner of liberty and imagination.

Prosaic France passed over to poetry. And everything changed.

Poetry ceased to be a game, even a serious one. Poetry ceased to be an occupation, even an honourable one.

Poetry became an adventure. The finest of human adventures . . . Its goal: clairvoyance and knowledge.

And so there was Baudelaire . . .

It is significant that many of Baudelaire's poems relate to the idea of a penetration of the universe.

> *Happy he who can with vigorous wings*
> *Mount to these luminous fields serene!*
>
> *The one whose thoughts, like larks,*
> *Towards the morning skies fly free,*
> *– Who soars over life and effortlessly sees*
> *The language of the flowers and dumb things.*[2]
>
> ('Elevation')

And in 'Obsession':

> *Yet even the shadows a canvas form*
> *Where, springing by the thousand from my eye,*
> *Live lost beings with familiar glances.*[3]

And in 'Travelling Bohemians':

> *Cybèle who loves them dons more green,*
> *Makes rock to flow and desert bloom*
> *Before these travellers to whom opens*
> *The familiar empire of future shades.*[4]

As for Rimbaud, literature is still feeling the tremors of the incredible seismic shock of the famous 'lettre du voyant':

*I say that we must be seers, make ourselves seers.*

Memorable words of distress and victory . . .
Henceforth the way is open for humanity's most illustrious dreams.
Henceforth there can be no doubt about the Mallarméan venture. The lucid audacity of what he wrote to Verlaine makes Mallarmé even more than the former (whose reflection is Paul Valéry) an especially important engineer of the mind.

Apart from those poems and pieces of prose of my youth and later similar ones . . . I have always dreamed of and attempted something else . . . A book, quite simply, a book that is a book, architectural and premeditated, and not a collection of chance inspirations, no matter how marvellous. I would go further, I shall speak of the Book (convinced that in the end there is only one) unknowingly attempted by whoever wrote it, even a genius. The Orphic explanation of the World, which is the poet's only duty. And the literary game *par excellence* . . . There's the confession of my vice.

To pass from Mallarmé to Apollinaire is to go from the cold calculator and strategist of poetry to the enthusiastic adventurer and leader of the pack.
Apollinaire was great because, between a popular song and a war poem, he was able – fundamentally – to remain one of those fearful workers whose advent Rimbaud celebrated.

### The Pretty Redhead

*You whose mouths are made in the image of God's*
*A mouth which is order itself*
*Forbear when you compare us*
*To those who were order's perfection*
*We who seek adventure everywhere*

*We are not your enemies*
*We want to give you vast strange lands*
*Where blossoming mystery is offered to anyone to gather*
*There are new fires there in colours never seen*

*A thousand imponderable phantasms*
*Which must be made real*

*We want to explore goodness the huge country where all is stilled*
*As well as time which can be banished or brought back*
*Have pity on us who are always fighting on the frontiers*
*Of the limitless and the future*
*Pity our errors, pity our sins.*[5]

I arrive, not without having skipped several stages, at André Breton. . . . It will be surrealism's glory to have brought down on its head all the avowed and unavowed enemies of poetry. To have decanted several centuries of poetic experience. To have purged the past, oriented the present and prepared the future.

It was André Breton who wrote:

In spite of everything it is from poets that, over the centuries, it has been both possible to receive and legitimate to expect the impulses capable of restoring man to the heart of the universe, momentarily to isolate him from his destructive adventure, to remind him that it is – for all the pain and joy external to him – an infinitely perfectible place of resolution and resonance.[6]

And even more significantly:

Everything leads us to believe that there exists a certain point of the mind where life and death, real and imaginary, past and future, communicable and incommunicable, high and low, cease to be perceived as contradictory. And it would be futile to seek in surrealist activity any motive other than the hope of the determination of this point.

Never in the course of the ages has such a lofty ambition been so calmly expressed.

This highest ambition is poetic ambition itself.

It only remains for us to examine how and under what conditions it could be realized.

At the root of poetic knowledge lies an astonishing mobilization of all human and cosmic powers.

The poet approaches the poem not just with his whole soul but with his whole being. What presides over the poem is not the most lucid intelligence, the sharpest sensibility or the subtlest feelings, but experience as a whole; all the women you have loved, all the desires you have felt, all the dreams you have dreamed, all the images – whether grasped or received, all the weight of the body, all the weight of the mind. Everything that has been lived; everything that is possible. Around the poem as it forms is the precious whirlwind: ego, self and the world. And the strangest combinations, every past, every future (the anti-cyclone forms plateaux, the amoeba loses its pseudopodia, extinct vegetations confront each other). All the flux, all the radiation. The body is no longer deaf or blind. Everything has the right to life. Everything is called. Everything is waiting; I mean everything. The individual whole is stirred up once more by poetic inspiration. And, in a more disturbing way, so is the cosmic whole.

This is the moment to remember that the unconscious, to which all true poetry appeals, contains within it the original relationships that unite us with nature.

Man of every age is within us. All men are within us. The animal, the vegetable and the mineral are within us. Man is not only man. He is *universe*.

Everything happens as if, before the secondary dispersion of life, there had been a knotted primitive unity, the bedazzlement of which poets kept for themselves.

Distracted by action, transported by what is useful, man loses the sense of this fraternity. Here the animal is superior. And, even more than the animal, the tree, since the tree is fixity, attachment and persistence in what is essential . . .

And because the tree is stability, the tree is also abandon.

Abandon to the vital movement, to the creative impulse. Joyful abandon.

And the flower is the sign of this recognition.

The superiority of the tree over man, of the tree which says 'yes' over man who says 'no'. The superiority of the tree which is assent over man who is evasion; the superiority of the tree, which is rootedness and depth, over man who is restless and corrupt.

And that is why man never blossoms.

He is not a tree at all. His arms imitate branches, but they are withered branches which, from having misunderstood their function, which is to embrace life, have collapsed and dried up, all along the trunk; man never blossoms.

But there is someone who saves humanity, someone who restores it to universal harmony, someone who marries a human florescence to universal florescence: this man is the poet.

What has he done to do this?

Very little, but it is a small thing which he alone could effect. Like the tree and like the animal, he has abandoned himself to primal life, has said yes, has assented to this immense life which exceeded him. He has rooted himself in the earth, has stretched out his arms, has played with the sunlight, has become a tree: he has blossomed, he has sung.

In other words, poetry is a blossoming.

A blossoming of man in the world's measure: a vertiginous expansion. And we can say that at a very mysterious moment all great poetry, without ever renouncing its humanity, ceases to be strictly human and starts to become truly cosmic.

Thereby – through the poetic state – two of the most agonizing antinomies possible are resolved: the antinomy of self and other and that of the Ego and the World.

'At last – oh joy, oh reason – I heard the azure from the sky, come from the darkness, and I lived, a golden spark of the light of nature.'

And so, pregnant with the world, the poet speaks.

In the beginning was the word . . .

. . . No one has ever believed this more fervently than the poet.

And it is on the word, a shaving of the world, a secret, unassuming slice of the world, that he gambles all our possibilities . . . The first and the last ones.

The word increasingly risks appearing as an algebraic notation that makes the world intelligible. Just as the new Cartesian algebra has allowed the construction of a theoretical physics, so the original handling of the word can make a new science (theoretical and impartial), of which poetry can already give us a fairly good idea, possible at any moment. Then the time will come again when the study of the word will be the condition for the study of nature. But here we are still groping in the dark . . .

Let us return to the poet . . . Pregnant with the world, the poet speaks.

He speaks and his tongue returns language to its pure state.

By pure state, I mean not submitted to habit or thought, but to the flow of the cosmos alone. The poet's word, the primitive word: a rupestral outline in sonic matter.

The poet's phrase: the primitive phrase; the universe that is played with and prospected.

And because in every true poem the poet plays the game of the world, the true poet wishes to abandon the word to its free associations, certain that it means once and for all abandoning it to the will of the universe.

Everything I have just said risks making us believe in the poet's disarmament. And yet it is nothing of the sort. If I make it clear that in poetic emotion nothing is ever as close to nothing as to its contrary, you will understand that no man of peace, no man of depth, was ever more rebellious and pugnacious.

The old idea of the roused poet should be applied to poetry itself. This is the sense in which it is appropriate to speak of poetic violence, poetic aggressivity and poetic instability. In this climate of fire and fury that is the poetic climate, currencies lose their value, courts cease to make judgements, judges to sentence, juries to acquit. Only the firing squads still know what to do. The further one advances, the clearer the signs of breakdown become. Regulations choke; conventions are exhausted. The Grammont laws for the protection of men, the Locarno laws for the protection of animals abruptly and marvellously renounce their virtues. A cold wind of disarray blows.

Unease upsets the most dependable assizes. At the blood-soaked end of mortal avenues an immense treacherous sun laughs derisively. It is humour's sun. And in the dust of the clouds, the ravens inscribe one name over and over: ISIDORE DUCASSE COMTE DE LAUTRÉAMONT.

And in fact Lautréamont was the first to integrate humour into poetry. He was the first to reveal the functional role of humour. He was the first to make us see that what love began, humour has the strength to continue.

It is not the least of humour's roles to cleanse the fields of the mind. To dissolve with a blowtorch the connections that, temporary as they may be, threaten to become encrusted in the mental pulp and harden it. It is humour first and foremost that, contrary to Pascal, la Rochefoucauld and many other moralists, convinces Lautréamont that if Cleopatra's nose had been shorter, the face of the world would not have been altered; that the sun and death can be confronted squarely; that man is a subject devoid of errors . . . that nothing is less strange than the contradictions one uncovers in man. It is first and foremost humour that convinces me that it is as true to say that the thief makes the opportunity as to say that 'opportunity makes the thief'.

Only humour convinces me that the most prodigious reversals are justifiable. Only humour alerts me to the other side of things.

But here we are being led into the crackling fields of metaphor.

One cannot think about the richness of the image without as a consequence imagining the poverty of judgement.

> *Judgement is poor with all the world's reason.*
> *The image is rich with all the world's absurdity.*
> *Judgement is poor[7] with all that has been 'thought' in the world.*
> *The image is rich with the whole life of the universe.*
> *Judgement is poor with all the rationality of existence.*
> *The image is rich with all the irrationality of life.*
> *Judgement is poor in complete immanence.*
> *The image is rich in complete transcendence.*

Let me explain . . .

One would struggle in vain to reduce analytical judgement to synthetic judgement. Whether you say that judgement assumes the putting into contact of two different concepts, insist on the idea of there being no judgement without X, that all judgement is a sublation into the unknown, and is transcendence, it is no less true that in all valid judgement the field of transcendence is limited.

The safety rails are up: the laws of identity and contradiction, the principle of the excluded middle.

Precious safety rails; but also singular limitations.

It is through the image, the revolutionary, distant image, the image that overthrows all the laws of thought, that mankind finally breaks through the barrier.

In the image A is no longer A:

> *You in whom so many raspberry laughs*
> *Are a flock of tame lambs.*

In the image A can be not-A:

The slab of the black hearth, real shoreline suns, ah! the well of magic arts.[8]

In the image, not every object of thought is necessarily A or not-A. The image maintains the possibility of the happy medium.

For Rimbaud again:

*The chariots of silver and copper*
*The prows of steel and silver*
*Beat the spray*
*Stir up the stems of the brambles.*[9]

Not to mention the persuasive complicities of the *found* world and the *invented* world which allow us to say *motor* for *sun, dynamo* for *mountain, carburettor* for *Caribbean* and so on, and to celebrate lyrically the connecting rod of moons and the breathless piston of the stars . . .

Because the image immeasurably extends the field of transcendence and the right to transcendence, poetry is always on the path of truth. And because the image ceaselessly sublates the perceived, because the dialectic of the image transcends antinomies, when it comes to it modern science may be nothing but the ponderous verification of a few wild images thrown up by poets . . .

Once the sun of the image arrives at its zenith, everything becomes possible once more . . . The complexes of the curse dissipate, and it is the time for the emergence of things . . .

What emerges is the individual essence: intimate conflicts, obsessions, phobias, fixations. All the ciphers of the personal message.

It is not a matter, as in the lyricism of the old days, of the *immortalization* of an hour of pain or joy. We are far beyond the anecdote here, at man's very heart, at the seething pit of his destiny. My past is there, showing and hiding my face. My future is there, holding out a hand to me. Rockets are set off. It is my childhood burning. It is my childhood speaking and seeking me out. And in the person I am, the person I want to be stands on tiptoe . . .

And what also emerges is the ancient ancestral essence.

Only the poetic atmosphere can bring hereditary images back to the light of day to be deciphered. A buried millenarian knowledge. The cities of Ys of knowledge.

In this sense all the mythologies the poet stumbles across, all the symbols he gathers and regilds, are true. And poetry alone takes them seriously. Which helps to make poetry a serious matter.

The German philosopher Jung discovered the idea of energy and its conservation in Heraclitus's metaphor of the eternally living fire, in medieval legends concerning holy haloes and in theories of metempsychosis. And for his part, Pierre Mabille regrets that the biologist believes himself 'ashamed to use the story of the phoenix to describe the evolution of blood corpuscles, or the myth of Saturn engendering children to devour them later for the functions of the spleen'.

In other words science loathes myth while poetry accepts it. This does not make science superior to poetry. In truth, myth is at once inferior and superior to the *law*. Myth's inferiority is one of precision. Myth's superiority is one of richness and sincerity. Only myth satisfies man entirely: his heart, his reason, his taste for the fragment and the whole, his taste for the false and the true, for myth is all of these at once. A hazy and emotional apprehension, rather than a means of poetic expression . . .

Hence love and humour.

Hence the word. Hence the image. Hence the myth . . .

With the support of these great forces of synthesis we can at last understand André Breton's words:

> Columbus had to set sail with madmen to discover America.
>
> And see how this madness has taken shape, and endured . . .
>
> It is not fear of madness that will force us to leave the flag of the imagination at half mast.[10]

It is not fear of madness that will force us to leave the flag of the imagination at half mast.

And the poet Lucretius foretold the indestructibility of matter, the plurality of worlds and the existence of the infinitesimal.

And in *Medea* the poet Seneca launched vessels in search of worlds:

> Centuries will come when the Ocean will burst the bonds by which it surrounds us. An infinite land will open up. The navigator will once more discover new lands and Thule will no longer be the last place on earth.

'It is not fear of madness that will force us to place the flag of the imagination at half mast . . .' And the painter Rousseau *invents* tropical vegetation. And the painter Chirico, unprompted, affixes to Apollinaire's forehead his future wound. And around 1924 the poet André Breton, unprompted, associates the word *war* with the number *1939*.

'It is not fear of madness that will force us to place the flag of the imagination at half mast.' And the poet Rimbaud writes the *Illuminations*.

And you know the result: strange cities, extraordinary landscapes, worlds that are twisted, crushed, torn apart, the cosmos turned to chaos, order turned to disorder, being turned to becoming, everywhere the absurd, everywhere the incoherent, the demented. And after all that, what awaits him? Failure? No. The searing vision of his own destiny. And the most authentic vision of the world if, as I persist in believing, Rimbaud was the first to feel, to the point of direct experience, to the very point of anguish, the modern idea of the active forces that slyly lie in wait within matter for our peace of mind . . .

No: 'It is not fear of madness that will force us to place the flag of the imagination at half mast.'

And here are some propositions by way of résumé as much as clarification.

### First Proposition

Poetry is that attitude that by the word, the image, myth, love and humour places me at the living heart of myself and of the world.

### Second Proposition

The poetic attitude is an attitude of naturalization brought about by imagination's demented impulse.

### Third Proposition

Poetic knowledge is that in which man spatters the object with all of his mobilized riches.

### Fourth Proposition

If affective energy can be endowed with causal power, as Freud has shown, it is paradoxical to refuse it power of penetration. It is legitimate to think that nothing can resist the unprecedented mobilization of forces which poetry necessitates and the multiplied momentum of each of these forces.

### Fifth Proposition

On the marvellous contact of the interior totality and exterior totality, perceived imaginatively and simultaneously by the poet, or more precisely within the poet, marvellous discoveries are made.

## Sixth Proposition

The sign of scientific truth is coherence and efficacy. The sign of poetic truth is beauty.

## Seventh and Final Proposition

Poetic beauty is not only beauty of expression or muscular euphoria. An overly Apollonian or gymnastic conception of beauty paradoxically risks puffing up or hardening beauty.

## Corollary

The music of poetry cannot be external. The only *acceptable* poetry comes from somewhere beyond sound. The search for music is a crime against poetic music which can only be the breaking of the mental wave against the rock of the world.

The poet is that very old and very new, very complex and very simple being who – within the lived confines of the dream and the real, day and night, between absence and presence – seeks and receives, in the sudden unleashing of internal cataclysms, the password of complicity and power.

[published in *Tropiques*, no. 12 (January 1945)]

## Editor's Notes

1. From *Do What You Will* (1929) London: Chatto & Windus, p. 41.
2. Charles Baudelaire, 'Elevation', in *Oeuvres complètes* (1975) Paris: Gallimard, p. 10 (our translation).
3. Baudelaire in ibid., p. 75 (our translation).
4. Baudelaire in ibid., p. 18 (our translation).
5. Apollinaire, *Oeuvres poétiques* (1956) Paris: Gallimard, p. 313 (our translation).
6. André Breton, 'Second Manifesto of Surrealism', in his *Oeuvres complètes*, vol. 1 (1988) Paris: Gallimard, p. 781.
7. Césaire actually writes 'rich' but this is presumably an error.
8. Arthur Rimbaud 'Veillées' in *Les Illuminations*, in his *Oeuvres complètes* (1955) Paris: Gallimard (our translation).
9. Rimbaud, 'Marine' in ibid., p. 196.
10. André Breton, 'Manifesto of Surrealism', in his *Oeuvres complètes*, vol. 1 (1988) Paris: Gallimard, p. 313.

RENÉ MÉNIL

# Evidence Concerning the
# Mind and Its Speed

## 1

THE CREATIVE SPIRIT is a bounding.

A bounding from the habitual to the extraordinary, from the familiar to the unfamiliar, in short from the known to the unknown. The mind boldly parts the boughs of mystery.

But all the unknown, all the mystery, of ourselves and of the world, is hidden in our unconscious. The prehensile faculty of the beyond (in the positive rather than superstitious sense of the term) is the liberating faculty of the unconscious – the imagination. And the image or metaphor is the act by which the mind, left to its natural movement, becomes aware of itself and the world to a point situated beyond common perception.

Far and away in the distance where we had been concerning 'life', at lightning speed and with a light flowing from its speed, the fire-spirit illuminates faces, countries and things springing up from broken habits.

## 2

The logic of the image is the logic of the absurd.

The logic of the absurd is the logic of fecundity.

Absurd is the seed that gives birth to the plant and the fruit that bears the tree.

Equally absurd is the mind in prey to metaphorical parturition.

Absurd is the transmutation of the metals of the mind.

Traditional logic? The logic of hateful sterility and solitude. A equals
A. No reality communicates with others. Metaphor, by contrast, boldly
affirms that this object, which until now has been defined in terms of
itself (a sorry tautology) could actually be defined as something else,
could actually be something else (A equals non-A). This negation of
logic closes certain curtains as it opens others: things start to become
interesting for the mind that had previously contemplated its own sterile
immobility.

Metaphor is irrational – or does not exist. Every metaphor affirms
a relation of resemblance and, ultimately, of identity between two
heterogeneous objects. This irrationality is either glaring:

> *This family is a brood of dogs.*
> Rimbaud

or else veiled:

> *The bells ring for no reason and so do we.*
> Tzara

The surprise provoked by the affirmation of such contradictions is the
unimpeachable sign that the idiotic circle of platitudes is finally broken
and that the mind is enacting its task as a fury that breaks idols.

### 3

From the point of view of life, the affirmation of such relations is no
surprise: the surprise is the isolation to which logic savagely condemns
thoughts and things.

From the point of view of life, everything is contained within the
whole, everything is related, there is a complementarity of everything,
everything resembles everything else – in an organic way.

The two terms of the metaphorical relation are simply joined back
together in their original unity under the active line of force that life
projects from the unconscious.

Metaphor breaks the solitude of ideas and things in the mind (a solitude we call rationality) and, as a result, discredits stagnant, putrefying
and idealist stabilities.

The film of the world is finally renewed under the impulse of life.
Water is a flame weighed down; the leaf is a bird that has taken root.

**4**

These lightning departures and arrivals reveal a fresh co-ordinate in the realm of thought: *the speed of the mind.* The slow mind is the prosaic mind. The only difference between prose and poetry is one of psychic acceleration.

Victor Hugo is merely a condensation or – what comes to the same thing – merely an acceleration of Racine's poetic genius as in the extraordinarily moving cinema visions that spring from the sufficiently rapid acceleration of trivial facts, such as the germination of haricot beans.[1]

**5**

In the mind as in nature changes in quantity give rise, at certain points of development, to changes in quality.

The proliferation of accursed poets (Nerval, Baudelaire, Poe, Rimbaud, etcetera) gave birth in 1924 – by a leap of thought – to a new poetry, that of surrealism. Artifice – which consisted, while flirting with God, in monstrously cultivating 'sins' like warts and in irritating the sensibility to the point of raging hallucinatory psychoses – needed to make way for the natural mechanism of psychic automatism which brings forth hidden images from the unconscious.

Breton, who was responsible for the heterogeneous transition, guided poetry from the realm of devilment and individual talent to the realm of the real functioning of thought (or, in other terms, the realm of a natural, necessarily specific, faculty).[2]

**6**

It is through its speed that the mind becomes clairvoyant.

Superbly mastering the distance between phenomena, it shatters the opacity of time and space.[3]

**7**

Contradiction in thought results from a clumsiness of mind. Contradictions (apparently irreconcilable in the eyes of logic) are only terms maintained in isolation by the inflexible mind.

One can escape contradiction, in other words the principle of identity, by means of the speed of the mind. (The irreducible images of a film are blended together by being thrown into motion.)

Aristotle's logic? A practice of things or corpses.
Thought is bio-logical – or does not exist.

## 8

Clarity does not reside in the object.
But in its relation with other objects.
In other words, the mind is fired through its movement like a shooting star.
The corollary is:
If the brilliance of the mind is proportional to its speed, the poetic image, which is our fastest form of knowledge, achieves its greatest possible clarity.

## 9

Dialectic of light.
What is logical has its light.
What is irrational has its light – it is just a different one.
In order to gain access to the one, you must deaden yourself to the other.
Against Reverdy when he says: 'as obscure as sentiment'.[4]
To proclaim the luminous pangs of absurd intuitions and dark dreams, this is the evidence:
That woman *was* an other, the room *was* the slope of a glacier, he *knew* that the door would open at the beautiful dead woman's touch. And the door opened.[5]

## 10

As psychoanalysis has shown that the collective unconscious is present within the individual unconscious (or vice versa), it follows that there is a universality of the irrational as there is of logical thought. In other words, the most 'absurd' insights of poets must find their resonance in all men on the same level on which they were found – that of the feelings.

## 11

Poetic tension is sustained only through the continuity of metaphorical movement, which always heads blindly beyond, beyond the beyond, *sic ad infinitum*. The lowering of tension, in other words, the prosaic, will appear whenever a tautology takes shape, whenever there is an explicit affirmation that was already understood or predictable from analysis. The mind stumbles over rational clarity which, taking the place of the clarity of the image, destroys the poetic atmosphere.

Corollary:

Memory and description are not poetic because they *enclose the mind beforehand*, making it turn in an already determined circle.[6]

### 12

If, by its speed and lightness, the mind can surmount contradiction and soar magisterially over the boundless plain of objects ready to make connections between the most disparate things and indefinitely multiply these relations, it seems certain that it is through the image that the mind attains its greatest power and can establish its dominance. In fact, once the so-called rational fixity is broken, once the paralysing armour of identity has been shed, the mind acquires a spontaneity, a fecundity, and the faculty to glide and leap, a means of departure and return that are equivalent to being all-powerful.

Here are possible these amazing relations which cast us astounded beyond space and time, beyond life's everyday routine: here is the emotional raptus that some have called the Absolute and we call poetry.

The quick mind is the sovereign mind.

### 13

Parochial conservatism, which comprises the life of 'civilized' societies, considers metaphor as a 'way of speaking', as a 'figure of speech', in short as a mere nothing. However, given that 'the natural world penetrates into the spiritual, serving it as fodder and contributing to effect an indefinable amalgam which we call our individuality', it is clear that our craziest fancies can have no other object than the very object of perception – namely the world.

Metaphor is an irruption of reality but of a reality that is unwonted, irrational and, for this reason, in practical terms useless. For how can one complain about the hawthorn in this poem:

> *I see the crests of the sun*
> *through the hawthorn of the rain*

except that it cannot be made into a bouquet?

However little one can supremely survey the two strands of the useful and the useless, perception and imagination, metaphor appears as an indispensable complementary means of knowledge of the world and of man.

## 14

Nothing is more real than the image considered as an image.

Nothing is more illusory than the image considered as life.

Illusion, having been created by life to give it a charming inverted image, turns against this life in hostility to demand an account of its poverty.

Thus the poet falls silent.

In the distance is the severe silhouette of Robespierre.

The ultimate destiny of poetry is to multiply itself, dialectically, into the bare force of a crowd.

### Notes

1. It goes without saying that to be poetically valid, this acceleration must be natural (images springing spontaneously from psychic automatism) and not rigged (by subsequently suppressing certain terms in the language expressed with a view to a stronger condensation). The latter eventually results only in the artificial thought of a Valéry. The natural leap of the mind – a leap by which the mind creates its object – has not taken place and thought, neither truly prosaic nor definitively poetic, loses all qualification.

2. Dalí continues the tradition of accursed poets in that he designates the spontaneity of the mind in perception in dangerously medical terms (paranoia). This amounts to certifying this society as healthy and maintaining that the real functioning of thought is a sickness and that those who think a bit too quickly are mad.

3. Reverdy: 'The more distant and precise the relation of two images, the stronger the image will be and the greater its emotive power and poetic reality.'

4. Beware of considering the savage attacks that poets make on stupidity as scientific data.

5. Poe: 'The Fall of the House of Usher'.

6. This is why the novel is normally (especially in France) so boring. It is too intelligent (static); even a mediocre reader has guessed everything from the first page. The novel will be saved through its velocity: it will be an impromptu tale, breaking its logical framework of boringly detailed whys and wherefores. The novel needs to be given back the spontaneity, movement and lightness of the story. Virginia Woolf's experiment should be encouraged, although she also begins by *enclosing the mind beforehand* (Mrs Dalloway). Further along this road lies Benjamin Péret and his tales.

[published in *Tropiques*, nos 13–14 (September 1945); reprinted in *Tracées*]

RENÉ MÉNIL

# Lightning Effect

T HE MOST RECENT interest of psychoanalysis and ethnography is
that they luminously reveal that the behaviour both of individuals
and of peoples cannot be explained by the reasons they consciously
give for their actions. The impulses in the absence of which action does
not exist (and in which it finds its energy) have their origin outside the
sphere of the reasons of our logic. These logical reasons constitute, in
relation to real causes, a deceitful phantasmagoria. Henceforth it
becomes perfectly obvious that all Socratic speculations about the
behaviour of individuals and peoples have been led miserably off
course into the stagnant pool of 'clear ideas' and constitute only a
game at best suited to the congenial exercise of the logical faculty.
Which explains the decorative, academic and quaint character of all
ethical systems until now.

The latest anthropological discoveries finally offer man access to
man, in other words they allow us to go beyond the ridiculous zone of
our false reasons and reach the line where the essential and vitally
absorbing energies are brought into play. It then becomes easy to conceive of a morality and a politics (no one who is serious will conceive
of anything more) supported on this precious centre of man which is
such that each of their imperatives, once articulated, releases the
desired action in an irresistible way because of the fact that impetuous
natural forces have been summoned. Human behaviour, once activated
by an infallible art whose laughable image we find in crude propaganda techniques, will develop outside the depressing atmosphere of
inevitably ineffective lamentations.

But the impulses that define our activity's frame do not appear to consciousness in all their furious nakedness. Physical and social prohibitions

force them to veil themselves. This is why they are not normally visible to the mind's eye except in the form of *vivid drama*. This is why they are known to us only as transposed into symbols and metaphors and why their play gives rise to the staging of dreams, reveries, stories, myths and so on. It is consequently in poetry and not in the mathematical chattering of Cartesian psychologists that we can read what matters to us, I mean what we live and die for. Any poem at all expresses human destiny more fundamentally than all the political treatises in the world.

Any system referring to human behaviour not inspired by the poetic conditions of action is consigned to a miserable fate as a harmless pastime of the mind. By contrast, everyone who really aspires to the difficult task of guiding himself and other people must act like a veritable magician of human energies. Such a man could only be considered a magician by a century imbued with the prejudices of logic and thus incapable of grasping the ins and outs of real human power.

This magic, which is a kind of dialectical sublation of contemporary formalist anthropology, arises out of a profound study of human inventiveness – an inventiveness that is a deformed image but still an image of our living possibilities. Knowledge so determined will be expressed in a language that will be able to have no common ground with the hasty, clumsy and primarily utilitarian language spoken in Cartesian eras. This language, the remains at the bottom of the melting pot, will have the very power of gesture, in other words it will be able to act magically. The spoken word, which is action, will now appear haloed with a terrible power, for it will be indissolubly connected to the secret impulsive movements of man or, more accurately, will be their faithful transposition.

In opposition to this century in which so many famous chatterboxes have been given the floor, we prefer to imagine this grandiose spectacle: a man armed with poetic power, standing tall above his people and overturning his country's social life with a single spoken word.

Only the poet has this word of deliverance at his disposal. But until now, distrustful of the transformations of the real, he has not sought to use the philosopher's stone he possessed (often without realizing it) with a view to refashioning the conditions of life completely. Unfortunately he has exposed a chasm between the realm of his inventiveness and the world in which he lived.

Ever since Hegel, such a divorce simply proves chimerical. The unity of dream and action (dream determining action and action determining dream) within man shows that not only is it possible to reconcile our life with our dreams, but that it is necessary, according to the decrees of a secret justice, to extract from the domain of dream the teaching that would allow clear-sightedness in this life and consequently perform the liberating transformation. At every moment the poet is unknowingly playing with the solution of all human problems. It is no longer appropriate for him to play childishly with his magical wealth; instead he should criticize the poetic material with the aim of extracting the sure formulas for action. No practical man can fight this critical-poet. Everyone knows that the word of the magus produced its effect with the certainty of lightning.

[published in *Tropiques*, no. 3 (October 1941)]

# The Great Camouflage

CRAMMED AGAINST THE islands are the beautiful green blades of water and silence. Around the Caribbean Sea is the purity of salt. Down there in front of me is the pretty square of Pétionville, planted with pine and hibiscus. My island, Martinique, is there, with its fresh garland of clouds prompted by Mount Pelée. There are the highest plateaux of Haiti, where a horse is dying, struck by lightning in the age-old murderous storm of Hinche. Nearby, his master contemplates the land he used to believe was solid and generous. He does not yet realize that he is participating in the islands' absence of equilibrium. But this outburst of terrestrial insanity illuminates his heart: he starts thinking about the other Caribbean islands, with their volcanoes, their earthquakes and their hurricanes.

At that moment a powerful cyclone starts to swirl in the open seas off Puerto Rico in the midst of billows of clouds, its beautiful tail sweeping the length of the Caribbean semicircle. The Atlantic flees towards Europe in great ocean waves. Our little tropical observation posts start to crackle out the news. The wireless is going mad. Ships flee – where can they go? The sea swells, this way, that way, with an effort, a luscious leap, the water stretches out its limbs as it gains greater awareness of its watery strength; sailors clench their teeth and their faces are streaming wet, and it is reported that the cyclone is passing over the south-east coast of the Haitian Republic at a speed of thirty-five miles per hour as it heads for Florida. Those objects and beings still just out of reach of the wind are gripped with apprehension. Don't move. Let it pass by . . .

In the eye of the cyclone everything is snapping, everything is collapsing with the rending sound of tumultuous events. The radios fall silent. The great palm-tree tail of fresh wind is unfolding somewhere in the stratosphere where no one will follow its wild iridescence and waves of purple light.

After the rain, sunshine.

The Haitian cicadas consider chirping out their love. When not a drop of water remains on the scorched grass, they sing furiously about the beauty of life and explode into a cry too vibrant for an insect's body. Their thin shell of dried silk stretched to the limit, they die as they let out the world's least moistened cry of pleasure.

Haiti remains, shrouded in the ashes of a gentle sun with eyes of cicadas, shells of mabouyas, and the metallic face of a sea that is no longer of water but of mercury.

Now is the moment to lean out of the window of the aluminium clipper on its wide curves.

Once again the sea of clouds appears, which is no longer intact since the planes of Pan American Airways pass through. If there is a harvest in process of ripening, now is the time to try to glimpse it, but in forbidden military zones the windows remain closed.

Disinfectant or ozone is brought out, but it hardly matters, you'll see nothing. Nothing but the sea and the confused lay of the land. You can only guess at the uncomplicated loves of the fishes. They stir the waters, which give a friendly wink to the clipper's windows. Seen from high above, our islands assume their true dimensions as seashells. The hummingbird-women, the tropical flower-women, the women of four races and dozens of blood ties, have gone. So too have the canna, the plumiera and the flame tree, the moonlit palm trees, and sunsets seen nowhere else on earth . . .

Nevertheless they're there.

Yet it was fifteen years ago that the Caribbean was disclosed to me from the eastern slope of Mount Pelée. From there I realized, as a very young girl, that, as it lay in the Caribbean Sea, Martinique was sensual, coiled, spread out and relaxed, and I thought of the other islands, equally beautiful.

I experienced the presence of the Caribbean once more in Haiti, on summer mornings in 1944, which was so much more perceptible in the places from which, at Kenscoff, the view over the mountains is of an unbearable beauty.

And now complete lucidity. My gaze, going beyond these perfect forms and colours, catches by surprise the torment within the Caribbean's most beautiful face.

Because the thread of unsatisfied desires has caught the Caribbean

and America in its trap. Since the Conquistadors arrived and their
technology (starting with firearms) developed, not only have the
transatlantic lands had their appearance changed, they have learned
new fears. Fear of being outdistanced by those who remained in
Europe, already armed and equipped; fear of being confused with the
coloured peoples who were immediately declared inferior in order to
make it easier to bully them. It was necessary initially and at any
price – be it the price of the infamy of the slave trade – to create an
American society richer, more powerful and better organized than the
forsaken but desired European society. It was necessary to take
revenge on the nostalgic hell which vomited its adventurous demons,
its convicts, its penitents and its utopians over the New World and its
isles. The colonial adventure has continued for three centuries – the
wars of independence being only one episode – and the American
peoples, whose attitude towards Europe often remains childish and
romantic, are not yet freed from the old continent's grip. Naturally it
is the American blacks who suffer most from the daily humiliations,
degeneracies, injustices and shabbiness of colonial society.

If we are proud to proclaim our extraordinary vitality throughout
the Americas, if it seems to promise us a definitive salvation, we need
the courage to say that subtle forms of slavery remain rampant. Here,
in these French islands, it still debases thousands of negroes, for whom
a century ago the great Schoelcher demanded, in addition to liberty
and dignity, the title of citizens. We must dare to point out, caught by
the implacable spotlight of events, the Caribbean stain on France's
face, since so many of the French seem determined to tolerate no
shadow of it.

The degrading forms of modern wage labour still find a plot of land
upon which to flourish unchecked among us.

Who will cast out, along with obsolete factory machinery, the thousands of sub-industrialists and grocers, that caste of false colonists
responsible for the human decline of the Caribbean?

As they drift along the streets of the capitals among their European
brothers, an unsurmountable timidity fills them with fear. Ashamed of
their languid accent and rough French, they sigh for the calm warmth
of their Caribbean homes and the patois of the black *da* of their
childhood.[1]

Prepared for any form of betrayal in order to defend themselves
against the mounting tide of blacks, they would sell themselves to
America (if the Americans didn't claim that the purity of their blood is
more than suspect) just as, in the forties, they proclaimed allegiance to

the Vichy admiral: Pétain being the altar of France for them, Robert had to become the 'tabernacle of the Caribbean'.[2]

Meanwhile, the Caribbean serf lives miserably and abjectly on the 'factory' lands, and the mediocrity of our market towns is a sickening sight. Meanwhile, the Caribbean is still a paradise with the gentle sound of palm trees . . .

That day the irony was that, a garment gleaming with sparks, each of our muscles expressed in its own way part of the desire scattered over the blossoming mango trees.

I listened very attentively to your voices lost in the Caribbean symphony which launched downpours to assault the isles, but could not hear them. We were like thoroughbreds, held in check but chafing at the bit, on the edges of this salt savanna.

On the beach were several 'metropolitan officials'. They stood there uneasy, ready to flee at the first signal. Newcomers have difficulty adapting to our 'old French lands'. When they lean over the baleful mirror of the Caribbean Sea, they see their own delirious image. They don't dare recognize themselves in that ambiguous being, the West Indian. They know the métis has some of their blood; that they both belong to Western civilization. Of course, 'metropolitans' are unaware of colour prejudice. But their coloured descent fills them with fear, in spite of the exchange of smiles. They didn't expect this strange burgeoning of their blood. Perhaps they would prefer not to respond to their Caribbean heirs who simultaneously cry out and do not cry out, 'Father.' Yet they have to reckon with these unexpected sons and charming daughters. They have to govern this turbulent people.

Here's a West Indian, the great-grandson of a colonist and a black slave woman. Here he is in his island, ensuring its 'smooth running' by his deployment of all the energies once needed by avaricious colonists for whom the blood of others was the natural price of gold and all that courage needed by African warriors in their perpetual struggle to wrest life from death.

Here he is with his double strength and double ferocity, in a dangerously precarious equilibrium: he cannot accept his negritude, but nor can he make himself white. Listlessness overcomes this divided heart, and with it come habits of trickery, a fondness for 'fiddles'; this is how that flower of human servility the coloured bourgeoisie blooms in the Caribbean.

Along roads bordered with glyciridia pretty black children, relishing the cooked roots – salted or unsalted – that they eat, smile at the posh car as it passes. They suddenly feel, in the pits of their stomachs, the

need one day to be masters of a beast so supple and shiny and powerful. Years later, stained with the fat of comfort, they can be seen
miraculously giving a quivering of life to rejected carcasses, in order to
sell them for a song. The hands of thousands of young West Indians
have instinctively weighed up the steel, considered the joints and loos-
ened the screws. Thousands of images of gleaming factories,
unwrought steel and liberating machines have swelled the hearts of
our young workers. In hundreds of sordid sheds where scrap iron rusts,
there is an invisible vegetation of desires. The impatient fruits of the
Revolution will inevitably gush forth from it.

Here among the mornes smoothed by the wind is the Free-Men's
Estate. A peasant, in whom the mechanical adventure still inspires no
excitement, leans against a giant mapou which shades the whole side of
the morne, feeling a dull thrust of vegetation welling up through him
from his bare toes as they sink into the mud. Turning towards the setting sun to see what the weather will be like tomorrow – the orangeish
red indicates that planting time is near at hand – and his gaze is not
only the gentle reflection of the light, but becomes oppressive with
impatience, the very one which stirs the Martiniquan earth – this earth
which does not belong to him yet *is* his earth. He knows that it is in
league with them, the workers, and not with the béké or the mulatto.
And when suddenly, in the Caribbean night decked out with love and
silence, the drum roll explodes, the blacks get ready to respond to the
desire of the earth and of dance, but the landowners, immured in their
beautiful mansions behind their wire gauze, appear like pale butterflies
caught in a trap under the electric light.

All around them the tropical night swells with rhythm, Bergilde's
hips have assumed, in the oscillations that surge from the chasms on
volcano flanks, their appearance of cataclysm and it is Africa itself
which, beyond the Atlantic and the centuries before the slave traders,
dedicates the look of solar lust exchanged by the dancers on its West
Indian children. Their cries proclaim, in a raucous and generous voice,
that Africa is here, present; that it is waiting, immensely chaste despite
the stormy, devouring colonization by the whites. And across these
faces constantly bathed in the effluvium of the sea around the islands,
across these bounded and small lands surrounded with water like huge
impassable gulfs, passes the remarkable wind that has come from a
continent. The Caribbean-Africa, thanks to the drums and the nostalgia for terrestrial places, lives on in the hearts of these island peoples.
Who will satisfy their nostalgia?

Yet Absalom's canna bleeds on the chasms and the beauty of the tropical landscape goes to the heads of passing poets. Through the shifting tracery of the palms, they see the West Indian blaze swirling over the Caribbean Sea which is a calm sea of lava. Here life is kindled by a vegetal fire. Here, on the warm earth that keeps alive geological species, the plant, through passion and blood, through its primitive architecture, establishes disquieting chimes surging from the dancers' chaotic loins. Here the liana, vertiginously balanced, assumes aerial poses to charm the precipices, hooking trembling hands to the ungraspable cosmic trepidation that mounts right through nights inhabited with drums. Here poets feel their heads reeling and, imbibing the fresh odours of the ravines, they seize the spray of the islands, listen to the sound the water makes around them, and see the tropical flames no longer revive the canna, the gerbera, the hibiscus, the bougainvillaea and the flame trees, but instead the hungers, the fears, the hatreds and the ferocity that burns in the hollows of the mornes.

And so the conflagration of the Caribbean Sea heaves its silent vapours, blinding for the only eyes able to see and suddenly the blues of the Haitian mornes and the Martiniquan bays fade, the most dazzling reds pale, and the sun is no longer a crystal that plays, and if the market squares have chosen the tracery of Jerusalem thorns as luxury fans to ward off the sky's ardour, if the flowers have known how to find just the right colours to make you fall in love, if the arborescent ferns have secreted golden essences for their croziers, coiled up like a sex, if my West Indies are so beautiful, it shows that the great game of hide and seek has succeeded and certainly that day would be too lovely for us to see it.

### Editor's Notes

1. *Da*: nurse.
2. Robert: Admiral Robert, who effectively governed Martinique on behalf of Vichy from 1941 to 1943.

[published in *Tropiques*, nos 13–14 (1945)]

# René Ménil

# Humour: Introduction to 1945

IN A SOCIETY in which the only quality commonly admired is prudent and ignominious application; where the beauty of the soul comprises such futilities as, for instance, giving 20 pence to a beggar and so solving the problem; where, sleeping on the rails of existence like a bee on the thread of instinct, man champs at the bit of the charity that degrades – there is a risk of bringing into existence quite a bit of conflict between the mind and that thing we call everyday life. If only we would awaken, if only we would awaken suddenly, as the sleeper does, to what is all around us.

Thus we can awaken and find life in a flash, the life of everyone, mine, yours, a life that in this society is determined here, there, on this day through force of circumstance. A life so profoundly rooted in the subordinate and accidental that normally the greatest hopes aren't worth a candle . . . when these hopes aren't quite simply insulting to man. And when, on that mountain of futile words and gestures that forms *this* life, we momentarily aim the cruel fire of the spirit, what appears, infinitely solitary and ridiculous, is a mouse. That's when we burst into laughter – as we convulsively, dizzily, stumble against what we were, in the face of emptiness and insults.

Humour's bitter laughter.

All deeply felt meanness is measured by the chasm separating what we are from what we imagine we should have been. Any protest against fate is measured on the same dial. But the leap of the mind that escapes the futility of everyday life is nothing but the very surge of the life instincts tugging away at and breaking the bridle of individual and social laziness. Humour is precisely the awareness of our diminished and restrained life as well as a revenge against this diminution and

restraint and the triumphant cry of the liberated mind. If we over-
whelm ourselves with subordinate stories, too bad for the marionettes
we are. But the mind screams its denial of any complicity. If, like pup-
pets, we are bent beneath the offensive authority of absurd tyrannies,
the mind withdraws from the race and reveals that it is not fooled by
the masquerade.

It is fairly clear that it is by means of an abrupt *withdrawal of love*
that the irreverence and irony of humour become possible and that this
magical transmutation of values is effected: what was important is no
longer so. And respect for a particular order of things becomes precisely contempt for that order. The investment we made of our feelings
has been submitted to a sudden transfer. We do a moonlit flit away
from our habits, our loves, our former virtue and from social humiliations. We're away and they no longer mean anything to us. We then
inhabit an astonishing climate of salubrity, the climate of our independence is rediscovered, intact. It is our own minds that we now invest
with the affective charge that establishes life's load. It is a narcissistic
return towards the self and a complete scorn for everything. But it is a
return to the highest part of the self, to the impalpable witness of the
self that the drama of our own life does not reach. A return to the critical spirit we never believed we had within us. The other perceptible
ego, our circumstantial, everyday ego compromised in the bloody farce
of everyday life – our anguished and diminished ego – swings in infinitely ridiculous estrangement. Freud tells us: 'The humorist's dynamic
attitude consists in the fact that he draws the psychic stress from the
ego and transfers it to the super-ego. Against the super-ego, exalted in
this way, the ego may appear tiny and all of its interests may seem
futile; it then becomes easy for the super-ego to stifle the ego's infantile
and passionate reactions.' This explains the bitter disdain one feels
both for oneself and for others and this invective that a good-hearted
man sometimes casts upon himself, as if on someone else: 'Yes, it will
amuse me to ridicule the odious being I call *myself*.'[1]

You can tell: the joker is giggling. Our own gravity collapses as does
that of the circumstances in which we find ourselves, and vanishes into
thin air, as vanity. The joker giggles and yet doesn't laugh: he recalls a
belittled life encaged behind the bars of brackish gestures. Even more
than this, he knows that such submission to a compromising reality
goes on and that the liberty he affirms is only imaginary, being only of
the mind. In fact, while the joker scoffs at reality, he does not change it
and his arrows are mere words. Humour is the triumph of irreverent
subjectivity and a safeguard of feelings. Nothing more. The drama of

social life that affronts the mind is not at all destroyed. And so a bitterness always enters humour: our anguish in the face of life is surpassed but not suppressed, and a vision remains instilled in the mind: of Prometheus bound. Of Prometheus who magnificently insults God but is bound.

Humour is a protest against our fall and a defence against the painful and unpleasant sensations resulting from the limitations imposed by men, things or chance on our natural grandeur. The energy in us that is able to generate suffering tends to transform itself and it does so partially into a source of pleasure. An abrupt safeguarding of our anxiety develops as we become aware of the repression of our most legitimate dispositions, and we then soar over the failures that once humbled our self-esteem. We regress vertiginously towards our childhood when harsh necessity was unknown to us and when all our narcissistic instincts were given free rein in the subjective and so easy geography of our games and pleasures.

Therefore, humour is not univocal.

It is dignity retrieved through a leap of the mind.

It is the mind crying out its disdain for a life far too tightly secured in the snares of compromise.

It is the hope that did not exist the moment before but that suddenly, in the light of liberated instincts, rises above conventions that have been denied.

But at the same time that humour trumpets the cry of the imaginary triumph of the instincts, it dispassionately sees real life being ridiculed. This vision chills laughter. The joker laughs through clenched teeth. And if, as today's sociologists know, God is only a mythical transposition of society onto an imaginary plane, then, given that humour is a protest against the life society imposes upon us, the giggling of humour will be irreligious, satanic and cruel. And supremely clairvoyant too. Because, *humour knows*. It is even supremely wise, having gone beyond the accidents of a life to reach the absolute of the Spirit.

From infancy, humanity has had to wield the sword of irony. But why has literature not retained Socrates's bitter laugh after his condemnation before judges whose bellies were stuffed with olives and lentils and whose judgement was made in accordance with the needs of the trade in olives and lentils rather than with the needs of the mind? And why does mythology tell us nothing about the convulsive and painful laughter that enabled Hercules to see himself, after Nemeus, after Lerne and after Augias, sweetly spinning the distaff like an amiable old lady?

It is because it is the task of modern literature to use and study the mechanism of humour in a systematic way.

Let's not mention Lautréamont and his black laugh and menagerie of lice, dogfish and assassins which make us ashamed with a shiver down our spines to be what we are while sharks, storms and men of violence exist. Let's not mention Raymond Roussel who, like a chess player, constructs such shrewdly sham worlds that a moment's sudden reflection is necessary to realize, in a flash, that all this is absurd and that it hides a crystalline mystification. These men have not learned what they know. They exist, impermeable thanks to a flawless literary perfection. But the literary explosion of 1918 that assumed the name of the Dada movement has illuminated the human attitude called humour in a sensational way.[2]

Let's recall the facts. This literary movement was born in 1916 and died around 1921. During and immediately after the First World War it was a protest against the bloody collapse of 'civilization' in the face of the bestiality into which a proud civilization had sunk and the palpable reduction of that culture, despite its pompous ideological trappings, to pure competition for plunder. Dadaist activity was a permanent revolt against art, morality, society and hollow values. It signified a refusal of the thoughts, customs and tastes that had led and continue to lead men to a life that was, for any thinking person, absurd.

The refusal of the whole of reality could develop only by a dictatorship of the spirit and this is essentially what characterizes Dada.

A dictatorship of the spirit that refuses to take seriously the pious works of culture as they united to form life around 1918. Marcel Duchamp, Picabia, Breton, Aragon, Soupault, Ribemont-Dessaignes and Tzara, the creator of the movement, meant to discredit the lived world totally: they proposed to 'disrupt the ritual' of social life, to create misunderstandings in order to make some people realize that in the end conventions are only conventions and that what is proper is merely what we have been told is such. An enterprise of wholesale demolition, that was Dada. An enterprise in the degradation and destruction of values. Ribemont-Dessaignes acknowledges:

There are no more privileged zones of human aspirations, and the basest values are as favoured as the most exalted. And the best strategy, since we always need to keep one eye open in order not to fall back on habits that have become natural in the wake of a long tradition, in order not to allow the fine, the noble, the high, the charming, the ordered, the perfect to find its feet, is to display a weakness for the baroque, the comical, the low, the vulgar, the unstable, the unexpected and the unformed.

The most well-founded values, the most sacred conventions, the thought most officially recognized as being true, no longer apply. The mind takes its revenge on what imprisoned it. The mind leads a regal game: everything that was constricted by importance founders in the ridicule brought, by a supreme justice, to the level of the valueless, but its lack of value was like that of a shooting star, returning to the sky of renown.

But this derision into which lived reality collapses can erupt only when referred to a higher reality: we can mock everything only through recourse to a supreme reason for laughter. And what could that higher reality be for people in whose eyes the spectacle of the world was collapsing into nothingness, indifference and scorn, but the mind itself emerging from its impregnable heart of hearts, the mind liberated of all those rules (of art, morality, logic and even science) that are merely disguised injunctions arising from social reality?

And so both in art and literature Dada reconstituted a world, with a rare casualness, zest and craziness. On what a merry dance were words, things, ideas and good habits led! Everything danced to the sound of the flute, sorry, to the sound of the dog whistle. Dada! An excellent word. A whole programme. But why use this word to indicate an attitude towards life and art? A gratuitous word like everything else, cast at the inanity of everything. Why Dada, you ask? But why not Dada, if you please? Does it matter? One of the movement's champions tells us:

I declare that Tristan Tzara discovered the word Dada on 8 February 1916 at 6 in the evening. I was present with my twelve children when Tzara for the first time pronounced this word which unleashed such legitimate enthusiasm in us. It happened at the Café Terrase in Zurich, and I was wearing a brioche in my left nostril. I am convinced that this word has no importance and that only imbeciles and Spanish professors are interested in dates. What interests us is the Dada spirit and we were all Dada before Dada existed.

To make the sensational discovery, Tzara had slipped a paperknife between the pages of a dictionary. This is the indifference and casualness of a mind no longer allowing itself to be exploited by anything at all (not even by the dictionary).

The same absurdity that presided at the birth of the movement is also found in the poems it inspired. Each poem shows us things, men and words leaving their everyday routine to pirouette and come to a halt, breaking with habit like letters one would throw randomly and that would suddenly come to rest to form a new language. A language that finally disorients us. Here is a short poem by Soupault:

### Flame

*A torn envelope enlarges my room.*
*I jog my memories.*
*We're off.*
*I had forgotten my suitcase.*

Or this one by Picabia:

### My Girlfriend

*Thanks I'm preparing a cyclone*
*To put laughter in my girlfriend's eyes*
*She's wrong to fear nothing*
*She needs to be frightened*
*In order not to be afraid*

etcetera, etcetera, etcetera.

The world is denied. The mind is rediscovered, freed. But bitterness accompanies this vision of devastation. We cannot break with our carnal habits, with the idiotic smiles that are still smiles, without tearing ourselves apart. And then, apart from this sadness behind the laughter, a supreme temptation lies in wait. Suppose you laugh at everything, absolutely everything – including laughter? Suppose you cut yourself off from the final deliverance, belief in the very value of the mind – if you were to mock the mind itself?[3]

What would remain to anyone undertaking such an operation? Nothing, absolutely nothing, not a single straw beyond the temptation of despair. It would become the laughter of mortal desolation. With the furious thirst of negation that dwelt within Dada, it was to be feared that it might end up denying itself and, as Dada took the mind seriously, such a negation would be equivalent to suicide. That's what happened. In 1919, shortly after the birth of Dada, Jacques Vaché, who knew the Dada spirit if not Dada, killed himself when faced with 'the theatrical and joyless uselessness of everything, when one knows', as he said. Dada itself put an end to its own existence in 1921, its elements dispersed to the winds. In 1920, Jacques Rigaut wrote in *Littérature*, the review of the Dadaist movement:

> There are no reasons to live, but nor are there any reasons to die. The only means open to us for testifying our disdain for life is to accept it. Life is not worth taking the trouble to depart it. By charity you can limit it for others, but for oneself? It's hardly worth making a fuss about despair, indifference, betrayal, fidelity, solitude, family, liberty, burdens, money, poverty, love, lack of love, syphilis, health, sleep, insomnia, desire, impotence, platitudes, art, honesty, dishonour, mediocrity, intelligence.

What thread attaches the writer of these dark lines to life? None, surely? Jacques Rigaut killed himself in 1929.

We can see that humour is a gun that goes off. But who should be the target? And as an ultimate gesture, should it not be against oneself?

Baudelaire had already made the inspired affirmation that the two fundamental literary qualities were supernaturalism and irony. And regarding irony, he said: 'The mingling of the grotesque and the tragic is pleasant to the mind, as discordance is to the indifferent ear.' In his *Préface de Cromwell*, Hugo – in a summary way it's true – initiated the idea of a poetry whose substance would be humour, but why did he restrict the explosive mixture of laughter and tragedy to the theatre alone, while pontificating so seriously in his lyrical 'great poetry'? In so doing, he conformed to the prejudices of the age and to his own. At the present time, it would be impossible to imagine a poetic work that does not, in a certain way, contain a greater or lesser comical element.

Poetry – whether surrealist or not – is necessarily, in as much as it achieves a certain sincerity, humorous.

The poetry of Breton, Eluard, Langston Hughes and Césaire is humorous.

The tales of Benjamin Péret and the novels of Faulkner or Steinbeck are humorous.

The jazz of Duke Ellington or Louis Armstrong is humorous.

The painting of Chirico or Picasso is humorous.

In architecture, art nouveau is baroque and so on . . .

Humour is a poetic attitude.

1. Because it desensitizes the poet in relation to the universe and so

allows the lightness of mind that is indispensable to poetic expression. The detachment of the ironist. Passion, which dramatizes and weighs down the slightest events, is an anti-poetic state.

2. Because it explodes the stagnant fixtures or institutions that immobilize (individual or social) life and, through the explosion, illuminated desires surge forth.

3. Because all humorous vision is a metaphor. The object of our perception is hidden by a grandiose hallucination compared to which it appears minimal, futile and impossible. This comparison or, more accurately, this identification, puts habitual logic to flight to give its poetical condensation.

4. Finally, because this metaphor, which ends in a degradation of the real finishing up as a shirt tail, triggers an antithetical exaltation of the mind. As reality falls away, the mind undergoes a vertiginous ascent.

It is fairly clear that humour proceeds with all the means of dream: condensation, displacement, hallucination, identification, etcetera, which are the very means of the poetic image.

How could Eluard have written this magnificent sentence without humour?

> I'm telling a well-known tale, a famous poem I'm reading again: I'm leaning against a wall, with verdant ears and lips burned to cinders.

And Breton?

> *Just before midnight near the landing stage.*
> *Don't be concerned if a dishevelled woman follows you*
> *It's the azure . . .*

I have not spoken about laughter in order to laugh, but rather to define, on the one hand, what merits laughter at this time and, on the other hand, the way the dangerous weapons of humour can be used against the ridiculousness of the age.

Beyond the greyness of the age comes the dawning of 1945. And throughout the grasslands of the West this year the world's most beautiful cabbages will burgeon alongside the daisies. These cabbages will have been nourished with new fertilizer. An excellent manure: MAN. You haven't yet worked it out? I mean, you realize, that it will have been man who has served as fertilizer and manure for these cabbages. Because on reflection man is, you see, the cheapest available at the present time on the world market. We are at the peak of a culture. Western culture is

Catholic, orthodox, Protestant, prudent, practical, economical and spiritualist. In fact the only culture, so we are told.

There we are – at the peak of a culture. Man has never been so good and useful for culture. I don't know if you like poetry, but in order to write these lines I feel the climbing flower of thrill running between my shoulders. Let's say we take man and put him in a park. There's a factory in the middle of the park and, around the factory, beautiful flowerbeds as far as the eye can see. Everything is beautiful in the factory because people are cultivated and have taste. Everything gleams, everything is white and hygienic. There are precision machines resembling amazing spiders or flowers of light and sometimes they give you signals like electrified stars. Around the park, there are thickets in which, under an admirable sky, flowers of electricity also sing. Let's say you take man and lead him into a room: you gently asphyxiate him. There is such sweetness in the air! And then you throw him into an incandescent oven. Oh, don't worry: all the ashes will be collected. Man is so useful that nothing of him must be wasted. You put man into the bags printed beforehand and use him to create the beautiful spring when the wind and the birds will quarrel in the trees, when the grass (it will be wild, this grass) will venture to grow beside the cabbages which aren't any more expensive this year because when it comes to it, in our civilization, we fortunately have some man whenever we want him and as much of him as we like, all for free . . .

So say the newspapers and people on the dawn of this new year. Happy New Year! Have a good time!

I will only situate this *news item* within the present civilization that is celebrated so highly – here and there – by republican poets. I can see nothing in it but the logical conclusion of this very civilization. Anyone who sees in such contempt for man simply a symptom of the war, or of the bestiality of a scapegoat population would be pretty crazy. War never affects anything concerning morality: it is, according to Clausewitz's definitive formula, merely the continuation of politics by military means. In a culture in which all ideologies, upon analysis, are directed simply towards a sordid cult of money, what other result is possible but the one we have shown? Throughout the century and a half and more that bourgeois 'nobility' has triumphed, has not man been measured precisely by the yardstick of the money he has or can produce, and are any values officially recognized and praised from on high by states, churches and academies other than commercial ones? What are the reasons for the war? In this age when each noble soul is distanced from its heart in order not to hear its anguished beating, what does a pope speak to us about but the respect due to money?[4] And what is the poetry current in the 'best circles' but those same utilitarian values wrapped, it is true, in a vicious confectionery of metaphors? This poetry won't lose its head in lyrical flight:

> *The worked earth in which seeds ripen*
> *Will ripple, joyful and sweet, with little billows*
> *Happy to feel in its underground flesh*
> *The fate of vine and fenced-in wheat.*[5]

Yes, let's rejoice that the owners of flour mills and vineyards will have had huge profits this year. For more than a century and a half, the limitless coercive power that money gives in present-day society has ensured that everything, within man, that is unable ever to pay its way (poetry, liberty, the spirit) is brutalized and degraded. And that those who during this time have devoted themselves, no matter how little, to true humanity have been hunted down, abused and martyred. In France alone, the land of liberty, we can cite the Marquis de Sade, confined in the Bastille; Hugo, exiled; Baudelaire, dragged through corrupt courts; Lautréamont, killed; Rimbaud, gnawed at by idealist vermin after his death; Zola, also exiled. And so many others. And others in whom the spirit burned whose lives were made so difficult because they were made to feel – oh so nicely – that this world was not theirs and so had the good grace to kill themselves: Nerval, Rigaut and others.

Therefore don't expect chauvinism to make us indignant about the brutalization of men in other countries, which is certainly no worse than ours each day as we jostle in the streets with the bestiality that is called modern culture. '*We who know*', as Vaché once said, 'have seen plenty of others.'

1945, as we have seen, has some excellent subjects in store for our enthusiasm. Prophesy is not required to appreciate what tomorrow will bring. Rather let's recapitulate:

The almost total crisis of critical spirit which characterises wartime mentality has an immediate impact upon the development of the arts and the play of ideas it brings in its wake. For several years now, like it or not, we have been forced to co-exist in a condition of edification, each of us witnesses to an extreme good to come, albeit by the paradoxical means of destruction and carnage. The coercive powers which today control the whole world are not content with taking

lives, they ask that every advanced method of judgement be sacrificed
to them: journalists make it their business to encourage thinkers to
repent their ways. . . . In the circumstances, it is not surprising that
regressive tendencies are coming to the fore in art: a taste for a return
to accepted forms and subjects, tombstone aesthetics, an attraction
for refuges of all types, arms insane enough to burden themselves
with chains and *fear*, a fear so great it could be completely mistaken
for its very object, that one sees desperately clinging to what engen-
dered it, a strange fear of the remedy rather than the sickness, a fear
of inspiration and imagination and, despite the denials of good or
bad faith, a *fear of liberty*.[6]

Yes, really, it might well be that those who seek liberty take the initial
precaution of putting their heads under the yoke.

Humour will flourish upon the brow of 1945.

It will be the year of gentleness. For the ransom of contemporary
bestiality will be the recourse to angelism. The best angels will be those
who will have been the most aggressive and the cruellest and they will
be the most gentle precisely because they will have totally purged their
aggressiveness and their cruelty. Thus a father of a family who sneaks
home from the brothel won't hear of anything but virtue being mentioned in the family. Gentleness will be a principle of government to
stupefy the mind and humiliate desire.

Reformers will finally come to testify on the temple parvis. They will
propose every possible social transformation and, if need be, they will
help to put them into effect. They will be prepared to change hearts,
heads, feelings and the physiologies of men and societies. Yes, really,
they will be ready for any sacrifice. ON CONDITION THAT IT DOESN'T
AFFECT MONEY.

The more inhuman the fate offered to man, the more vibrant the
protest of consciousness will become, and humour will most approach
its ideal conditions. No one could deny that, all things being equal, in
the part of the globe in which we live[7] we risk finding a degradation
of man greater than elsewhere. It can be imagined, without any displaced vanity, that we think we in the Caribbean are not badly placed
to contribute significantly to a literature of humour.

Humour, at least humour conscious of itself and its means, has
barely taken root in our soil, but it will quickly ripen because it has
taken the ultra-rapid short cut of poetry. Listen to Aimé Césaire in his
*Notebook of a Return to My Native Land*:

I refuse to pass my swellings off as authentic glories.

And I laugh at my old childish imaginings.

No we have never been amazons at the court of the King of Dahomey, nor princes of Ghana with eight hundred camels, nor doctors at Timbuctoo when Askia the Great was king, nor architects at Djenné, nor Madhis, nor warriors. We do not feel in our armpits the itch of those who once carried the lance. And because I have sworn to conceal nothing of our history (I who admire nothing so much as a sheep grazing of an afternoon in its own shadow), I wish to confess that we were always quite undistinguished dishwashers . . .[8]

It needs to be acknowledged that among Caribbean peasants a humour has always existed, which is generally unperceived but whose everyday expression is to be found in the jokes and songs in which blacks take themselves as the butt of their gibes. They even, so great is the excellence of their moral health, rise to the purificatory summits of effrontery. On the other hand, in supposedly 'cultivated' Caribbean circles, a natural insincerity prevents any awareness of human stupidity, something certainly more aggressive here than elsewhere. Its pretension numbs the mind, solemnity curbs derision, sentimentality fossilizes feelings, and self-importance prompts stiff gestures whose ridiculousness somehow escapes their authors. A wild conviction and unshakeable complacency prevent any self-reflection or revision of social values. The Caribbean intelligentsia does not even suspect that one can turn over, as fishermen do octopi, any idea of reality or of oneself we have formed at a given moment. It is unaware of the play of ideas and words. It believes in what is 'reasonable', and rest assured it has no difficulty in finding what is reasonable: it is the geometrical mean between two extremes as the centaur is no doubt more reasonable than man and horse which are, poor things, extremes. Incapable of the slightest aggression towards itself that would unsaddle it, or against events to call in their accounts, it understands nothing about poetry, before which it offers the excuse: 'But what use is it?' Society, if it has no awareness of humour, if it doesn't appreciate the poetic element it might use in order to envision itself mounted on stilts and imperturbably ruling over grains of dust (everyone being king of some trifle), nevertheless is part of objective humour.

This lugubrious gravity thanks to which everyone in this small world takes themselves seriously and imposes the same seriousness on their neighbour has obviously held back Caribbean spiritual evolution for nigh on a century, because you penetrate into this land only through detachment, lightness and even effrontery, which are means for *self-detachment* and the transgression of your own limits through embracing the groundswell of blind sincerity.

There is no shortage of reasons for laughter in one part or another of the globe.

The age is singularly advantageous for an art of humour: the decline of societies and the accompanying difficulties present ideal conditions for it. Institutions deteriorate and by themselves fall lower and lower. By itself, history turns into a sinister farce in which man becomes a caricature of man. What is at stake? Our taking of revenge on this masquerade by erecting the ideological defeatism that precedes fresh beginnings. It is a matter of demoralizing this society, discrediting it, ridiculing it, and making it feel ashamed of itself. In the final analysis we must cause it to lose consciousness of its rights, among which is its right to exist, and make it dance hypnotically like a bear to the sound of its own tune.

Art is capable of this feat of strength.

We will reinvent Dada but in a dialectical way in order to sublate it.

Dada was absolute negation and killed itself according to an implacable logic. It made a short circuit of its humour within which it placed itself and its death resulted from this electrocuting force. It isolated itself in the *desolate circle of its subjectivity* and prospected this supreme islet of imaginary liberty through humour.

We are people for whom the external world exists and it is not a matter of generalizing mockery to the point of making a desert of our faith.

There are questions about which we have refrained from joking. Liberty, life, poetry.

And we see the image of this liberty beyond the false reality of the age.

And we see this life dawning above a bestial life.

And this poetry gleams through the living eyes of History.

And by being steadfastly bolstered by these sur-realities, we shall sustain, over everything, the salvo of atrocious humour.

### Notes

1. Stendhal, *The Red and the Black*.
2. I am considering Dadaism only from the literary perspective, although from the start it equally gave itself a social and political dimension. Moreover, the Dada spirit has strongly inspired other arts, for example painting and music.

3. Thanks to their contempt for logical and aesthetic forms, the Dadaists already revered nothing but the mind's bare fury and ranked the genius on the same level as the idiot. Which also ruined a certain dignity (conventional, it's true) of the mind.

4. At present there is a crisis of the spirit. But Pope Pius XII thinks such things can always be sorted out. He attends to what is most urgent, immediately using words calculated to threaten those who might be tempted to scorn commercial values: 'We officially wish to remind you that the common doctrine of the Church is that property is the cornerstone of the social order.' And to control the strongest-willed, he upholds the thesis of the divinity of money: 'It's God who is master of all things [meaning wealth]. . . . Those whom God has confided with its management are accountable only to him and no one can claim the right to deny that private property stands above everything . . .' and so on (official communication of 1 September 1944). Such is the sordid morality of what represents the Spirit in our society. Does it surprise anyone if we abandon this spirit to those who are possessed by it?

5. Madame la Comtesse de Noailles.

6. André Breton, January 1944.

7. The colonies.

8. *Return to My Native Land* (1969) Harmondsworth: Penguin, p. 66–7.

[published in *Tropiques*, no. 12 (January 1945); reprinted in *Tracées*]

RENÉ MÉNIL

# Concerning Colonial Exoticism

THERE IS AN exoticism founded in nature resulting from a particular form of human relation. Finding myself in a foreign land,
I am disoriented and perceive the manners, practices and customs of
the native as picturesque and marked with signs of alienness. And as
the relation is reciprocal, the native of the land will have a similar, if
inverse, vision of me. For him I am as alien as he is for me: he has an
exotic vision of me and I have an exotic vision of him. Things cannot
be otherwise. Montaigne in Italy, the Marquis de Custine in Russia,
Leiris in the Caribbean were moved and amazed as they stumbled
upon manners new to them. The Italians, the Russians and the
Caribbeans saw them as travellers 'from somewhere else'. Human
relations in exoticism are those of two different consciousnesses
brought face to face and seized with a sense of the difference
between their respective customs. The exotic vision is a view of man
taken 'from the other side', from outside and beyond geographical
frontiers.

Unfortunately, the natural tendency in exoticism is to miss the 'seriousness' and authenticity of the drama (of the other) and to confine
oneself to an idyllic and superficial vision. This is because the first
impulse of consciousness surprised in a new situation is to examine the
scenery, external picturesqueness, and people as part of the scenery, as
objects and as decor (landscapes and costumes).

It is only through breaking the bounds of this idyllic consciousness
that the stranger can approach the stranger in his own circumstances, as
a profound and rich subject. Exoticism is thus a first movement in the
relation between countries and peoples. But this moment needs to be

overcome and negated to reach the truth of the person who until then had been perceived only in the exotic vision.

But besides this normal exoticism, there exists another form of exoticism which constitutes the object of the present examination – colonial exoticism. Next to that kind of exoticism resulting from the very nature of a particular form of human relationship – 'I am exotic for a foreigner and he is exotic for me' – there looms the monstrosity of an exoticism unique of its kind. It is not without stupefaction, in fact, that upon analysis we notice that, in poetry as in painting, the Caribbean people have an exotic vision of themselves and offer up an exotic expression of themselves. It is not someone from abroad – such as the mainland French person – who portrays the Caribbean as picturesque and ornamental. He himself is the one who describes himself from a distance – externally and superficially – without involving his personal circumstances.

Let's think about this: for there to be exoticism, there needs to be two humanities facing one another in which one party appears alien to the other – in other words, *exotic*.

What conditions could have caused Caribbean society to become exotic – in other words foreign – to itself? The condition for such an aberration can be nothing but the colonial situation.

The fundamental characteristic of human existence in colonial society is separation from oneself, exile from oneself, alienation from oneself. This phenomenon of cultural oppression, inseparable from colonialism, will determine within each colonial country a suppression of its particular national soul (its history, religion and customs) to introduce into this collectivity what we can call the 'soul-of-the-mainland-other'. Depersonalization and alienation follow. I perceive myself as a foreigner, as being exotic. Why? Because 'I' is consciousness, 'the other' becomes the self. I am 'exotic-to-myself' because my view of myself is the view of the white person having become mine after three centuries of colonial conditioning. Exoticism – a means of expression for the Caribbean person when he recounts his life in literature and painting – expresses separation and exile. This expression is superficial and false: it belongs to the psychopathology of colonial life. Vision, instead of springing from a genuine West Indian consciousness (to be conquered or re-conquered) is imposed from outside by white colonialist consciousness. This exoticism results from the distance our society finds in relation to itself within the colonial system.

Do not, therefore, be amazed by the tenacity of Caribbean exoticism – it is a phoenix eternally reborn from its own ashes. After the old exoticism of the period of ascendent imperialism (Duquesnay and Thaly in Martinique), there now appears a rejuvenated and preened – surrealist – exoticism which is an aspect of the current anti-colonialist struggle.

But if we consider it without complacency, we see the wrinkles of a familiar old age behind the newness of form. In spite of the poet's resolute intention to escape the insignificance of exoticism, he is inevitably and despite himself tempted to return to it for the simple reason that the basis of the poetic process is the very structure of the colonial regime. *Exoticism is a constant of colonial consciousness centred – economically, socially and culturally – outside itself, on the mainland.* The embellishments of colonial poetry, despite an attempted humanism discernible among our best poets today, are woven on a similar canvas: a collective consciousness that, even in revolt, suffers from a tragic dispossession. For the historian, exoticism (whether it be of renunciation or revolt) remains exoticism – the literature of the colonial period. The sickness within Caribbean poetic consciousness, which desperately aims to assume possession of itself but is drawn outwards by a cultural system founded on the negation of individual characteristics, will vanish only when the colonial system itself is shattered and the colonial structures are replaced with human structures.

Once the philosophical critique had allowed Caribbean poets to become aware of the colonial situation and the falsity of the vision of the world resulting from it, poetry in the Caribbean became characterized by a continual effort towards the most authentic expression possible of Caribbean man. Poetic expression will henceforth be a constant struggle progressively to rid the poem of its exotic elements.

For exoticism is not a *quality* (a homogeneous and static unity) but, like all styles, is a collection of multiple and active (psychological and social) resolutions such that, even forewarned against it, it is not unusual for the poet, while avoiding certain of its aspects, still to fall prey to one or another of its insidious manifestations. The struggle against exoticism is the reverse side of the struggle for the conquest of truth and the richness of colonial consciousness.

The problem of exoticism is thus connected to historical development and will only be resolved as the level of collective and personal involvement in the political struggle rises. This is why the very qualification of exoticism is relative: what in our eyes today appears true and authentic can tomorrow suddenly, cast in a harsher light, be shown to be formal, external and exotic.

At the current time, poetry illuminates many aspects of colonial reality. This luminous core is perhaps what is most valuable within the world's poetry, which is hardly surprising. Since, of all peoples, those in the colonies most heavily bear the weight of modern history – let's say of 'Western civilization' – do they not have a greater responsibility than others to reveal the reality of the world? The misfortune of the poets of imperialism is to be cut off from the inconsequential conditions of their lives by the practical activity (the forced labour) of colonial peoples. And this causes them to transform the hard brilliance of things into distant stifled echoes. And this is why they tend to succumb to insipidity and verbalism.

But it is still the case that the limitations of the genuine colonial poem are revealed in its very core and that the conflict between the elements of truth and the elements of exoticism emerges. It is the case that exotic elements of life can sneak in beside the authentic cry in a formal and external way (sometimes it is the race that is shown as being picturesque, sometimes elements of folklore or mentality, sometimes the tropical landscape, etcetera). It goes without saying that race, tom-toms, witchcraft, and luxuriant vegetation do exist and must be integrated into the poem. But it is enough that they are *treated in themselves* (for example evoked for their strangeness) instead of being subordinated to and seen through the historical human drama for them to shoot forth in decorative visions and exotic play. Let's point out in passing that to evoke aspects of life because of their strangeness and because they are part of the existence of 'distant lands' implies the use of trickery on the part of the metropolitan Frenchman since the colonial artist's own land is *neither distant nor strange for him*.

Thus the struggle against exoticism assumes different forms in the course of history in proportion to the enrichment of Caribbean consciousness as it raises itself to higher degrees of critical reflection. Thus we can today perceive a subtle form of exoticism. It can be called *anti-exotic-exoticism*.

The naïve exoticism of the period of assimilation (Duquesnay, Salavina, Thaly, to mention only the 'more modern' poets who even today are still working this apparently inexhaustible mine) is just the exoticism of the white colonizer accepted without critical examination by these assimilated writers. These 'bards' turn themselves exactly into the ignominious idea that the white colonialist has forged for blacks, in order to pursue his enterprise of piracy with a clear conscience. Once given the signal for revolt, a struggle against this degrading exoticism begins. But here is the astonishing thing: *this struggle (which continues today) sometimes assumes the form of an anti-exoticism that unfortunately is itself situated in exoticism.* The majority of our poets today believe they are completely outside exoticism and they act in good faith. But good faith concerns only the subjective relations of consciousness with itself.

Let us analyse some of the mechanisms of this new error.

If we examine the poetic works published in the French Caribbean during the past twenty years, we will notice that sometimes poetic method, by being defined as a struggle against the image colonialism has formed of us, creates a negative of this image, in the photographic sense of the term. Which means *we assume the same image for ourselves and simply embellish it differently. Usually, we are content with simply reversing the colours and qualities whilst maintaining the colonialists' image.*

We therefore start from a false image of ourselves – a product of the colonial system – and believe we can transform its fraudulence into authenticity by two poetic procedures:

We may, like children overcome by a bout of contrariness, proceed by mechanical contradictions (saying black where colonial mentality said white; courage where the colonialists said laziness; nobility when they said abjection, and so on). From this point of view, a good proportion of today's black poetry is outmoded: it represents bravura with neither truth nor depth and consequently with no power of conviction.

For Senghor, white becomes synonymous with malignancy: '. . . white like ennui, like poverty and like death'.

Otherwise, using humour, we boldly assume all the ignominy of the degraded image the colonialists conceive, rejecting it through the very act of expressing it in an ironic way. The poet will say: 'I wish to confess that we were always quite undistinguished dishwashers, small-time shoeshiners, at the very most fairly conscientious witch-doctors . . .'[1]

Admittedly, to depict the negro with qualities opposed to those the white man uses to define him is already poetic, already revolutionary. Certainly, to transpose the 'ill-mannered' negro into humour is already an important step on the path of self-awareness.

However, such poetic expression is still internally contradictory, insufficient and tainted with spuriousness. And this is why poetic expression today tends towards a truer expression.

If we think we can recapture the image of us that has resulted from colonial culture and use it for our own benefit simply by reversing its colours and qualities, we are making an error.

The fact is that if we are not what the white man, in his colonial delirium, would like to think us, we are no more the contrary of his idea of us. We are not the 'opposite' of our colonial image, we are *other* than this image.

We are not the reverse side of colonial error. We define ourselves adjacent and outside, which is something altogether different.

To use Kant's vocabulary, Caribbean poetic consciousness is still characterized at present, at its heart, by heteronomy, that is by external dependence. The image of us that colonialism intends to propagate, and which its culture circulates, is false, but its contradictory nature is determined by its alien origin: either way, we are encased in alienation.

The foundation of colonial exoticism resides in this.

Determined from the start to express the Caribbean soul decisively in its authenticity thanks to heroic sincerity, our modern poetry is nevertheless far from escaping exoticism. We have examined the historical causes of this deviation.

But *critical causes* also exist: the poet will be all the more vulnerable to exoticism if he fails to subject the colonial situation to preliminary examination. Such a critique reveals the colonial situation as a concrete totality of multiple relations connected with the mainland and such that, even when one struggles *against* it, one still remains *inside* it. This does not mean that all struggle is illusory, but rather that, in order to keep its distance, it must be aware of these theoretical foundations, failing which we risk simply floundering within the framework in which colonialism holds us imprisoned at the very moment we believe we are triumphing over it. Even worse, we risk, through tacit complicity, developing myths of exoticism in a sort of division of labour whereby one aspect will be expressed by whites, the other by blacks.

Thus we must go beyond anti-exotic poetic expression which is contaminated by the very thing it wants to oppose.

The conquest of autonomy in poetry – which is inseparable from political autonomy – will destroy the duality by which we appear as strange and strangers to ourselves. Only then, by engaging integrally with ourselves, will we cease to be picturesque in our own eyes and simply *exist*, able seriously to live out our drama which is assuredly not the antithetical shadow of the colonialists'. For at last we will be ourselves – to be invented, it's true.

## Editor's Note

1. Aimé Césaire, *Return to My Native Land* (1969) Harmondsworth: Penguin, p. 67.

[published in *La Nouvelle Critique*, 1959; reprinted in *Tracées*]

# PART III

# AN ENCOUNTER FROM

# the OTHER SIDE

# André Breton and André Masson

## *Creole Dialogue*

— L ook at that white splash up there: you'd say it was a huge flower, but perhaps it's only the underside of a leaf: there's so little wind. The night here must be full of traps and unknown sounds. But the most beautiful thing, because it's least imaginable, remains daybreak. Everything that you won't forgive yourself for having missed.

– The forest envelops us: we knew the forest and her spells before we arrived. Do you remember a drawing I called 'Vegetal Delirium'? That delirium is here, we can touch and participate in it. We are one of those layered trees that holds a miniature marsh in the hollows of its branches, with all its parasitic vegetation grafted onto its central trunk: rising, falling, active, passive, and rigged out from top to bottom with star-flowered lianas.

– You more than anyone else feel at home here, in fact. Everything has been like this for so long. In the end surrealist landscapes will be seen as the least arbitrary ones. It is inevitable that they should find a resolution in those lands where nature has not been tamed at all. What a Rimbaudian dream of alternating planes that waterfall into the valley is, with the ultimate whirlpool device roaring at its base.

– Yes, everything exists in the world, and I can think of nothing so ridiculous as that fear of the imagination that crushes the painter. Nature and its profusion put him to shame:
*Find the flowers that would be chairs!*
But we've almost got them here in front of us!

– One might wonder to what extent the paucity of European vegetation is responsible for the flight of the mind towards an imaginary flora. Is what we want to escape today perception in general, or just the specific perception of what reaches our senses when we return to less favoured places? Some people have quite deliberately left Europe for that very reason. It is striking to think that Gauguin, among others, passed through Martinique and thought of settling here.

– Exoticism, one could mistakenly say, exoticism, a most careless word. But what does exoticism mean? The whole world is ours. Just because I was born near a weeping willow is no reason to devote my art to this rather limited liaison.

– Besides, we are not totally limited to the view from our window just because we are condemned to live in a particular place: there are the illustrations in childhood books, from which so many visual memories spring up scarcely less real than others. But all the same don't you find that the need for something more is less keen here than elsewhere? Nothing could really be added to this spot to perfect it. I wouldn't dream of reinstating imitative art, of course, but it would seem more justified here than elsewhere.

– What is not justifiable, to my mind, is to impoverish what exists. As youngsters the engravings of the *Magasin pittoresque* set us dreaming, and later on we loved the virgin forests of the Douanier Rousseau, which you found again in Mexico, I believe.

– Perhaps Rousseau would be even more at home here. You know that whether he saw America with his own eyes is often disputed. It's a problem of the greatest importance, in my view. The arguments on either side are impressive. Apollinaire was adamant that the Douanier did his military service as a musician in Mexico. And yet, in a biographical note in Rousseau's own hand, written in 1892, there is no mention of this visit. Who should one believe? That would be a fine advanced examination question to set art critics (don't you think they should be made to sit exams?): does Rousseau's painting prove that he had or had not been to the tropics?

– In fact, critics have barely considered this important question. It challenges all the byways of dream. Whatever the answer, you were talking to me the other day about *La Charmeuse de serpents*, that painting in the Louvre that's so fascinating. Since our arrival, we pass it on our way every day. It has lost nothing of its mystery and enticement.

– That's just what's extraordinary. That black man we just passed in the undergrowth, brandishing his sword – no, it was his cane-cutting cutlass – could have been related to her! If Rousseau had never left France, one would then have to admit that his primitive psychology led him to discover entire primitive places which *conformed to reality*. So there would have to be, beyond all the obstacles civilization puts in the way, a mysterious, *second*, communication that is still possible between men, based on what originally united, and divided, them. It deserves more than the insubstantial investigations so far devoted to the subject.

– You are touching on something that moves me profoundly. You have always argued for the poet or the artist to have something of the quality of a medium. In fact one could argue that Henri Rousseau was the repository of dreams and ancient desires. The longing for an Edenic life is striking in him: I consider the one revealed in Fra Angelico's *Paradises* to be far less profound, for example.

– You were telling me about Cook's *Voyages*, which I haven't read. I'd like you to tell me more about this work which has an important place, it would seem, in the history of the discovery of distant – poetically distant – islands.

– I was particularly struck by the episode of the encounter between a sailor and a beautiful island girl. Lacking a common language, these two people in love managed to tell each other *everything* in an invented language, made up of nothing but caresses. For me it is this tale that drives the whole protracted reverie prompted by the work. The Europeans, the English in this case, show themselves in a pitiful light. In a space such as this, where your gaze endlessly follows a sinuous line, it is hard not to evoke those young girls crowned with flowers, swimming off to meet the boats. Love, when we say that it must be reinvented . . .

– Everything must be reinvented. I believe it, and I think about the intolerable lack that would result from too great a unification of the world. A world where nothing was left to reinvent? It would be the end of the world.

– Listen . . .

– Our friends call it the mountain whistler, listen: there are several of them, and their combined songs compose a melancholy aura around the beautiful star-shaped liana flower, which we will find hard to pick.

– Melancholy . . . The interval between each modulation and the next is painful. In that time there's nothing there for action. In *White Shadows*, perhaps only the exchange of kisses could have withstood such an accompaniment. But the liana flower is also too slender, too white, to be a star: it could only slip from a sylph's letter. When you manage to make out their forms in their entirety, these lianas – I'm talking about those that are so upright, so tall – are truly the harp of the earth. And have you tasted the little apple that follows this star? An apple for an Eve who would be a serpent. . . . What else might so melt in the mouth: poison and cantharis honey, if that were possible?

Our friends the great malefactors of the late nineteenth century would only have wanted to bite into such fruits while lying on a black couch, listening to the poems of Levet.

– *White Shadows*, how distant and yet so close. Around the same time I was reading *Typee*, Melville's book, which shows how you can acclimatize yourself to a cannibal Eden with the help of women, all of them having something of the sorceress about them . . . But see: there on the bed of the stream, that little pool of strangely yellow water and those hissing bubbles, it's a hot-water spring. The volcano is never far away on this island.

– It really knew how to say what it had to all in one go. Damn it, what an idea, to spare only the prisoner! How pleased Sade's magnificent hero Rodin would have been. Besides, this volcano certainly hid its intentions. This story isn't bad: an old priest, who had spent his whole life on Martinique, had been called away just before the catastrophe. Just as he was about to take a break for coffee, he was joined by a brother, all aflutter. 'Come at once, the Father Superior wants to speak to you.' 'Never mind that,' he thought. 'It can wait.' A second brother addressed him in the same way, and then a third. 'But what's this all about? Can't I drink in peace!' 'I've promised not to let on,' replied the other, 'but I think there's been an eruption in Martinique.' 'Well, in that case I can take my coffee. There's no volcano in Martinique.'

– An excellent story. It shows how there will always be heroes of incredulity. No volcanoes, no prehistory either, isn't that so, despite those blossomings of giant umbels of the arborescent ferns and the petrified trees in the south of the island. Fortunately there are still the exhibits in the 'volcanography museum' (what a wonderful idea: a museum of catastrophe) which we visited with all due solemnity. Those perturbed objects teach us above all that the turn-of-the-century style – the eruption occurred in 1902 – needed the finishing touch of elemental fire. Don't you find that the volcano improved those rather affected lamps, that glassware that's not yet contorted and varied enough? I know how much you admire the iridescence produced by lava, so much brighter than that which a ceramicist's kiln could produce.

– A marvel. A litre bottle, a 'common' litre bottle seized with such convulsions and caressed so perfectly by all the colours of excavated glassware that it would have made Mr Gallé, so dear to Barrès, die of jealousy. One wonders whether it was art nouveau or the earthquake which came first and which set the other going. But what I wouldn't give to open the little perfume bottle, so carefully exhibited, which we admired at the museum, this bottle which was so hermetically sealed that only the container was set in motion! The devil himself, smelling of jasmine.

– What do you think now of Wilde's quip about nature imitating art?

– The last to take it up would still be architects. You could line up every cathedral, blow a few of them up, reflect it all in a lake and make the onlookers take belladonna, and you still wouldn't come close to the entanglement of those trees that specialize in high-wire gymnastics, which play piggy-back into the clouds, jump off precipices and, moaning, describe an arc like beloved sorceresses beneath the cups of sticky flowers that are acetylene lamps, arc lights designed to light up maternal crypts in the shadows of the heart of private regions, which open up and close again on our life.

– It's true, there every form is confronted and every contrast magnified. In the *heart* of the forest, how I love that expression! Yes, our heart is at the centre of this prodigious entanglement. What ladders for dreams these implacable lianas are! And these branches, what bows drawn for the arrows of our thoughts!

– And how deep the space is too, how enticing in comparison to those thickets that surround it! The stone you just dropped from up on the bridge just keeps falling, and stands for something in us too. For a second I was that stone. All the same you would rather throw yourself off this bridge than the one on rue de Rome. I have trouble returning to the track. We will have left something imperceptible behind, a very faint, very fleeting premonition of death, but death went by none the less: beware, the soil is damp and slippery, the leaves are shiny.

– Yes, precipices, abysses: this splendid sylvan wood is also a well. And humidity reigns over everything. See, those explosions of bamboos seem to be wreathed in smoking vapours, and the summits of the mornes are turbaned with such heavy clouds.

– We're a long way from the avenue du Bois.

– We're a very long way from contrived vistas here. Nature in the open dislikes straight avenues and won't allow symmetry, which is mankind's traditional prerogative. Modern avenues, the alignments of the megaliths at the dawn of history, the planting of rigid scenery: always symmetry. 'The sadness of such vast monumental perspectives', as Beckford said. And for Pascal, symmetry is simply based on the human form.

– Take it away from man and I really fear he would have to forgo deciphering what he views. It's true that what you enjoy is what you least decipher. You know the experiment that shows that the eye, choosing from two possible shapes – white on a black background or black on a white background – selects the symmetrical shape to the exclusion of the other, without preference for black on white or white on black. If two asymmetrical objects of different substances were separated by a symmetrical gap, everything suggests that it is the gap that the eye would read, that the gap would become real, while the objects would vanish, would fade into the background.

– The theory of privileged structures has taken up all my attention. If the human mind enjoys certain constructions and geometries, it is no doubt because they are reassuring. We think we can abandon ourselves to the forest with impunity and then all of a sudden its meandering obsesses us: if we escape this green labyrinth, won't we be at the Panic Doors?

– Fortunately we won't have to look far for the antidote. Without falling into the irrevocability of *Paul and Virginia*, it's enchanting to imagine that the south of the island contradicts and exorcises what is perilous in this landscape. Sometimes nature too likes symmetry: it likes it in crystals, and man has only had to take it as a model in order to release, purely from its dust, the complete light that lurks in the diamond. Don't you find it at the same time extraordinary and necessary that the rock of the island that leads to the open sea should be called precisely Diamond Rock?

– I see in it the very promise of a deliverance. Yes, we are smitten by the force of vegetation and yet what could be more significant than the overwhelming need we have felt to maintain regular forms in a place of nature where it is precisely the formless, I mean the lack of framework, that seems to predominate?

– Let us symbolically bear away from it a canna flower, as beautiful as the circulation of blood from the lowest to the highest life forms, its calices filled to the brim with this marvellous residue. May it be the heraldic expression of the reconciliation we seek between the graspable and the desperate, life and dream – it is through a whole lattice of these flowers that we pass so as to continue our advance in the only valid way there is: through the flames.

[published in André Breton, *Martinique, charmeuse de serpents*]

ANDRÉ BRETON

# A Great Black Poet:
# Aimé Césaire

APRIL 1941. THE view was blocked by the hulk of a ship, sealed with madrepore to the sand of the beach and probed by the waves (at least the little children could not have dreamed of a better place to frolic all day long), which by its very fixity gave no respite to the exasperation of only being able to move a few measured paces, between two bayonets: the Lazaret concentration camp, in Fort-de-France harbour. Released after a few days, with what avidity did I plunge into the streets, in search of all the never-before-seen things they had to offer, the dazzle of the markets, the humming-bird accents, the women Paul Eluard, on his return from a trip around the world, had told me were more beautiful than anywhere else. Soon, however, I discerned a discovery that threatened to take everything over once more: this city itself was coming apart, seemingly deprived of its essential organs. Its trade, all on display, assumed a disturbingly theoretical character. All movement was a little slower than might have been necessary, all sound too distinct, as if something had run aground. In the delicate air the continuous, distant tolling of an alarm bell could be heard.

It was in these circumstances that, chancing to buy a ribbon for my daughter, I happened to leaf through a publication on display in the haberdashery. Very modestly presented, it was the first issue of a journal that had just been published in Fort-de-France, entitled *Tropiques*. Needless to say, knowing what a year of intellectual degradation had led to, and having experienced the lack of any discretion characteristic of police reactions in Martinique, I approached this collection with extreme suspicion . . . I could not believe my eyes: what was being said was exactly what needed to be said, not just in the best way but with the greatest force! All those mocking shadows were torn aside and dispersed; all the lies and derision fell in tatters. It was proof that, far from being broken or stifled, here the human voice rose up like the very shaft of light. Aimé Césaire was the name of the one speaking.

I make no apology for an immediate feeling of some pride: what he was expressing was far from foreign to me, the names of the poets and authors cited alone would have been firm collateral, but above all the tone of these pages of the sort that does not deceive, attesting to the fact that here was someone wholeheartedly committed to the adventure who at the same time possessed all the means for the foundation, not only on an aesthetic but also on a moral and social level . . . (what am I getting at?) to make his intervention necessary and inevitable. The accompanying texts revealed people who clearly had the same attitude, whose ideas were truly one with his. In complete contrast with what had been published in France during the preceding months, all bearing the stamp of masochism if not servility, *Tropiques* was continuing to carve out the regal pathway. 'We are the kind', Césaire announced, 'who refuse the shadow.'

This land he was revealing and which his friends were helping to explore, yes, it was my land too, it was *our* land which I had wrongly allowed myself to fear was fading into darkness. And one sensed his revolt and, even before gaining a deeper understanding of his message, one realized that, how can one say it, all the words he uttered, from the simplest to the most unusual, were laid bare. This resulted in his work culminating in concrete realization, in that endlessly *superior* quality of tone that allows such easy distinction between great and minor poets. What that day taught me was that the instrument of speech had not even gone out of tune in the turmoil. The world must not have been sinking after all: it would regain consciousness.

The Martiniquan haberdasher, by one of those additional acts of chance that indicate propitious moments, lost no time in introducing herself as the sister of René Ménil, the principal animator of *Tropiques* with Césaire. Her mediation would ensure the quickest conveyance of the few words I hurriedly scribbled on her counter; and in fact less than an hour later, having searched the streets for me, she gave me the arrangements for a meeting on her brother's behalf. Ménil: the height of culture in its least ostentatious sense and impeccable correctness, but in spite of that also vigorous and full of nervous excitement.

And the next day, Césaire. I can recall my quite basic initial reaction at finding him such a pure black in colour, masked all the more at first sight by his smile. In him (I already know, and see what everything will subsequently confirm) is mankind's crucible at its greatest point of fermentation, where knowledge, here moreover of the highest order, interferes with magical powers. For me – and I don't just mean on that day – his appearance, coloured by the countenance he has, assumed the value of a *sign of the times*. Thus it is that, single-handedly challenging an age in which one might think we witness the general abdication of the mind, when everything being created seems to aim at perfecting death's victory, when art itself threatens to solidify into outdated notions, the first fresh, revitalizing breath of air, fit to reassure us, comes from a black man. And it is a black man who handles the French language as no white man today can. And it is a black man who is our guide today through unexplored territory, establishing as he goes, as if it was a game, the ignition points that permit our advance, spark by spark. And it is a black man who is not only a black but a *total* man, who expresses all his questioning, all his fears, all his hopes and raptures, and who will assert himself ever more in my mind as the prototype of dignity.

We would meet in the evening, in a bar that the outside light turned into a single crystal, after the high-school classes he was then teaching about the work of Rimbaud, or at gatherings on the terrace of his house whose enchantment was made complete by the presence of Suzanne Césaire, as beautiful as the flame on a bowl of punch. But most especially there was an excursion right into the interior of the island: I shall always recall us perched perilously high over the Gouffre d'Absalom, as if over the very materialization of the crucible in which poetic images powerful enough to move worlds are formed, with no other landmark in the tide of frantic vegetation than the great enigmatic canna flower, a triple heart quivering on the end of a spear. It was there, and under the auspices of this flower, that the mission assigned in our day to man to break violently with the ways of thinking and feeling that have led him to the point of no longer being able to tolerate his existence, truly appeared to me in its complete imprescriptibility; that once and for all I was convinced of the idea that nothing will be gained so long as a certain number of taboos have not been lifted, so long as we have not managed to purge human blood of the fatal toxins kept in circulation by the – ever more indolent – belief in a hereafter, the solidarity absurdly attached to nations and races, and the supreme abjection that we call the power of money. Nothing can change the fact that, during the past century, it has fallen to poets to crack this iron brace which stifles us, and it is significant to observe that posterity tends to sanction only those who have gone furthest in this task.

That afternoon, with all the sluice gates of vegetation sumptuously thrown open before us, I experienced all the reward of feeling in such close communion with one of these poets, of knowing him, amongst all men, to be blessed with free will, and of being unable essentially to distinguish his will from my own.

And of holding him to be, with ample evidence, a man of complete accomplishment: a few days earlier he had made me a present of his *Notebook of a Return to My Native Land*, a limited special edition of a Parisian journal where the poem must have passed unnoticed in 1939, and this poem was nothing less than the greatest lyrical monument of our time. It brought me the richest certainty, that which one can never expect from oneself alone: its author had gambled on everything I believed right and, incontestably, he had won. What was at stake, taking into account Césaire's particular genius, was our common conception of life.

What one will first recognize is this most effusive animation, this exuberance from the shoot to the bouquet, this ability endlessly to rouse the emotional world from top to bottom until it is turned upside down, which is the characteristic of authentic poetry as opposed to false poetry, simulated poetry, the poisonous kind which constantly proliferates all around it. *To sing or not to sing*, that is the question, and there can be no hope in poetry for someone who does not *sing*, even if the poet must be asked to do *more* than just to sing. And I need hardly say that, for those who do not sing, the recourse to rhyme, fixed metre and other baggage would seduce only the ears of Midas. Aimé Césaire is above all the one who sings.

When it moves beyond this first absolutely necessary and non-sufficient state, poetry worthy of the name is evaluated by its level of abstention, by the *refusal* it implies, and this quality of negation demands to be seen as constitutive: it is repelled at the thought of allowing through anything that might already have been seen, understood or habitual, or at using what has been used before, unless it be to misappropriate it from its previous use. In this respect Césaire is one of the most *obstinate*, and not only because he is the soul of integrity but also to the extent that his knowledge is vaster, that he is at once one of the best and most widely informed.

Finally – and here, to dispel any ambiguity as to whether *Notebook of a Return . . .* is exceptionally a poem 'with a subject' if not 'an argument', I can specify that I am referring just as much to those poems (of a quite different order) published since: the poetry of Césaire, like all great poetry and all great art, is of the greatest merit due to the power of transmutation it activates, and which – starting from the most discredited of matter, amongst which must even be included monstrosities and slaveries – consists in producing what we well know to be no longer gold or the philosopher's stone, but liberty itself.[1]

It would be too presumptuous to want to attribute the gift of song, the capacity for refusal and the power of particular transmutation that has just been mentioned to a certain number of technical secrets. All one can validly believe about it is that all three possess a greater common denominator which is the exceptional emotional intensity when faced with life's pageant (bringing with it the impulse to act on it in order to change it) and which, for the time being, remains irreducible. The most the critic may do is account for the most striking events in the formative years of the person in question, and shed light on what is significant about this development. It should be acknowledged that in this way, where Aimé Césaire is concerned, and *for once*, we shall emerge at full tilt from indifference.

*Notebook of a Return to My Native Land* is in this respect a unique and irreplaceable document. The understated title of the poem is alone such as to place us at the heart of the conflict which its author must feel most keenly, that conflict which he considers vitally important to overcome. In fact, he wrote this poem in Paris, when he had just left the École Normale Supérieure and he was preparing to return to Martinique. His native land: of course, how could one not be seduced by its skies, its siren sway, its all-cajoling accents? But just as quickly shadows gather: you need only put yourself in Césaire's shoes to appreciate what assaults this nostalgia might be exposed to. Behind these florid patterns lie the misery of a colonial people, their shameless exploitation by a handful of parasites who flaunt even the laws of the land they are dependent upon and yet unrepentantly dishonour, as well as the resignation of this people whose geographical disadvantage is to be sparsely planted seedlings in the middle of the sea. And even beyond that, just a few generations back, is slavery, and here the wound reopens; it reopens from all the magnificence of a lost Africa,[2] from the ancestral memory of suffering abominable treatment, from the consciousness of a monstrous and forever irreparable denial of justice whose victim was a whole community. A community to which the one who is leaving belongs body and soul, enriched with all that the whites could teach him and at that moment all the more torn.

In the *Notebook* it is only natural that such claims pitch him against feelings of bitterness or even of despair, and also that the author should expose himself to the most dramatic self-examinations. One cannot stress too much that these claims are the most well-founded in the world, so much so that for the sake of equity alone white people should long to see them realized. But that day is still too far off, even if it is now tentatively beginning to be put on the agenda: 'In the former colonies, which should be submitted to a new system and whose evolution to liberty will become a matter of international concern, democracy must put an end not only to the exploitation of coloured peoples but also to the social and political "racism" of the white man.'[3] It is with the same impatience that one awaits the day when, outside these colonies, the great mass of coloured peoples will cease to be kept at an outrageous distance and kennelled in employment that is at best subordinate. If the international settlements that will come into force on the conclusion of the present war fail to satisfy this expectation, one would be forced to subscribe definitively to the view, with all it implies, that the emancipation of coloured peoples can only be the work of these peoples themselves.

But if we were to be content with this more immediate aspect of his claim, no matter how deep-seated it may appear, it would be to reduce unforgivably the scope of Césaire's intervention. In my view the former is invaluable in that it constantly transcends the anguish that a black person associates with the fate of blacks in modern society and, making common cause with all poets, all artists and all thinkers worthy of the word but, providing a contribution of verbal genius, embraces everything about the conditions most generally imposed on *mankind* by this society that is not only intolerable but also infinitely curable. And this, writ large, is what surrealism has always made the first article of its programme: the firmly resolved will to deal a fatal blow to so-called 'common sense', whose impudence has been such as to claim the title of 'reason', and the overriding need to have done with this mortal dissociation of the human spirit, one of whose constituent parts has managed to allow itself every liberty at the expense of the other, and which moreover cannot fail to exalt the latter by dint of trying to frustrate it. If the slave traders themselves have vanished from the world's stage, one may be certain that in return they rage on in the mind, where their 'black ivory' is our dreams, more than the plundered half of our nature, that unripe cargo which can all too conveniently be sent to rot in the depths of the hold. 'Because we hate you, you and your reason, we claim kinship with dementia praecox with flaming madness with tenacious cannibalism. . . . Accommodate yourself to me. I won't accommodate myself to you!'[4] And suddenly comes this transfiguring stare, the blue bloom on the embers as if on the promise of a redemption that might no longer be a fraudulent one: he whom both Césaire and I hold to be the great prophet of times to come has just walked past, I mean Isidore Ducasse, the Comte de Lautréamont.

*The poetry of Lautréamont, as beautiful as a warrant of expropriation*. . . . He accumulates a pale, lyrical scattering of the death trumpets of a comedy of philosophy – as the fingers of the tropical pear tree fall off in the evening gangrene – which raises man, hands, feet and navel, to the dignity of the marvel of a hierarchical universe – a clamour of bare fists against the barrage of the sky. . . . The first to have understood that poetry begins with excess, immoderation, forbidden pursuits, in the great blind drumbeat right up to the incomprehensible rain of stars.[5]

The word of Aimé Césaire, as beautiful as oxygen being born.

*New York, 1943*

### Notes

1. To look at the reverse side of the coin, I had not expected this declaration in *Lettres françaises* (nos 7–8, February 1943): 'I imagine poetry to be primarily a sort of writing which, obeying not only the constraints of prose but also those others unique to it (number, rhythm, the periodic repetition of sound) must also however surpass it in power. . . . In this way I require poetry to possess all the qualities sought in prose, of which the most important are nakedness, precision and clarity. . . . The poet must want to express entirely and solely what he desires. Ultimately there should be nothing ineffable, nothing suggestive, no evocative images, no mystery. . . .', etcetera. Roger Caillois, often more inspired than this, expresses himself here like a perfect philistine.

2. Leo Frobenius, with reference to the observations of the European navigators of the late Middle Ages, writes: 'When they arrived in the Bay of Guinea and landed at Vaïda, the captains were astonished to find well laid-out streets, flanked with a double row of trees for a distance of several leagues; for days on end they crossed a countryside covered with magnificent fields, inhabited by men wearing dazzling costumes whose cloth they had woven themselves! Further south, in the kingdom of the Congo, they found a teeming mass of people, dressed in 'silk' and 'velvet', well-ordered states, down to the smallest detail, powerful sovereigns, opulent industries. Civilized to the very marrow!' (Quoted in *Tropiques*, no. 5, April 1942.)

3. Pierre Cot, 'Les Différents Types de constitutions démocratiques', *Le Monde libre*, no. 2, December 1943.

4. Editor's note: Aimé Césaire, *Return to My Native Land* (1969) Harmondsworth: Penguin, pp. 55–62.

5. Aimé Césaire, 'Isidore Ducasse, comte de Lautréamont', *Tropiques*, nos 6–7, February 1943.

[originally published in *Tropiques*, no. 9 (May 1944), and then as a preface to Aimé Césaire, *Memorandum On My Martinique* (1947) New York: Brentano's, the first English-language edition of the *Notebook of a Return to My Native Land*; reprinted in André Breton, *Martinique, charmeuse de serpents*]

PIERRE MABILLE

# *The Jungle*

## On the importance assumed by art criticism in the contemporary age

TEXTS ABOUT PAINTING, to consider only those, have proliferated
since the middle of the last century with such speed that today
they constitute a substantial library. This proliferation has many
causes. On the material level, I would cite the increase in the number of
art magazines which goes hand in hand with an improved reproduction
of pictures, thanks to modern mechanical methods. This technical
progress allows a large public to get to know works that were formerly
scattered and hidden away in distant museums and private collections.
In the future this will have profound repercussions for popular mass
culture and will inevitably have an effect on painting itself.

Another, this time regrettable, aspect of the problem is that easel
painting has become a commodity submitted to unbridled speculation
leading to an exploitation of producer and buyer. Public auctions have
become transformed into veritable stock exchanges where share indexes
are fixed. From the time money was subjected to incessant fluctuations,
a painting has been considered a safer investment than the banknote.
In this way capitalism pays involuntary homage to what its rational-
ization cannot produce. As a by-product of this art market, most
criticism is scarcely different from other advertising literature: a
pseudo-philosophical vocabulary in which the emptiest words mingle
with hyperbolic praise is the cover for sordid mercantile schemes. It is
not the least nauseating form of literary prostitution.

The increase in criticism has other, deeper reasons: painters, musicians, poets and philosophers feel the need to band together in groups
driven by a shared ideal and aiming at a common goal. Such formations
are characteristic of contemporary intellectualism. The Pre-Raphaelite

brotherhood was a good example; surrealism has been the most recent one.

Such spiritual families offer the artist a receptive climate favourable to his work. These little circles have quite aptly been dubbed sects or chapels. The willingness of the adepts to join together at all costs through provocative attitudes capable of excluding the profane and shocking the bourgeois world has been emphasized, often in order to deride it. This behaviour reflects a profound feeling that innovation in art constitutes a powerful element of subversion, effecting the interior transformation of man and consequently being akin to certain mystic impulses and initiation practices. Each school has felt the need to assert itself through manifestos and writings that alternate polemic with self-justification. We know how fragile these enthusiastic groupings have proved. The shortcomings of their programme, their utopian character and the development of personal ambitions account for their dissolution. The painter quickly complains about the writer's level of understanding which he feels is inadequate and seeks to free himself from this tutelage; he keenly feels the difference in technique – that of the brush and that of the pen; he intends to offer his pictorial message in complete freedom and express his emotions in an individual way. The literary interpretations his works provoke annoy him. He wants his works to reach the spectator's sensibility directly without aesthetic discussions.

The painter's hope of entering into immediate contact with the public is generally frustrated. A detailed study of the mechanism of visual perception reveals why. Man does not perceive the totality of what his eye sees in the reality that surrounds him but only what his mind is looking for. He distinguishes the forms he is accustomed to, which remind him of known objects. He *recognizes* more than sees. He perceives that which responds to an inner interrogation, which accords with his fears or desires. Thus perception proves to be a function of a prior sensorial and intellectual education and reflects internal life as much as external reality. For more than half a century now the painter has renounced the reproduction of familiar images composed for the spectator's enjoyment; he has devoted himself to the destruction of traditional forms; he has ceased to act as a narrator so as to become a constructor, an explorer.

Considering this modern painting which shocks and perplexes the public, the writer feels the need to fill the gap, to draw attention to canvases whose importance seems primordial to him, to place the spectator in frames of mind that offer the possibility of understanding and feeling.

The fact that in the contemporary age art has ceased to be a source of pleasure for the use of a privileged class, a means of pleasantly embellishing any leisure time they still have, the fact that it has been devoted to the *aims of disruption*, place the painter and the poet in the advance guard of a battle unprecedented in history. The artist is a lone fighter subject to his personal necessity but his internal drama is a testimony, a manifestation of the general drama of the world: his life and work are often more characteristic than many collective movements whose interpretation is made difficult by the combination of contrary forces that they represent.

If it is a cliché to insist on the breadth of the revolution we are witnessing today, it is another to admit our incompetence at mastering the whole situation and perceiving the resolution of conflicts it represents. Plunged into this disheartening obscurity, the writer spontaneously brings his attention to bear on the few luminous images that shine out and which he interprets as responses to his inner anguish. He interrogates certain paintings more anxiously than ever.

## About Wifredo Lam

During the three centuries following Columbus's discovery, the Caribbean was the far-off paradise where Europe's dreams became reality; bewitching islands where life escaped the moral and material restrictions that the structure of the bourgeois economy increasingly imposed on the old continent. It was truly the poets' Eden, with its unknown trees, its monstrous, heavily perfumed flowers, its perpetual summer and its infinite riches waiting to be gathered. The descendants of a nobility emigrated there, eager to reconstruct a feudal system that had vanished forever in its native land somewhere far away: the lost children of Nantes, Cadiz and Amsterdam, keen to indulge their appetite for violence, sensuality and indiscipline.

Such paradises imply the existence of penal colonies. With the original Indians extinct, negroes were imported to maintain the garden of Hesperides. In their stinking holds, carvels transported an entire people whose only wealth was a nostalgia for their native Africa and the memory of a most ancient civilization from which they had been brutally torn, a people who were to be submitted without explanation to the customs and religion of the masters who were buying them. In these West Indies, through the magic of the soil, the European little by little lost his original characteristics and became Creole. The black man, too, transformed himself: he veiled his deep hatred and his desire for revenge with the indolent acceptance that suggested an infinite taste for happiness. Under a complicitous sun, he hid his atavistic fears behind raucous laughter and kept the rhythms of his race unbroken. And so the West Indies waited, in a heavy atmosphere where pimento mixes with sugar as, forgotten by zoological evolution, the iguana of the Île des Saintes, the agouti of Cuba and the anachronistic cayman of Ester and the Artibonite, waited, species suspended in time, dream images that faded away on awakening. Awakening, that is what the steamboat's siren heralded. The gardens fell prey to new arrivals, avid for trade and exploitation. With slavery nominally abolished, a less recalcitrant and more efficient workforce was supplied by an over-populated Asia.

Across the sea conquered by machine the route that girdled the globe was traced, linking the hemispheres, to become ceaselessly tra-versed with ever-increasing speed, a speed that today has become dizzying and negates space. Along this great world route, replacing the old Asian trade routes, lies Havana. From Caribbean Cuba, woven with cane fields, fanned by palm trees, sprang up one of those places of encounters, intersections and minglings that are the great international ports, places where everything comes together and separates again, from where one can leave for anywhere, return from anywhere, where continents greet each other as the liners set sail. Havana, the crossing of the ways, is at the same time also the capital of a state that has con-structed its independence. A unique city, with its white Capitol, the mark of America, its banks, its palaces, its luxurious European shops. In the Vedado quarter, comfortable private mansions shelter rich descendants of the Spanish colonists who keep a watch on sugar prices on the New York stock exchange while their wives, so white, scintillat-ingly elegant, prepare to leave for Europe and the centres of luxury and pleasure.

Behind the Capitol, in the very heart of the city, the Chinese quar-ter brings together a large, industrious community, with a passion for gambling, trembling with the strange rhythms of its theatre and cine-mas, a community that experienced extremes of hardship nearly a century ago and overcame them, which now has its banks, its pawn-brokers, its restaurants, which has lost none of its ancestral customs and has retained its links with Asia.

And immediately around Havana, from La Regla to Marianao, there is Africa singing, being born and dying with the same frenzy to the sound of the drums, taking fright and defending itself in the magic huts.

1902 . . . As an immense wind of liberty set Cuba on the road towards the realization of national independence, in the provinces, in the middle of an ocean of sugar cane, at Sagua la Grande, Wifredo Lam was born. His father was a 77-year-old Chinaman, still in the prime of life: he would die in 1928, aged 103. Not a coolie, but a cultivated figure, a public scrivener respected by everyone. He knew the thousands of characters of the world's most complex written language; people came from far and wide to consult him while he remained mysterious and secretive, in an almost complete silence. He first married a white woman whom he renounced, in accordance with ancient practice, because she was barren. His second wife was a beautiful, lively young negress, who bore him nine children and showered them with that affection that African women reserve for their young. Her own mother, moreover, was born in the Congo; imported to Cuba, the good fortune of a marriage to a well-to-do mulatto had delivered her from her servitude.

Wifredo's youth was the avenues of flame trees that disappear into the vast expanses of sugar canes, the great heat in which muted presences shimmer in the noonday air, shaded corners where disquieting forms float. Strange lights flickered in the eyes of the men living around the child: the flames of hope and of disquiet, a hope for liberty, a violent desire to put an end to the age-old oppression, a desire to rise to the ranks of men, to participate in what European culture imposes as an ideal of beauty; a disquiet faced with the vicissitudes of local politics in which, by the paths of corruption, oppression assumed new forms. On some evenings, whilst his father joined his compatriots at the Chinese casino, Wifredo heard, coming from the far reaches of the plain, the echoes of the ceremonies by which the blacks, his mother's blood brothers, asked the forces of the earth, through the power of the herbs, for beneficent support and the means to gratify their vengeance.

Lam's father was a civilized man. He knew, better than those gentlemen of the sugar companies, the value of intelligence and the excellence of the power of sensitivity. He allowed his son to embark on a career as a painter, without trying to discourage his vocation; on the contrary, he had the presentiment that light would emanate from his son, and often called him 'Lucero'. The latter began his studies in Havana and, with a modest travel grant awarded by his home town, arrived in Madrid in 1923. At the time this voyage was an obvious necessity. Despite the political independence so painstakingly achieved, the Latin American republics have remained up until the last few years in the grip of a yearning for their culture's birthplace and of the spiritual guardianship of Europe.

Wifredo's stay in Madrid lasted fifteen years. He has only told me about the most general stages of his evolution there. His life there, which was dramatic, would merit a detailed analysis, whose elements I hope his wife, Hélène Lam, might one day assemble. It seems that during the first period he set out to conquer European tradition with considerable good will, good faith and even complete enthusiasm, and that everything appeared to be going well. He married and had a child. But, almost immediately, the storm burst that destroyed his plans for integration into Madrid life: his wife and child died. Wifredo found himself plunged into total despair; he stopped painting. Nothing mattered to him any more, he wanted to understand, but as yet knew only what he had to reject: he rejected the paintings he had done, those being made around him, and the stifling social order, the source of his unhappiness. His attitude was entirely one of disgust and revolt, of nonchalance and pessimism. He emerged with difficulty from this state only around 1934; transformed by this inner crisis, through his readings, he was now conscious of his ancestral reality, which he no longer had to hide or deny and which was not in any way inferior. He started to become interested, in an as yet imprecise way, in what he called the 'cosa negra'.

At this time Madrid was plunged into an atmosphere that I well recall, in which the ever-present threat of a fascist *coup d'état* was counterbalanced with the dizzying hope of a final conquest of social and human liberty, an atmosphere at the same time weakened by the detestable qualities of the Republican powers and strangely invigorated by the will to win the battle that one could rightly foretell would be decisive. It was clear to me at the time, and today nobody disputes this, that the fate of Europe was at stake in the Spanish Civil War. It is highly significant that Lam, like many Cubans and American sons of Spanish descent, descendants of the oppressed, should have from the first moment spontaneously found common cause with the Spanish people whose lives were threatened by the oppressive coalition that was the most frantic, most brutal and best-organized the world had ever known: the coalition of every political and social reaction contained within fascism. And, alas, what a contrast the lucidity of Lam and of his brothers was to the blindness of the masses of the old continent!

It was in Madrid that Wifredo saw negro masks and sculptures for the first time. For him, as for all coloured West Indians, it was through the intermediary of European anthropologists and collectors that contact could be resumed with the ancestral art from which other Europeans had brutally separated them. It was again in Madrid, in 1936, that he first attended an exhibition by Picasso, the artist who was to have such great importance for his future development. Lam's tribulations were to follow step by step the phases of the West's tragedy: Madrid at war, Barcelona, Paris in 1938, where he met both Picasso and the surrealist group, then the retreat to Marseilles and the laborious return journey by way of Martinique, Saint-Domingue and Havana.

### On the singular events that took place in Paris at the turn of the century

When the doors of the International Exhibition of 1900 closed, one of the things that seemed most certain was the definitive triumph of the modern form of European civilization, of which Paris for many centuries seemed to be the established centre. This was clear to those Cubans who, having dined at the Café de Paris, went to spend a few hours at the Longchamp and Auteuil races before returning, at the end of the afternoon, to visit the art exhibitions in the rue du Faubourg Saint-Honoré and to finish the evening at the Opéra or the Boulevard theatres. It was also clear to the Americans of every persuasion who knew the streets of the Madeleine district better than the provinces of their own country, and to all the European intellectuals whose favourite haunts were Montmartre or the Latin Quarter. Today we have difficulty imagining the cheerful optimism and naïve confidence which reigned at that turn of the century: science's progress was little by little to guarantee men mastery over nature, to prevent wars and famines: a gradual social evolution would progressively bring the whole of humanity to participate in civilization's benefits.

In painting, impressionism reigned supreme. Painters had rejected the old complicated techniques, freed themselves from preparations and glazes, and turned their backs on large-scale compositions. They were content to express the emotion provoked by light momentarily reflected on a woman's cheek or irradiating a seashore in the morning. Just as the novels in which naturalist descriptions were married to meticulous psychological dissection proliferated in bookshop windows, so the canvases accumulated on the picture rails of the ever more numerous salons. An avalanche of still lives where Cézanne apples vied with Provençal porcelain vases, old Breton churches, Concarneau harbours, young women bathing or languorously stretched on sofas, met the rising tide of bursting bouquets, portraits of industrialists or of politicians. This geometrical progression continued right up to 1939, and only the present scarcity of oil paint, I believe, has managed to put an end to it. Impressionism had undertaken the colonization of the whole world and set up a flourishing line in exoticism. Gauguin was in Tahiti and the Fauves amassed the first collections of African, Indian and Oceanic art.

Yet amidst this general euphoria a few worrying symptoms were breaking out. In poetry it was becoming clear that one could not continue to rework the age-old alexandrine, to polish ever more precious images. Having issued his aggressive message, Rimbaud, reduced to voluntary silence, had gone off to lose himself in the torrid exile of Abyssinia. The howl of Lautréamont had been crushed by a desperate death.

Despite all the efforts of Mr Viollet-Le-Duc and his followers, nothing of any value could be added to the Gothic style. The colonnades of the Madeleine and the Chambre des Deputés were worthless copies of Greek and Roman temples.

The multiplicity of exhibitions of painting gave proof, for many young people, of a real sensibility, but prolonged the first impressionists' discoveries to no advantage.

In the pictorial domain the sensational event, in 1906, was Picasso's affirmation that the time had come to cease considering the so-called primitive arts (in other words those not belonging to the European tradition) as curiosities, but to understand that a beauty comparable to that of our greatest masterpieces and a lesson of far-reaching consequences sprang from them. It was learned that Art was not limited to Venuses and Madonnas, that it was not linked to progress in knowledge and even less to that in material comfort. This was the beginning of a revolution whose development will not stop and of which we are today still experiencing only the initial phases. From that moment on, the artist once again questioned not only taste but also traditional norms of perception, the representation of reality, the interrelations of objects and their significance in man's eyes.

At the height of its colonizing power, Europe suddenly ceased to enjoy the curiosities of exoticism and the affirmation of its reason and superiority in peace, and for the first time had to submit to examination by the slave, who spoke to it from behind a Dahomey mask. Picasso, a man of the Mediterranean, the son of the Malaga drawing teacher, the man of his age who best understood the deepest reasons of time-honoured tradition, would henceforth oscillate between the need to continue this tradition and the desire to destroy it, to find in its foundations, laid bare, the possibilities of a transmutation. He is at the same time both the direct heir of Cézanne the architect and the ally of the savage, whose still-intact forces threatened to overcome the tired old master.

Anyone visiting the exhibition mounted at the Ambroise Vollard gallery in 1909 could say with all certainty that the world was bound for radical transformations; and when 3 August 1914 arrived, he could forecast that things were not going to resolve themselves so easily by a reannexation of Alsace-Lorraine and a change in ownership of a few colonies. The war put an end to the last hopes for a progressive evolution by which the values of all orders could be safeguarded. In fact, social revolution broke out in Russia, plunging the international bourgeoisie into a consternation that continues to this day, and amazing the Western masses who slumbered in evolutionist organizations for social democracy. The armistice, as it brought the armed phase of the conflict to an end, only served to clarify the conflict and to situate it in all its amplitude. It is interesting to note that in 1919–20, Picasso returned to realistic representation and entered his neo-classical period as though he was suddenly recovering a belief in tradition; it was the period of his collaboration with the Ballets Russes and his friendship with Jean Cocteau. This period was brief and Picasso soon resumed his researches.

Shortly after the war, the avant-garde was constituted by the Surrealist Group. With it, the foundations of poetry and painting were brought into question more severely than ever before. It was no longer a matter of aesthetic debates and technical refinements, but a question of penetrating to the very origin of inspiration, of reaching emotion at its source. Surrealism supported its approach with the findings of psychoanalysis. This gave more detailed information about the nature of the human, which surrealism could use to seek what, behind social frameworks, aesthetic formulae and the habits of perception, lies at the origin of artistic creation. It applied itself to what, in childhood emotion, in madness, in man's passion, is found to have an identification with mechanisms that society obliges us to censor in order to turn us into obedient citizens. At the place where inspiration springs forth, communication becomes possible between all people, and it is precisely at this point that the transmutation can take place that sublates the redundant stages of traditional form.

Whilst these – I grant unequally successful – experiments were being undertaken, the global crisis was reaching its peak. A former painter, an advocate of 'health in art', was to seek to resolve all problems by setting up concentration camps.

### On the return to the native land

If ever a meeting could stir the soul, it was the one that took place in Paris between Lam and Picasso. The Master, in the prime of his genius and glory, still powerfully marked by the revelation of negro art, saw standing before him a black man who had known Western values, had immersed himself in them but who, far from having been absorbed by Europe, had gradually regained an awareness of himself and his own means; a man who had arrived at forms similar to those that he himself had expressed, by a route exactly the inverse of his own. Picasso was not mistaken about Lam's value, whilst the latter in his turn strongly felt the seduction and magnetic charm of the Andalusian master.

I remember Wifredo in Paris, arriving at the Deux-Magots café, reserved, a little awkward, gesticulating with his long thin arms. He had come from Spain, and bore the traces of the struggles he had undergone. But he spoke little about that and amazed us more by the depth of his culture, the philosophical aspect of which was no less remarkable than the artistic side. He showed us drawings of an extraordinary elegance and an astounding freedom.

I saw him again in Marseilles, worried, seeking the weak points of the cage like a captive eagle, and then at Ciudad Trujillo, having succeeded in bringing from a Europe that had gone up in flames a few Picasso reproductions, a few issues of *Cahiers d'art* and *Minotaure*, all the wealth he had been able to amass in the course of seventeen years of work. His reintegration into his native land was not without severe difficulties. I regret not having been with him whilst he painfully regained contact with the Tropics of his birth after so many years.

When I met up with him again in 1943, he had just finished the work that, in my opinion, marks the decisive turning point of his career: *The Jungle*. Rightly or wrongly, I see in this painting an event whose importance may be compared to that of Paolo Uccello's discoveries in perspective, discoveries so crucial that all subsequent painting, and with it the whole of Western sensibility, felt its influence. I think I should explain my train of thought. For as long as man has existed, he has always observed that distant objects were seen as smaller than those nearby, and that parallel lines all seemed to converge on a point called the vanishing point. If this observation is immemorial, European perspective is, for its part, relatively recent; it consists of the wish to emphasize this sensory phenomenon and organize the whole composition around such a central point (no matter, furthermore, if this centre is in the middle or in one of the corners of the painting). What the traditional painter understood by composition was precisely the organization of the different elements of the canvas around this centre or focus. Such a concept infinitely exceeds the realm of painting; it expresses the general idea of the organization of the world emanating from a single God, of social organization emanating from a supreme leader. A series of laws or relations strictly determines the position of the peripheral parts in terms of the centre. Whether it be the rite of the Mass where all eyes converge on the officiating priest, the social pyramid whose summit is the father, or the parades of the masses where the leader controls the assembly of disciplined cohorts, the same *laws of perspective* are at work. Other laws order the composition of *The Jungle*.

### A Night on the Haitian plain

Near the dwelling hut, a little room made of beaten whitewashed earth displays the objects of the cult: the houmfor. On the altar, also made of earth, covered pots enclose the souls of the initiate faithful while others contain divine forces, and bottles filled with liquors and perfumes have been left for the use of the gods; on the walls are flags, sabres and coloured prints representing Catholic saints under whose effigies the African gods are venerated. The sacred vestments are packed in a trunk.

Outside is the bower held up by the middle post which, I believe, symbolizes the *arbre mystère*. This is where the ceremony will unfold: tonight a score of hounsies dressed in white form the choir. Three drums beat as the mambo or priestess directs the ritual. Contrary to what has been written about voodoo, its ritual is fixed and is identical in every houmfor. This is proved to me when a neighbouring houngan arrives and as a mark of honour he is asked to officiate instead of the mistress of the house and in collaboration with her. Immediately he is fully in harmony with the hounsies, as though they are the ones who normally attend him. The change in officiant does not result in the slightest hesitation. The succession of chants and prayers will be what I already know well, having often witnessed it elsewhere. The ceremony is addressed to the Congo loas (this is the name for the gods, which are also sometimes called 'esprits' or 'mystères'). There are many of these loas, more than twenty, with no hierarchy among them. Whilst in the pantheist cults of antiquity each divinity had its own temple, priests and particular cult, here the celebration is a general invocation. In some houmfors, several rites are celebrated (the Congo rite, the Pedro rite, etcetera) but here tonight we are in a community that only knows the Congo rite. Despite the wealth of the African pantheon, each of the hounsies, as indeed each of the assistants, is only subject to a particular loa. In general, the believer is linked to his god through family tradition, but it can happen that a divinity claims the devotion and worship of a specific individual. This happens in the course of a ceremony when the god, incarnated in a dancer, has made its will known in an unquestionable way: it would be unwise to ignore it. No proselytism exists at all; no one takes pride in serving one loa rather than another.

. . . Now they begin. Legba is invoked, the god of the barrier and the door, he who precedes the others and introduces the spirits into the presence of the people. Everyone dances (if, to describe what I see, I can use a word that elsewhere evokes couples in a dance hall or those combined spectacles where a ballet corps mimes a classical theme). Here, everyone dances for themselves, tensing each and every part of their body to prepare to receive the god. He appears, possessing one of the women serving him. She loses consciousness, shaking with convulsive movements. André Breton's expression goes through my mind: 'Beauty will be convulsive.' The recollection of a book about hysteria obsesses me. The woman struggles frantically. What is a happy event for her, since it signals the divinity's favour, does not preoccupy the other dancers at all. At most, one or two of those next to her take off her shoes (for the loa must be honoured barefoot) and prevent her from hurting herself during her disordered movements. The drums beat faster, another woman is seized in her turn. The houngan, approximating the dance steps so as to catch the rhythm, completes his ritual duties, to which no one seems to pay attention: he traces magic drawings on the ground with flour; he salutes the cardinal points, pouring a little water in the four directions. He only intervenes in the possessions if the god shows the desire to hail him and to pass on an oracle, or if the possession, by its violence or duration, seems excessive to him; in this case using appropriate frictions, cabbalistic words and, if need be, by leading the woman to the houmfor altar, he will quickly bring the god's excesses to an end.

The chants change. Now it is Aisan that the hounsies invoke: the same scenes are repeated. The possessions succeed each other, multiply, grow confused, with no perceptible emotion or fear among the audience.

The preparations for the sacrifice come to an end: here are the cockerels whose feet have been broken and whose heads are torn off with a single blow. Three hounsies pluck them, three others fan the hearths, the cauldrons get hot; the ritual cooking continues without the chants ever being interrupted, without a moment's respite. The drums, which have been resounding for over two hours, will continue like this all night. The ceremony is everywhere; to understand it, one would have to be able to follow every member of the audience, each one of whom has their precise role, knows what they must do and acts on their own part. All the actions have an equal value; they are synchronized by the music, or more precisely by the rhythm. What distinguishes this music from European symphonies is that the different instruments are not constrained by the obligation to maintain by their playing a melodic line that follows its course as a more or less complex pattern. In the voodoo ceremony, the melody exists; it is contained in the chant, but it develops on its own account, like all the other elements of this ensemble, like the ritual and the possessions, according to the rhythm of the drums. Thus it is the latter that serves as a link between all the simultaneously unleashed phenomena. A closer analysis of the beating of these drums proves that the rhythm is obtained by the interweaving of different measures, just as, in the life of a human organism, the individual's rhythm springs from the composition of the particular measures of its heart, its breath, its muscular movements, and other deeper, unknown measures.

In relating certain striking aspects of the ceremony that took place that night, on the Haitian plain not far from Port-au-Prince, I do not intend to produce an ethnographic document. I am giving an example of a collective manifestation, one that was overwhelming for me, and far more overwhelming still for those taking part, a perfectly ordered ceremony but which progressed in a way totally opposed to that with which the European is familiar, and which embodied not the slightest perspectival concentration towards unity. Such a process reminds me of the extraordinary composition of William Faulkner's book *The Sound and the Fury*. Here it is no longer a question of an empire with an all-powerful monarch at its head, of a structure dependent on a single centre, but of a vast space, without gaps, all of whose parts act at the same time, all equally free and equally dependent on the totality, unaware of any external hierarchy and oriented towards their own destiny: a living whole, knowing no other laws than those of the rhythm.

The immense value of Wifredo Lam's canvas called *The Jungle* lies in its evocation of this kind of universe, in which the trees, flowers, fruits and spirits cohabit thanks to the dance. For my part, I see a total opposition between this jungle where life explodes on all sides, free, dangerous, gushing from the most luxuriant vegetation, ready for any combination, any transmutation, any possession, and that other sinister jungle where a Führer, perched on a pedestal, awaits the departure, along the neo-classical colonnades of Berlin, of mechanized cohorts prepared, after destroying every living thing, for annihilation in their turn in the rigorous parallelism of endless cemeteries.

*Havana, May 1944*

[published in *Tropiques*, no. 12 (January 1945)]

ANDRÉ BRETON

# At Night in Haiti

A T NIGHT IN Haiti, lines of black enchantresses carry, three inches above their eyes, canoes from the Zambezi, the synchronized fires on the mornes, belfries topped with cockfights and the dreams of Paradise which shamelessly flutter around atomic disintegration. It is at their feet that Wifredo Lam sets his 'vèvè', in other words that marvellous and ever-changing gleam that falls from the improbably wrought stained-glass windows of tropical nature onto a mind freed from all influence and predestined to bring forth from this gleam images of the gods. In times like ours, no one will be surprised to see the loa Carrefour (Eleggùa in Cuba), here adorned with horns, spare no effort in blowing on the wings of doors. A unique and ever-trembling testimony, as if weighed out on scales of leaves, egrets taking wing from the brow of the pool where today's myth is being cast, Wifredo Lam's art spreads from that point where the vital source reflects the *arbre-mystère*, I mean this race's resolute soul, to shower with stars the BECOMING that must be human well-being.

*January 1946*

[published in André Breton, *Signe Ascendant* (1949) Paris: Gallimard]

PART IV

# HAITI 1946:

# SURREALISM AND REVOLUTION

PAUL LARAQUE

# *André Breton in Haiti*

I WON'T GO back in time to the child's struggles with the demon inside him, but I refuse to banish the adolescent who hasn't stopped dreaming. I am not prepared to forget what I am testifying since it concerns a no doubt unique experience in the life of an unknown poet: that of having encountered, at the age when hope stirs within us like a flame, one of the rarest of men who, for my part, I can only call 'my dear Magus', since his intransigent generosity brought him as close to me as a friend, and since at the same time he incarnated in my eyes the very magic of the Word.

## Port-au-Prince, Haiti, Autumn 1945

The journal *La Ruche*, the organ of the revolutionary youth, was leading the struggle against the dictatorship of the reactionary government of Elie Lescot. Thanks to the progressive ideas coming to light in the most backward countries at the end of the Second World War, this opposition struck a chord with the liberal bourgeoisie and began to win over the people. By one of those instances of objective chance, whose invisible threads we are still exploring, it was at just this moment that André Breton arrived in Haiti. I had been informed of this in advance by the Haitian poet René Bélance. Dr Pierre Mabille, then the cultural attaché at the French embassy in Port-au-Prince, a personal friend of Breton and the author of important works such as *Le Miroir du merveilleux* and *La Construction de l'homme*, wanted to gather together a few avant-garde poets and writers to greet the eminent ambassador of Poetry delegated to us by France, so dear to us. A short time before, thanks to Mabille and above all to Bélance, I was given the opportunity to get to know Breton's work fairly well, in addition to surrealism in general, which was little known among us before the luminous breach opened by Césaire, with the exception of a few intellectuals who, for the most part, moreover, showed only slight interest in it; others, on the contrary, recognized in it the vitality of the great movements that have stirred universal literature: such were Philippe Thoby-Marcelin, in reality a harvester of other fields, and Magloire-Saint-Aude, who, at the risk of his reason and his life, made himself its lone sentinel – even if his poems, whose elliptical beauty aims at the quintessence of poetry, do not seem in their creation to be the pure products of automatic writing. It should be said that what was for us the living example of Aimé Césaire during his stay in Port-au-Prince (then the capital of the night as it announces the dawn), and the crystallizing presence of Mr and Mrs Mabille, had clearly opened the way to Breton. On 4 December, we made up a group of numerous admirers waiting at the airport for the poet. Among us was the great Cuban surrealist painter Wifredo Lam, who had arrived a few days earlier. With leonine head, a mane of sun, Breton stepped forward, a god begotten by lightning. To see him was to grasp the beauty of the angel of revolt. The shadows became sources of light. The storm of a life was shot through with bolts of light whose flashing blades, burst from the scabbard of night, tore through the veil of time, and restored the lost paradise of innocence to love. Putting all mysticism aside, one then felt that mankind's supreme ambition is twofold: to banish hell from the earth and to integrate heaven into it. In the poet's shadow, or rather as if at the edge of his shadow, was a long silhouette of clarity whose prism of reality only just reproduced the colours of dream: the rainbow of hope, which was how, in a miraculous smile still besieged by tears, Elisa Breton the child–woman of *Arcane 17* appeared.

With the first contacts made, we agreed to meet again that same evening at the Savoy café–restaurant. Magloire-Saint-Aude, a bohemian who lived on the margins of society and shunned literary gatherings on principle, trailing his despair and his 'cat's laugh' in working men's bars, arrived a little late. In the form of a welcoming speech, with that 'bearer from the prodigious isle' accent, he proclaimed his poetic profession of faith, which was none other than the definition of surrealism formulated by Breton some twenty years before: 'Surrealism, pure psychic automatism, by which it is proposed to express, either verbally, in writing or by any other means, the real functioning of thought. Dictation of thought, in the absence of any control exercised by reason, beyond any aesthetic or moral preoccupation.' Breton was visibly overwhelmed with emotion, as he was to admit publicly in his first lecture on surrealism: 'By singular good fortune, the definition I proposed of the word surrealism has gone around the world, and on the very day of my arrival in Haiti, I listened with intense emotion to the great poet Magloire-Saint-Aude quoting it by heart to some of you.'[1] The first impression Breton left was that of an Olympian strength. However, the man was courteous in the extreme – and the word, turning back time, regained its original meaning, evoking all the images relating to the notion of courtly love, with a hint of preciosity and, dare one say it, of mannerism. Then, to tell the truth, you were pleasantly surprised to find him to be of such a simplicity that, with all shyness gone, you found yourself on an equal footing with him. You felt him wanting to establish, beyond words, a profound communication with others, mindful of drawing out your own best qualities.

On 7 December, a great banquet was arranged in Breton's honour by the intellectuals of the avant-garde and the revolutionary youth. And the poet spoke: in a voice that separated the wheat from the tares, he recalled the movement's fundamental principles, which are inseparable from the guidelines of his own life. He reaffirmed his unshakeable faith in youth whose calling is to make 'its own daring solutions prevail over everyday routine'. From the Magus's first words, the atmosphere became electric and would soon set off the mines laid by the young revolutionaries of *La Ruche*, whose meeting with Breton at the Savoy at the beginning of December 1945 turned our banquet into a crossroads of poetry and a sort of prelude to battle. Things had come full circle. *The Magnetic Fields* was no longer just the title of a book, it was the lived surrealist moment: Breton's magnetism irresistibly drew into its field all those who, unknown to them and even temporarily, deserved election, everything else being violently rejected or burned on the spot. The two poles of surrealism – poetry to make you lose your breath and unconditional revolutionary action – joined together, revealing the very object of the surrealist quest: 'a certain point of the mind where life and death, real and imaginary, past and future, communicable and incommunicable, high and low cease to be perceived as contradictory'. The surrealist climate was created. Thus when Jean Brierre, whose interventions, by word or deed, marked the greatest periods of our destiny as a people, wished to link Breton's name with *La Ruche*, by asking for exclusive rights to publish the poet's address, it was clear to everyone that an explosion was imminent. The shadow of Jacques Roumain, the poet and novelist of international fame, founder of the

Haitian Communist Party, who had died at thirty-seven, the idol of Haitian youth – the shadow of Jacques Roumain was not absent since Breton, who along with his wife had just finished reading *Gouverneurs de la rosée* with tears in his eyes, took care to allude to this moving masterpiece, in that magisterial language whose key he alone held: a fire sprung from the dark transparency of waters. . . . At the end of the banquet we all signed the menu card and presented it to the guest of honour, in homage to his genius and, for some of us, as a sign of our total adherence. On the suggestion of Jean Brierre once again, we arranged regular Friday meetings with Breton. So we adopted the habit of gathering at the Savoy and it was at one of these intimate meetings – although it was a public place – that I brought Breton the collection of poems by my friend Hamilton Garoute, a collection published during that year and which had provoked something of a stir in Haitian literature. The introduction I had written for *Jets lucides* pleased Breton and perhaps it will be surprising that he was sensitive to that measured tone that, it seems, has always been my characteristic and which he noticed at first glance. No doubt it would be wrong to believe that a human being, whoever he is, can be cut from a single block. He presents a thousand facets, some of which appear contradictory. Some people reproach Breton with having been too intransigent; others with not having been intransigent enough. What is certain is that he was, in all senses of the word, incorruptible; even whilst being very broad-minded, he never to my knowledge compromised his principles. On another evening when we were urging Breton to let us hear one of his poems, he partially acquiesced to our request by reciting, as I felt no one else could, *El Desdichado* by Gérard de Nerval. Breton, as we know, did not reduce poetry to form. 'To sing or not to sing, that is the question, and there can be no hope in poetry for someone who does not sing, even if the poet must be asked to do more than just to sing. And I need hardly say that, for those who do not sing, the recourse to rhyme, fixed metre and other baggage would seduce only the ears of Midas.'

Meanwhile, politics was dominating the national scene. In the midst of a situation becoming more threatening from one day to the next, Breton's presence was the only other event to attract the literate public's attention. On 13 December Breton's interview with René Bélance, which Breton was to reprint in *Entretiens*, was published, causing a great stir. On the 20th of that month Breton, introduced by Mabille, delivered his first lecture at the Rex theatre, which was packed to bursting. The Haitian journalist Roger Gaillard, in an obituary article published in the journal *Conjonction* (December 1966), evoked the unique atmosphere of that unforgettable evening. The audience was made up above all of young people: students, poets, artists, nonconformist writers, etcetera. But the President of the Republic was also there, surrounded by high-ranking civil and military officials. The orator first paid homage to Haiti and its people. 'I do not want to talk about surrealism in Haiti without first of all casting a highly respectful glance at what conditions your country's inalienable enthusiasm for liberty and its affirmation of dignity above all obstacles. But some of you already know, and others are destined to discover, that here surrealism verifies one of its fundamental propositions, namely that the first condition of a people's persistence, as of a culture's viability, is that both can endlessly re-immerse themselves in the great affective currents which bore them at birth, without which they rapidly collapse.'[2] He then traced the movement's history, up to the encounter between surrealism and the Marxism professed by the university students guided by *La Ruche*: 'It is now that we arrive at dialectical materialism as the only rampart against national selfishness, as the sole promise of universal concord and harmony.' Quoting Maurice Blanchot, Breton clarified his opinion still further, making his position so close to that of our young revolutionaries as to make them indistinguishable. 'Through the fault of the capitalist state, man is not only oppressed and limited, but sees himself as other than he is.'[3] He nevertheless had one essential reservation which those above all whom poetry or art had led to revolution would remember:

> Besides the economy, whose importance I would not wish to underestimate, there is a lyrical element which to some extent conditions the psychological and moral structure of human societies, which has always conditioned it, which will continue to condition it. One has only to look at Haiti to convince oneself that this lyrical element, far from being merely a matter for specialists as it is elsewhere, emerges from the aspirations of the entire people. The other problem we are set is that of social action, action which we believe possesses its own method in dialectical materialism and in which we can all the less lose interest for holding man's liberation to be the *sine qua non* of the liberation of the mind.[4]

Enthusiasm rose to fever pitch, and at the end of the lecture the speaker left to a standing ovation, but without paying his respects to the head of state as is customary in Haiti. This gesture, considered a public affront to the government, served to enhance the poet's prestige still further in the eyes of the political groups and especially of the youth, which was hostile to any compromise.

At the end of December a collection was made among the Friday habitués in aid of a special edition of *La Ruche* in homage to Breton, on the occasion of the New Year. The issue of *La Ruche*, which reproduced Breton's speech at the Savoy *in extenso* and on the front page, was seized by the police. Some of the leaders were arrested, others pursued. Among the youngest one should mention René Depestre, the journal's editor-in-chief, a child prodigy and *enfant terrible* of Haitian poetry, author of *Étincelles* (1945), a volume of poems which literally put a match to the powder keg, and the medical student Jacques Stephen Alexis, who signed his violent *Letters to the Old Men* with the pseudonym Jacques la Colère and who, some years later, at the height of his literary glory, was to give his life to the revolution. After his first novel, *Compère Général Soleil* (Gallimard 1955), some critics placed him above Pierre and Philippe Thoby-Marcelin, the winners of the Inter-American Prize for literature in 1944 and whose latest work of fiction, *Tous les hommes sont fous*, was recently published in the United States under the title *All Men are Mad*; it is astonishing that a French edition has yet to appear. But let us return to what we like to call the Revolution of '46. Public demonstrations were organized against police repression, against the government's ineptitude and in support of the liberation of political prisoners. A general strike was called: the insurrection had reached the City gates. Then the army intervened and ousted the government, exiling the most revolutionary students by awarding them grants to study in Paris, transferring suspect young officers (amongst them the author of these lines) and draining the hope of the revolution. But in the meantime I had managed to see Breton again several times: at the Institut Français, at the Law Faculty where he gave two more lectures, the second with colour slide projections of modern painters, and at the Centre d'Art, at the exhibition of paintings by Wifredo Lam, who opened a mysterious door of art for our wonderment, and one of whose gouaches, *The Jungle*, is in the Museum of Modern Art, New York. Moreover, I had the pleasure of receiving a farewell letter from Breton who, having become an undesirable, soon left Haiti accompanied by his wife, the Mabilles and the Lams. So much for an anecdotal account. Yet I cannot end without saying what Breton 'bestowed upon us to see', both on myself personally, as I was flung headlong into the great adventure, and on the whole of my generation.

What surrealism represented to us above all was the leap into the unknown. In a world that, in the name of logic and reason, condemned them to choose between lies and despair, in a world that left those who 'refused the shadow' no way out but madness or suicide, the surrealists opted for the disruption of traditional values. Beginning from total negation, it was no longer a matter of creating or inventing but of discovering. Man had been presented to himself in one of his guises to which, without any justification, he ascribed not only primacy over the other but his exclusive attention. It seemed there was a shameful part of himself which could not be talked about. The honour of the surrealist set, striking out on the trail laid by Freud, is to have relentlessly prospected mankind's subsoil. For us the surrealist coming to consciousness corresponded to the *revelation* of Breton's personality, spiritually by the mediation of his works but above all, in a way that cannot be gauged, by an entirely physical attraction. My own debt to Breton lay, above all, in his having brought me lucidity. The further I entered myself, the more the columns of shadow rose up into the light. I was not unaware that at a certain level everything is in danger of confusion but, without a doubt, there is the lance which runs it through. Little by little, I became decipherable to myself, and the world became clearer. In this sense, Breton was truly a bringer of light.

Heir to the beautiful blaze of Dadaism, which left nothing but ashes, surrealism constituted itself at first as anti-art. The contradiction of such an attitude – to combat art with art – recalls that of the ancient myth of the monster who tries to devour himself. How many problems became falsified by being defined as eternal? Nevertheless, the surrealists' experiments led to a virginal means of expression which made a clean slate of the moral conceptions and aesthetic forms to which some fossils, weakened from maintaining their threatened privileges, desperately clung. It is possible to speak of the failure of automatic writing, pivot and key method of surrealist activity, in so far as it was accorded an absolute power; but it is henceforth impossible to deny that it may have prompted the discovery of a new world that straying navigators had hitherto only glimpsed. I would not be able to forgive myself if I didn't cite Aragon on this, whose evidence cannot be questioned. This is what he wrote in *Les Lettres françaises* (May 1968) on the subject of the first surrealist document:

*Les Champs magnétiques* has become the work of a single author with two heads, and the double aspect alone allowed Philippe Soupault and André Breton to advance along the path where none

had gone before, speaking boldly from out of that darkness. This was
how this incomparable text came to be – which must really be
considered today just as I had the presentiment that it would be even
before it was completed: as the point, at the dawn of this century, at
which the whole history of writing turns, not at all the book with
which Stéphane Mallarmé wanted the world to end, but the one with
which everything begins.

As for surrealism itself, it has not only broken the barriers of the
subconscious, it has in consequence extended the realm of dream and
the imagination. It has changed Western artistic sensibility. It has
planted desire in the midst of life. It has married poetry and revolution in the heart of mankind. It has exploited the luciferian power of
black humour just as it wanted. It has revitalized notions of love and
liberty. It has put forward a fine defence in support of women, fighting against the repeal of affective forces, kept under the yoke – forces
that woman incontestably incarnates. It has laid bare certain arcana
of the collective unconscious and taken a decisive step towards the
psychic liberation of mankind. When all is said and done, this liberation can only be total after the social and economic liberation of all
the world's peoples. But there could be no question of poets and
artists waiting passively for this to happen, nor of handing the task
over to others who are not called to do it. Here and now they must
trace out new paths and cast the seeds of the future, in the field that
is their own. Surrealism has put the mind on trial: its avowed aim is to
create a 'new human understanding'. It has accelerated – following
Mallarmé, driven back to the glass wall of silence – that wonderful
work of the self-destruction of language, that phoenix ever more
beautifully reborn from its ashes. If the part of the road travelled
with the French Communist Party was surrealism's Calvary, it none
the less remains true that Breton's voice combined the irresistible call
of Marx – 'transform the world' – with the impassioned cry of
Rimbaud – 'change life'.

Beginning with the theory of the image expounded by Reverdy,
namely 'that it cannot be born of a comparison but from a bringing
together of two more or less distant realities', and going back to
Lautréamont, surrealism has pushed to its ultimate limit the shock
power of the image, all the more beautiful for its elements being unexpected and even contradictory. 'It is from the in some way fortuitous
bringing together of the two terms that a particular light has sprung,
the *light of the image*, to which we show ourselves to be infinitely

sensitive.' That this bringing together is therefore not premeditated cannot be too firmly stressed: it is involuntary. Moreover, Breton specified that the image that is 'strongest is that which offers the highest degree of arbitrariness'. The surrealist image is strictly speaking perplexing: it sets something other in motion, something within being that is deeper and darker. 'Beauty', as Breton also said in *Nadja*, 'will be convulsive or will not be.'

Rejecting the concept of the continuous and harmonious development of nature and man, surrealism everywhere explodes the contradiction that is within us as much as within things. So what it offers to sight – without for all that causing us to lose consciousness of relentless daily reality – is the other aspect of things, the other face of man, the other bank of the river of life. The history of surrealism did not take place in a sealed container; it was made in a laboratory, in the magic system of 'communicating vessels', but also in the 'open air of the street', Breton whispers to us, in a voice that, beyond death, is more alive than ever since it is the very course of eternal youth. To be convinced of this, one has only to listen to the record on which he reads one of his finest poems, *L'Union libre*, in which one image emerges from another in a mad profusion and where words, liberated at last, make love.

Passing through Martinique in April 1941, Breton discovered Aimé Césaire: 'In him (I already know, and see what everything will subsequently confirm) is mankind's crucible at its greatest point of fermentation, where knowledge, here moreover of the highest order, interferes with magical powers. . . . Thus it is that, single-handedly challenging an age in which one might think we witness the general abdication of the mind . . . when art itself threatens to solidify into outdated notions, the first fresh, revitalizing breath of air . . . comes from a black man. And it is a black man who handles the French language as no white man today can.' Of the *Notebook of a Return to My Native Land*, Césaire's first work, he says that this poem is 'nothing less than the greatest lyrical monument of these times'.

Passing through Haiti in 1945, he discovered Magloire-Saint-Aude, the alchemist of words, who transposed the silence of Mallarmé into the verbal explosion of surrealism. This is how he presents the Haitian poet in *La Clé des champs*: 'Twelve or fifteen verses, and no more, I understand your desire: the philosopher's stone or very nearly, the unexpected note that stills the tumult, the single tooth where the wheel of anguish meshes with ecstasy. One searches for he who, since the Sphinx, within such limits, had managed to halt the passer-by. In

French poetry, on occasion, Scève, Nerval, Mallarmé, Apollinaire. . . .
But you well know that today everything is much too *lax*. There is a
single exception: Magloire-Saint-Aude.'

It is not my intention here to study the influence of surrealism on
Haitian literature, but in order to illustrate the vistas it opened up perhaps one particularly enlightening example will suffice: that of René
Bélance, whose work marks a decisive turning point in modern Haitian
poetry in the French language. Constantly progressing beyond itself,
his work is concerned with the synthesis and surpassing, through surrealism, of the other principal tendencies of Haitian poetry:
indigenism, negritude and revolutionary humanism. A surpassing of
the level of folklore where, according to Anthony Lespès, the drum all
too often hides the man; a surpassing of the exclusively racial awareness that, in the political domain, leads to further racism and to the
exploitation of negro by negro; a surpassing of the stage of pure
protest where revolutionary slogans, necessary at the level of action,
are worth nothing in terms of art – but a surpassing without disavowal
since there has been an integration or rather an internalization of the
different tendencies – from Jacques Roumain to Magloire-Saint-
Aude – to the point where they are now a part of the substance of
being. For Bélance, man always stands tall, whether he descends into
his own darkness the better to see himself more clearly, or whether he
rises up into the light to see the universe more clearly. Even when desperate, he never gives up the struggle against despair and the causes of
despair. What characterizes him is the power of negation. Automatic
writing reveals the poet's deepest self, his subconscious – and this subconscious is that of a man whom the conditions of existence, that is the
Haitian environment, of the black race in the grip of colonialism or
imperialism, and of the organization of society on a world scale, have
led to take a stand for the total liberation of man, a material as well as
spiritual liberation. With *Epaule d'ombre* above all, where the means of
exploration and discovery go back to the very source of speech, of the
word-only thing in the world, as Francis Ponge says, which could be
internal and external at the same time – there can be no question of
differentiating form and content. An explosive poetry, made up of hallucinatory images in succession with a dizzying rhythm, in which
formal logic would recognize no coherence. Henceforth, attention centred on language – a language freed from the tutelage of Cartesian
reason and from all formal constraints; a language that liberates misunderstood or unknown forces; a language that reveals '*the other side
of the mirror*' where the unwonted part of the real rubs shoulders with

the marvellous of dream; a language that creates another world – the supreme quest of poetry – and that according to Paul Eluard, whose word has the authority of crystal, is nowhere else but within our own. Bélance passed the key to the magnetic fields of poetry to new generations. This is no doubt why, already more than twenty years ago, René Depestre, 'his people's commissioner of poetry', chose the patronage of this colleague to bring together, in a single shower of blood and of light, liberty and love, dream and reality, poetry and action.

In his *Panorama of Black-African Poetry*, Edouard Eliet underlines the close ties that exist between negritude and surrealism. Quoting Sartre's famous words, namely that 'black poetry in the French language is the only great revolutionary poetry of our time', he adds: 'revolutionary because it is surrealist, one might wonder. . . . But itself surrealist because it is black.' As Eliet himself recalls, Léopold Sédar Senghor, one of the most prominent advocates of negritude, had already noted in his presentation of the finest *Writings of the French Union* (1947): 'But what moves the Black is not the external aspect of the object, it is its reality, or more accurately (since *"realism"* has become sensualism) its *"surreality"* ' (my emphasis). The fate of poetry in French is equally in the hands of black poets, poets of an accursed race – on a poetic as well as a racial level. For a final proof of this I need only mention the discovery by Alain Bosquet of Davertige, a young Haitian poet he introduces with these words:

> Once every ten years or perhaps less it happens that, reading an unknown poet, we receive a shock that suddenly makes us aware of the difference between studied, intelligent literature, worthy of every praise, and genius in its raw state. . . . *Idem*, which was published in 1962, contains a dozen poems of an extraordinary verve, of an ever-dazzling originality, with imagery to make the reader tremble. Already Davertige is one of our great poets.

The new generation follows the paths opened by surrealism with its own means, in the realm of the imagination and the senses as much as in that of language. Personally, the values that remain essential to my life are not exclusively surrealist, but only surrealism has been able to unite them in such a shower of lightning flashes:

> poetry that 'blows on the wings of doors' and effects the crossing of the mirror;

love 'as it rises to invulnerability between two beings';
and liberty 'the colour of man'.

There can undoubtedly be no question of making surrealism a point
of arrival, but one cannot prevent it from being a point of departure –
at least in poetry. On the level of action, as we have seen, it has once
and for all recognized its limits. The most important movements that
succeeded it (existentialism, structuralism) took shape outside the
poetic realm. The only poetic movement of the century – historically
situated between two world wars and two abortive attempts at verbal
destruction (Dada and lettrism) – it extended and renewed itself in
negritude, which could have been its coloured child. Certainly, the
ivory tower has been abolished – along with the notion of utilitarian
art. The writer's problem is writing, in other words that by which he
reveals himself and reveals the world as he changes it within himself. So
he does not reflect reality; he transposes it, he contests it, he discovers
what is hidden behind it or what may be born from it, he metamor-
phoses it, in short he makes it other. The work is an end in itself and
could not in any way be a means without denying itself. The prophesies
of the poet–magi are coming true. However high genius rises, the
summit from which the Word thunders remains accessible to the slow,
violent ascent of man.

### Editor's Notes

1. André Breton, 'Le Surréalisme', lecture given at the Rex theatre, published in
*Conjonction*, no. 1 (1946), reprinted in *Conjonction*, no. 194 (1992).
2. Ibid.
3. Ibid.
4. Ibid.

[published in *Nouvelle optique*, no. 1 (1971); reprinted in *Conjonction*, no. 193
(1992)]

RENÉ DEPESTRE

# André Breton in Port-au-Prince

IF YOU CONSULT the *Surrealist Ephemerides* from 1919 to the present day, you will discover at the end of 1945 a rather mysterious reference to André Breton's activities in Haiti, shortly before his return to Paris after his years of exile in the United States.

> In Port-au-Prince, Haiti, where he met up again with Mabille and Lam, Breton gave a series of lectures. As a result of the first of these, the journal *La Ruche* issued a call for insurrection which resulted in a student strike, which soon took the form of a general strike. The Haitian National Palace was stormed and the members of the government taken prisoner.

These sibylline words describe an event that assumes ever greater importance with hindsight, since it was an encounter between André Breton's surrealism and one of the most luminous episodes in the struggle of the Haitian people in the twentieth century for freedom and human rights. The most objective of those chance events so dear to the author of *Nadja* brought to life an exceptional adventure for my generation, in the aura of the wondrous life and knowledge surrounding the works and the days of the French intellectuals 'of great human fraternities' that André Breton and Pierre Mabille remain in my eyes.

At the end of 1945 I was nineteen years old. Thanks to the 'fame' that the publication of *Etincelles*, my first book of poems, brought me in Haiti, I founded *La Ruche*, an avant-garde literary, artistic and political weekly, with Théodore Baker, J.S. Alexis and G. Bloncourt. That year, as forty-five years later, all kinds of collective misfortunes had restricted Haitian horizons. Public opinion immediately welcomed our journal as a breath of fresh air for the country's asphyxiated lungs. Our articles invited both young and old to unite and rally around the democratic and anti-colonial hopes that the immediate aftermath of the war had ignited on every continent.

We then wanted to demystify a society that was still fundamentally subject to a colonial heritage that the Haitian Revolution (1791–1804) had not managed to efface from our national life. We illuminated our youthful revolt with ideas hastily borrowed from poetry, the novel and the rare Marxist texts that fell into our hands in the desert of theory in which we lived, isolated and cut off from everything by the dictatorship of the tyrant Elie Lescot.

On 4 December 1945, the news of André Breton's arrival in Haiti inflamed our imaginations. Our enthusiasm was all the more incandescent in that Aimé Césaire's stay among us, a few months earlier, had prepared us to receive the *culture shock* of André Breton. Thanks to the author of *Notebook of a Return to My Native Land*, one of the first bedazzlements of our lives, we knew that surrealism was that movement of the spirit and sensibility that, in the course of the twenties and thirties had, with unprecedented verve, denounced the mystifications, the hypocrisies, the moral relativisms, the mockeries and the debaucheries that everywhere stood in the way of the emancipation of the best faculties of the human condition.

During the inter-war period surrealism, under Breton's dazzling authority, had effected a veritable revolution in poetry and modern art. Its refreshing mythology, irrigated with a sense of the marvellous, had given pride of place to love and humour as well as to revolt and tenderness, which were called upon to fill (in men's minds and behaviour alike) the prime position in modernity's values, in the face of the formidable political and social realities of a world constituted around the power of money alone, set up everywhere as *raison d'État* and as the decisive criterion of civilization *itself*.

For the angry young men that we were, Breton and surrealism could only be welcome. The great poet would not disappoint our expectations. His personal magnetism fascinated us. His leonine head, his noble and majestic bearing, his air of a prophet, the sobriety of his gestures and the sumptuousness of his French tongue were to make a lifetime impression on all those like me who, thanks to Pierre Mabille, had the honour and the poetic exhilaration to share his company in private and during the lectures he gave in Port-au-Prince.

André Breton was simple, open and warm with each one of us. He spoke to the Haitian people of Victor Hugo, Baudelaire, Nerval,

Mallarmé, Lautréamont, Rimbaud, Jarry, Apollinaire, Picasso, Matisse, Chagall, Klee, Duchamp, Max Ernst, Miró, Masson, Seurat, Rousseau, Wifredo Lam (who was also staying in Haiti at that time), Brauner, Giacometti, Matta, etcetera. To listen to André Breton was to realize that he, in the twentieth century, was the man possessed of the most elevated and intense sense of poetry and art, and at the same time had the strength to win his listeners over to the idea that there is more beauty in the world than human imagination will ever be able to exhaust to its limits.

Breton's first lecture took place on the evening of 20 December 1945 in the auditorium of the Rex theatre in Port-au-Prince, in the presence of Haiti's principal authorities and more than seven hundred intellectuals and university students. Pierre Mabille, who was the cultural attaché of Free France, had the pleasure of introducing his lifelong friend. Some of Mabille's brief words still ring in my ears as though it were yesterday evening.

'I wish to emphasize the absence of all compromise in André Breton's life. His resolute refusal of all opportunism is a very rare thing in literary circles . . . Breton has played an essential role in the transformation of contemporary sensibility. Young people from all corners of the globe have gathered around him, having in common a fundamental dissatisfaction with the conditions placed on mankind in our times; he has been a point of crystallization for artistic concerns throughout the past twenty-five years. But he has been more than this: on meeting him, in the ambience of his personality, in the magnetic field which forms around him, people have given their best, vague and uncertain gifts have developed magnificently, and if one was to name those familiar with his studio in the rue Fontaine, one would have to enumerate all of the famous names of modern poetry and art . . .'

Sitting in the first row of the audience were President Lescot, his ministers, senators and members of parliament, military chiefs and import–export businessmen, who knew nothing whatsoever about Breton and surrealism. Before having heard Mabille extol the speaker as the 'extraordinary centre of spiritual forces', they thought they were in the presence of one of those fine pillars of tradition and received ideas who came to talk about 'the role of latinity in the Americas'. Great was the consternation of these gentlemen and their wives when Breton began to unleash the gems and fruits of his thought in that electrified auditorium.

'I do not want to talk about surrealism in Haiti without first of all casting a highly respectful glance at what it is that conditions your country's inalienable enthusiasm for liberty and its affirmation of dignity above all obstacles. But some of you already know, and others are destined to discover, that here surrealism verifies one of its fundamental propositions, namely that the first condition of a people's persistence, as of a culture's viability, is that both can endlessly reimmerse themselves in the great affective currents that bore them at birth, without which they rapidly collapse . . . Besides the economy, whose importance I would not wish to underestimate, there is a lyrical element which to some extent conditions the psychological and moral structure of human societies, which has always conditioned it and will continue to condition it. One has only to come into contact with Haiti to convince oneself that this lyrical element, far from being merely a matter for specialists as it is elsewhere, comes from the aspirations of the entire people.'

This vigorous message from Breton, right over the heads of the disconcerted officials, enlivened the imagination of the young people who filled the theatre. They applauded fit to burst, they stamped their feet, they soared on Breton's contagious lyricism like birds discovering that the tree in which they have landed is a marvel of music and liberty. The scandalous and subversive atmosphere that had characterized surrealism in the heroic period of its Parisian era was created at the Rex. From the moment André Breton began to speak, we knew that the time was ripe in Haiti to unleash, before the event and *mutatis mutandis*, a terrific May '68 in the tropics!

From this memorable 'surrealist' evening, the *La Ruche* team decided to dedicate a special end-of-year issue in homage to Breton, Mabille and surrealism. This edition was an event. *La Ruche*'s success was unprecedented in the history of the Haitian press. Around Breton's words, which occupied the whole of the front page, surrealism was celebrated in effervescent articles. *Insurrection* was equally celebrated as the legitimate violence that every enslaved people has the duty to exercise when the legal forms of its long-suffering have been removed. André Breton's speech served as the backdrop for a pure and simple call to national insurrection!

Lescot's response was swift. A presidential decree ordered the confiscation of the special issue of *La Ruche* and forbade its future publication. Théodore Baker and myself found ourselves in prison. From 7 to 11 January 1946, the student strike launched to demand our release immediately turned into a general strike. All Haiti's nerve centres were paralysed. The brutalities of Lescot's cops, far from intimidating the demonstrators, contributed to the creation of an insurrectional climate in Port-au-Prince and the main provincial towns. Within a few days the *La Ruche* affair assumed the proportions of a torrent of democratic objection that engulfed Elie Lescot's power.

But this national movement which saw off the dictatorship was subsequently torn apart by all kinds of subsidiary disputes and failed at the very point of leading the Haitian people to destroy the old structures of oppression and install a rightful state. The army took control of the country and set in motion the social and political process that, a few years later, would allow François Duvalier and his tontons-macoutes to reduce Haiti to the *animal condition* which still characterizes it in 1991.

One of the 1946 military junta's first measures was to expel Breton and Mabille from Haiti. The presence of the great surrealist guide served as a pretext for an official campaign of vilification against Pierre Mabille. The army instigated a wild accusation against our marvellous friend: that he had been liaising with revolutionary centres in Mexico and Havana which had allegedly given him large sums of money to help the Haitian youth to put an end to the scandal of tyranny!

On the strength of these calumnies, the Military Executive Council demanded that Paris recall its cultural attaché. With tears in their eyes, the young people of my generation watched heavy-hearted the departure of two men of great combustion: the two most eminent minds ever to have lit up the blue haze of French intellectual embers in the life of a country of the Caribbean or Latin America.

*Lézignan-Corbières*
*10 July 1990*

[published in *Opus international*, nos 123–4 (April–May 1991), devoted to André Breton and surrealism; an earlier version of this essay was published in René Depestre, *Bonjour et adieu à la négritude*]

# CLÉMENT MAGLOIRE-SAINT-AUDE

# *A Record about Surrealism*

. . . ACCEPTING THE EXPLICABLE is the lot of the mob. For the common herd, being is the ruminant's function. For the poet, to exist is a wonder. The poet is the one who engages strangeness. He is unable either to yield to the crowd's formulas or to aspire to the logic of rhythmic phrasing. The poet descends into the darkest corners of the Unconscious. This marvellous world is the source of the creations from which spring the unchained images of the impossible and of wonderment.

Symbolists and surrealists glorify the subconscious and dream. Mallarmé was a 'master of the dream', Saint-Pol-Roux said, 'We are the colonizers of the beyond,' and E.L.T. Mesens said, 'We are tireless even in sleep.'

Symbolism is a reaction against Parnassus and naturalism. It liberates the possibilities of the internal world.[1]

Surrealism rejects the conformist main course and allows no limits to the mind's horizons.[2]

Surrealism could find no sympathy among superficial minds. It entices rebels, Baudelairians, those who have not been forced to behave.

The stylistic exaggerations in which the hangers-on of surrealism have indulged cannot invalidate the radiance of a political school whose masters are venerated by disciples of every race.

### Notes

1. 'There was no means of stopping the mind that had begun to function unchecked in the direction of every dream and every temptation and to construct dazzling worlds' – Jean Cassou.

2. 'In the end surrealism is a poetry freed from critical sense. It is the search for liberty' – Pierre Montal.

[published in *Haïti-Journal* (25 April 1941)]

# CLÉMENT MAGLOIRE-SAINT-AUDE

## *Surrealism: What It Is*

T HE CHATTERING OF in-crowds and salons, the lyricism of tirades
could not be fit food for people torn beyond mere words.

Roxane's smile, the worn eyes of beautiful marquises, fine vague
regrets are facile subjects that disgust men forged by the violence of
existence.

. . . Life is unsatisfactory. Yet we are not resigned to it. We refuse to
be fooled. We fear nothing: being misunderstood, being criticized,
being labelled 'jokers' or 'madmen', suffering, life or death – nothing.
We are neither dreamers nor idealists nor unrealistic . . . Surrealism is
an attitude of reaction, defiance and distrust. A distrust of the illusory
philosophies at the level of the naive, a distrust of unctuous and
sonorous morals . . .

. . . No genre is obscure . . . So as not to be overloaded with rhetoric
or cloying sincerity, the poet's message is no less a song in which
emotion's modesty dismisses fine transports.

. . . Hermeticism and 'concentration' is Modesty's final stage. The
poet is the one who engages strangeness. Disdaining the beaten track,
his immediate concern is the negation of all that is merely sentimental
afflux, senility or the prattle of an inconsolable soul . . .

[published in *Le Nouvelliste* (26 January 1942)]

## Jacques La Colère

# *Letter to the Old Men*

**Port-au-Prince, 1 December 1945**

I SHALL REFRAIN, gentlemen, from all your patinated formulas as I
take up that dangerous weapon the pen, to write to you about everything on my mind. I know, gentlemen, you share those Competencies,
those Experiences, those Eminences, that willingly take up Louis XIV's
phrase: 'What will our descendants say . . . ?' Well well! I believe I am
one of them, and so I'm sending you this letter which the news-vendors
will cry out and cast on the bitter winds of time, in everyone's direction,
towards the Old Men as towards the fine Young Men. Indeed, I affirm
that men can only be young or old, with no in-between state.

I can already see you stating your ages and some of you even, like
old coquettes, saying to us: 'I'm still in good shape, don't you
think . . . ?' But we're not gigolos. We know, to our sorrow, all your
intellectual rheumatisms, all your frailties of the heart. We see them in
the sickly effluvia of the air you have breathed in time's inexorable
march turned against you despite you. And on those paths you have
followed where you stand rooted, worm-eaten and infirm, an ill-
omened vegetation. You are certainly Eminences, Experiences,
Competencies; we know because you were born centenarians and it
doesn't upset us to hear tell that we are Impertinences, Imprudences,
Conceits . . . Thanks . . .

No, my problem is not mine alone, and it's my right to connect it
with that of the suffering populations of the world. I can already see
you affirming it as 'simply the effect of the war'. Correction: not the
war but a simple effect, the effect of the hoar frosts and April moons of
Reaction against the burgeoning forces of youth.

You want the traditional world? We want the rational world.

You affirm history's repetitions? We affirm history's dialectical evolution.

You seek truth in old millenarian books? We demonstrate it by means of science applied to life and societies and in the great open book of world reality.

Oh yes, gentlemen, we are non-conformists! Your beards tremble before the affirmations of modern consciousness. This is no longer the affirmation of an élite caste like all the others. Modern consciousness is no longer an élite consciousness but a mass consciousness.

You affirm, messrs Old Men, the specificity of the Haitian situation; we affirm the identity of human situations. You are afraid of your humanism, and when in Art for example we reveal new beauties you spit on what we consider to be the only altars. We scandalize you, don't we? But every new Beauty appeared at first as a scandal. The new Art will be one of the banners of our non-conformism.

You wish to win us over by renewing soporific Dogmas. They are all guilty of Embezzlement. We affirm that the essence of scientific method is established once and for all. For the first time spiritual energies will not be enticed into empiricism and fantasy.

You threaten us with the cosmic dangers with which you juggle. We too are armed, for the only weapon in the world is the life within Young Men. Contrary to you we reject the prophets, but see in the world's material laws the signs marking the end of traditional historical cycles.

I know that your response will be to hurl your reactionary yelps at the very tops of your voices in pursuit of us, in pursuit of me for having dared. But I enjoy maintaining this correspondence. I'm only a Young Man suffering the world's old age that you perpetuate, and I'm excited by the certainty of the display to come . . .

Goodbye, gentlemen; I add to these worrying truths all the good wishes one can have towards Old Men.

Jacques La Colère

PS. See you soon!

[published in *La Ruche* (7 December 1945)]

PART V

# APPRECIATIONS

# OF HAITI

/

HENDRIK CRAMER

# Extract from a Letter to
# Monny de Bouilly

An incident

AT PORT-AU-PRINCE, IN the rue des Miracles, there is a house of education for young boys (a Catholic boarding school). In 1903, in November, the rumour went round Port-au-Prince that a horseless carriage was traversing the city during the night. No one dared look at this carriage. Two boarders, little boys aged about eight or nine, resolved to disobey the rule not to get up during the night and watch the horseless carriage. When they heard the sound of wheels coming closer, they got up and opened their window shutter. But at the moment the carriage went past one of them took fright. The other watched. He was never seen again. He had vanished both from the room and from the boarding school as though borne away by the horseless carriage. And none of the searches for him were successful. However, his parents undertook all the ceremonies[1] in order to find him, because they had been told[2] that the child was not dead. One day they did find their child at Léogane[3] under the mapou tree[4]. He was an old man. They questioned him: the old man[5] could not remember having lived.

A ritual

When someone dies, the houngan[6] is immediately called to extract the loa.[7] The soul has gone, but the loas are still attached to the mortal remains. These loas should be extracted so that the body may return to the mother[8] in a virgin state. A ceremony takes place before the corpse is embalmed. This ceremony is done by the houngan among his intimate friends. He is attended by his 'little leaf'.[9] Some of the relatives and friends present reply to his chants by performing a backwards dance[10] around the corpse. They have their backs bent and hold a stick between their legs.[11]

Dear Monny, I know you well enough to know how you will appreciate these two 'observations' about magic. But believe me when I tell you that, personally, it is not for their beauty or fantastic qualities that I value them. I want one day to be able to prove that the human body is sacred, *that our actions have repercussions in the Invisible, and that the word, the song and the mask are means of invocation and are absolutely magical.*

## Notes

1. Magical ceremonies.

2. That is, the spirits invoked during the ceremonies.

3. A small town a few hours from Port-au-Prince.

4. A colossal tree with elephant-like bark, which is one of three sacred trees: the mapou, the médicinier béni and the accursed fig tree.

5. The old man's name was known, but is missing in my notes.

6. Voodoo priest.

7. Spirit.

8. The earth.

9. The name of one of the houngan's initiated assistants who deals with everything to do with magic leaves, healing, etcetera [translator's note: that is, the hounsi].

10. By taking positions contrary to those taken during ordinary invocations so that the 'loas' (or 'spirits' or 'angels' or 'mysteries') realize that they are not being invoked and are being asked to leave.

11. I don't yet know what this action signifies and don't want to 'suppose'.

[letter written from Haiti, during a visit by Cramer. Monny de Bouilly was a Yugoslav surrealist who had participated in the Surrealist Group before gravitating toward Le Grand Jeu. Cramer, who was Dutch, wrote the letter in hurried and slightly clumsy French. The letter is published in Hendrik Cramer, *Vizioen en Geboorte* (1974) Amsterdam: J.M. Meulenhoff BV]

PIERRE MABILLE

# Memories of Haiti

THE PORT-AU-PRINCE BUREAU of Ethnology has two departments: one of pre-Columbian archaeology, the other of Haitian folklore. The latter is far richer, a collection of ceremonial clothing, flags, statuettes, ritual necklaces, pottery, decorated calabashes, notebooks of songs and prayers and a record library, in short an immense documentation which one day will allow a complete study of voodoo, its origins and evolution from colonial times to the present day, and an understanding of the various factors that make this syncretic religious phenomenon – despite its similarities with Brazilian macumba, Cuban locumis rites and the cult of Ethiopianism – a fundamentally Haitian form.

If so many ethnologists (whether professional or amateur, foreign or native) have failed to encompass the totality of the problem and have until now only accomplished incomplete, more or less fanciful, accounts, it is because such a study is infinitely harder and more extensive than one imagines on arriving in Haiti.

It is childish and false to talk about a black, white or yellow soul, as though the various communities of these essentially heterogeneous races correspond to fixed biological and psychological unities. Nevertheless, I cannot think about black people without the image of the forest being conjured up in me like an obsession. When I think of the forest, I mean the sum total of the contradictory, confused sensations it leaves in tangible memory and which the popular language expresses. Don't we speak of 'plunging into the forest', don't we talk about its depths, as we would about the depths of a mine or an ocean, and yet it has neither a surface nor a skin, but an edge, a border. Language, confusing the part with the whole, often evokes the *heart of the forest*, doubtless suggesting the meaning of 'heart of the tree', of a centre. But the point is that the forest does not have a centre; it is everywhere and nowhere.

The considerable importance of the vegetal world in the religion, medicine and art of black peoples, their ability to appear or disappear as if a tree was ever-present to act as a screen, fully justifies the connection formed in my mind. Among them I rediscover that impression – experienced again and again as I cross the forest – of feeling myself lost, seized with a wild terror with no precise cause, but also feeling calmed, protected and relaxed by the safe keeping of the 'guardian' branches. A strange feeling of being spied upon by a thousand eyes, mocked by the birds, pursued by the snake or some other terrible animal, garotted by the lianas and thorns, surrounded by an active and *watchful* life, and yet of finding oneself so perfectly alone that no cry would elicit the slightest rescuing response, not even the simple and reassuring reflection of the wave of vibrations offered by the valley or even the cave.

To study voodoo is precisely to plunge into the forest and brave its traps. At the instant you think you are furthest from your goal, you find you are only separated from it by a thin curtain of trees, and when you think you're close, you can walk for hours only to find yourself led 'to the border' without encountering anything. While the reading of Judaic, Christian or Islamic texts often makes one think of the seduction of the *mirage*, it is the *labyrinth* that invariably comes to mind once you try to penetrate into voodoo. How can you be sure you haven't passed right by the hidden sanctuary, the thing you *had* to see?

This uncertainty, easily understandable on the part of a foreigner, likewise disturbs my Haitian friends, to whom these ceremonies are nevertheless familiar and who, one would think, should have every reason to understand. So the Bureau of Ethnology takes on informants. Their task is to inform us of the place and date of cultural events in the Port-au-Prince region. Apart from the relatively fixed dates, such as those of Christmas, All Saints and Easter, on which more or less similar services are celebrated every year, the meetings respond to specific needs (family obligations, illnesses, the initiation of a hounsie[1] and so on), known only to those living in close contact with the families or houngans.

It must be remembered that, although voodoo is the actual religion of the majority of Haitian peasants and of many people who profess it, in theory it is forbidden and in practice is only tolerated. In fact, the Concordat of 1864 guarantees apostolic Roman Catholicism as the only official state religion. Those who wish to hold a voodoo celebration to obtain the help of the gods or appease their anger must request authorization from the rural police, who may refuse for no other reason than that the local officer is hostile to the cult or simply ill-disposed towards the celebrants. In any case, official approval must be bought. There could be no question of avoiding this, since the ceremonies are accompanied by the beating of drums and noisy dancing that one could hide only by going off into the mountains or very far beyond the cane fields, as they had to do in colonial times. Voodoo's semi-clandestinity is thus a first obstacle to overcome before dealing with the secrets inherent in any religion based on mysteries.

One of our informants, bearing the high-sounding name of Dieu-Loué, told us that a major sacrifice was to be celebrated the following Saturday at the home of one of his aunts, a maman loa living in the Léogane plain, during which in addition to chickens, kids and other animals, an ox would be offered to the loas. It would be an important event. We decided to attend this ceremony, leaving at noon on Saturday in my car. The expedition was made up of an officer of the guard who was passionate about the study of voodoo, and a director of the Bureau of Ethnology, a colourful character of the handsomest black, who only ever went out in a dark suit, with a felt hat on his head and a gold-knobbed cane in his hand, all attributes recalling the splendour of the Haitian bourgeoisie of some thirty years earlier. Before 1915, the date of the North American military occupation, no one wore linen clothes, shorts or open shirts, and they pretended not to notice the tropical heat so as to conform to a dress code as rigorous as that of the most outmoded French provincial bourgeoisie. Moreover our friend's refined language, adorned with sonorous adverbs and outdated turns of phrase, recalled the pure notarial style of the eighteenth century. Two hounsie canzos accompanied us: one, a pretty girl, a very pale mulatto, the mistress of a foreign businessman, seemed more suited to profane merry-making than ritual functions; she had the inestimable advantage in my eyes of speaking an easily understandable Creole and even fairly often French.[2] Her friend, Miss Caméla – or Carméla – had a less flattering physique: as broad as she was tall and of a thorough blackness with frizzy hair, she was furthermore blessed with such a confusing accent that I had trouble understanding her. Lastly there was Dieu-Loué, our guide.

We took the Bizonton road out of Port-au-Prince, first crossing the crowded suburb where tumbledown, teeming huts crowd together.

Then, between two rows of trees, we were soon skirting the sea which was warming itself in the most beautiful bay in the world, at the foot of the high mountain bordering our road on one side. It was very hot, and after about four miles a tyre burst. I fitted the spare wheel and, fifteen hundred yards on, the same tyre burst again. This time it meant a breakdown. Haitian roads are never deserted: lines of peasant women go by endlessly in poor patched tunics made out of coarse canvas or old flour sacks on which the brand names can still be made out. These women carry baskets or wooden trays on their heads piled up with veritable mountains of fruits or vegetables, walking barefoot one after the other, singing, shouting out, sometimes even dancing, invariably hailing each other in a loud voice. More often than not they are accompanied by donkeys heavily laden with charcoal, calabashes or breadfruit; with their incessant cries and volleys of blows with sticks they try to rouse the lazy donkeys. The lashings, gallopings and spilled loads clutter up the road.

Dieu-Loué noticed a young boy passing on horseback dressed in a blue cloth smock with a red scarf around his neck, as worn by country folk on their way to town. He explained our dilemma and procured a lift as far as the Port-au-Prince suburbs to take the wheel for repair. The only thing for us to do was wait for him in the stifling heat. The hounsies sang us voodoo-style tunes. A highly serious and very lively conversation set in, theologically oriented, about the limit of houngans' powers over malevolent beings such as loups-garous. From this I learned that the houngan's power and protection was only maintained inside his houmfor.[3] Outside, he can be overcome by evil forces. At home, reinforced by the magnetic chain of his hounsies, he is impregnable. It should be pointed out that the Catholic clergy also share this doctrine.

A rickety old coach halted, down got Dieu-Loué, and we could get going.

Worried about these two successive punctures, I stopped a few hundred yards on. While the other tyres were merely hot, the one that had just been repaired was roasting again. There was no explanation for the phenomenon, since the pressure was correct, the brake was not rubbing and the hub was recent. A mystery of mechanics or of the gods! In fact we had to stop every five hundred yards to let it cool down and sprinkle it with water when we could find some. In this way the journey was hardly progressing. Half seriously, half in jest, we decided to invoke Papa Legba, the god of crossroads, who is called upon at the start of all voodoo worship, in whose honour the cockerel is sacrificed at the garden *barrière*[4] so he will allow the other divinities to participate in the ceremony. We also hailed Ogoun-Feraille who, for his part, is more specialized in matters of fire, mechanics and at the same time certain branches of medicine; he represents the survival of the blacksmith god whose cult is still widespread in Africa. With no possibility of setting out offerings for these supernatural powers, our hounsies spiritedly chanted invocations reserved for them. Either because the heat had abated, because something had clicked and changed the mechanical situation, or else because the loas had been appeased, I noted an improvement in the state of my wheel and we reached the Léogane plain. Unfortunately, it was now six o'clock; we only had an hour left before night would abruptly fall, with no dusk.

Dieu-Loué was highly optimistic. According to him, the hut which he knew well was nearby. We would be there in less than a quarter of an hour. We left the car on the road and set off along a footpath. First we crossed several cane fields, then reached some rice plantations by crossing, with some difficulty, the innumerable little irrigation canals that give this part of the plain an extraordinary fertility. After half an hour of exhausting walking, Dieu-Loué's confidence quickly diminished; he was less and less certain about the direction to take and we had to ask the way at a hut.

On the doorstep, an extremely old white-haired negro was majestically smoking a little clay pipe. Our intrusion in his garden caused an old woman and a swarm of children to come out. These bewildered people all looked us over anxiously. I let my companions start the conversation, enquiring about where the Flampin lady lived (I cannot be at all sure about her precise name, which was probably deformed by the Creole pronunciation), the presumed aunt of our devoted Dieu-Loué. As a white man and a foreigner, I kept my distance. I had the impression that the conversation had started badly. There's a book to be written about ceremonies of social contact in different countries . . . Either because the minds of the old man, whom I considered to be at least a hundred years old, and his wife were profoundly affected by age, or because, terrified by our presence and by the nature of the question (the address of a maman loa), they preferred not to reply. If they were to be believed, they had never heard of this woman and, in any case, we had come the wrong way. We retraced our steps, found the car and postponed our expedition until the following day. Our return to Port-au-Prince was incident-free.

*Sunday morning.* The departure was arranged for half past eight to give me time to stop off at the garage (nothing wrong was found that

might explain the previous day's incidents). I invited along a
Frenchman, a Parisian who had been living in Port-au-Prince for several years, having married a woman from Haitian high society. He had
long burned with desire to attend a voodoo ceremony and finally see
the country in a different light to what was offered by the Turgeau
tennis courts, sparkling receptions, fashionable balls and bridge parties
that were his usual activities. Being furnished with two cars I hoped,
this time, we would have luck on our side.

Our friend the ethnographer was the last to arrive, a little out of
breath but decorous as ever. He recounted the reason for his delay: he
had received a visit concerning us that worried him. Miss S. was his secretary at the Bureau of Ethnology, a highly proficient typist who spoke
fluent French and English and came from a cultivated background.
During the night this woman had been possessed by Ogoun-Feraille. It
really was a case of possession and not a dream or nightmare. Her sister confirmed this as she related the event: the two young women,
sleeping in adjacent rooms, were separated by only a thin wooden partition. She was awakened first by sighs and then gasps. She went to see
what was happening and saw S. in prey to extreme convulsions, strug-
gling on her bed, violently bumping against the partition and singing,
in a voice not her own, the songs that every Haitian recognizes as those
of Ogoun. This was not a family that frequented voodoo ceremonies,
which was why the thought of a possession hardly occurred to the
young woman. At first she feared an attack of fever or a stroke. But she
had to yield to the evidence: the state had lasted more than half an
hour and when, exhausted, S. regained consciousness, she recounted
that the god had mounted her, that he was very angry, that he had
shown her her boss (the ethnographer), the officer and myself, that he
had told her that we were forbidden to attend the ceremony on pain of
exposing ourselves to the gravest danger. She had judged it necessary to
warn us in order to dissuade us from leaving. Naturally, such advice
could only increase our desire to make this expedition.

I expected fresh mechanical problems or some conclusive breakdown.
Nothing. Today the car ran merrily along in the clear Haitian morning.
What an enchantment of light and trembling joy! The night's possession
had singularly excited my companions who were only too pleased to
thus prove to me that the mounting of loas, as the hallowed expression
puts it, was not, as had so often been written, the result of hysteria provoked by being drunk on alcohol or the diabolical beating of drums
maintained at a rapid rhythm for hours. In fact, these attacks of possession, happening unexpectedly during sleep outside any abnormal

excitation, infinitely extend the problem without for all that altering its fundamental basis. They attest particular aptitudes for convulsive attacks and an exceptional facility for dissociation of the psychic personality, tendencies whose origin must be sought in both the biological constitution and in the influence of the social environment.

As on the previous evening we left our car, but instead of plunging into the rice fields, this time we followed a beaten earth track very occasionally bordered by wooden huts nestling under the palm trees; each little villa had its porch where, shaded from the sun, old men and women rocked in dodines[5] while clusters of practically naked children played noisily. We managed to get some directions: Maman Flampin lived much further on, two or three hours' walk away (contrary to the information supplied by Dieu-Loué)! It would be better to procure some horses, which we soon did. Now our convoy looked splendid. I was living a childhood dream drawn from my favourite books: tales of Louisiana, *A High Wind in Jamaica* and *Treasure Island*. Everything I had imagined during my adolescence, in my dark Parisian bedroom, suddenly came true.

We had gone less than a mile when, all of a sudden, a diluvian rain battered down on us; we just had time to shelter in a nearby hut. Tropical rain is totally different from the most violent downpours we get in Europe. The water does not fall in drops but in streams, to such an extent that you have the impression that nothing will be able to survive, that no refuge will do, and that the earth will be submerged, as if by the flood of a river that has suddenly burst its banks. The trees bent under the weight of the water. The black children, screaming with joy, went out naked into the avalanche, running around frantically. The noise was so loud that the collective delirium quickly reached its height, as at the culmination of a festival. It was the water mother, the great fertility. What for us is terror is for them intoxication.

We took advantage of this enforced halt to open up our provisions: *grillots* and *bananes pesées*, all washed down with a delicious Haitian rum. Out of discretion our hosts would not accept a share of our snack; they were watching over the crowd of brats – who were using our presence as a new source of excitement – making sure they did not disturb us. Our French friend would have preferred a good glass of fresh water to rum; he asked for it and we soon saw a little girl eight or nine years old carrying a glass and an earthenware jug like an alcarraza on a mahogany tray with a lace cloth. He filled his glass and saw, to his horror, that the water was completely muddy, more or less the same reddish yellow colour as the torrent now streaming down the road. He did not know how to avoid drinking this dangerous liquid without giving offence to our hosts.

This scene encapsulates all the reality of the Haitian countryside. The inhabitants of this hut, made of wicker, earth and wood, were unquestionably very poor and yet they insisted on presenting refreshment to their guests with an etiquette and a solemnity that recalled the pomp of the eighteenth-century French nobility. These peasants slept on a straw mattress, yet they owned the tray and the tray cloth to honour their visitors. This deference was not the result of our status as strangers, or the presence of white men; if a barefoot mountain peasant woman had knocked on the door, she would have been welcomed as ceremoniously. This formality, it seems, is authentically African; it has only been reinforced and shaped by the customs of the French masters during the colonial period. The liberated former slaves made it a duty to preserve the fine customs to prove themselves worthy of their conquered liberty. Unfortunately the water in the jug was muddy because no water supply existed; wells are scanty and contaminated, which accounts for the shocking spread of intestinal parasites, typhoid and so many other epidemics. Despite his idealism and lace, despite his dignity which places him among the most civilized beings, the poor peasant lives on the land like a primitive animal. It would be more accurate to say that he lives more in, by, for the land than on it. He is incorporated into it, submitted like it to the rain and drought, shaken by the same cosmic forces.

With great cowardice I left our friend to extricate himself from his difficult situation and, with the officer and the ethnographer, considered the next stage of the adventure. It would be impossible to continue on foot; we had to try and get back on the horses. They moved forward with difficulty, slipping in the thick red, clay-like mud at every step. The urchins following us sank in up to their knees. Even though the rain had stopped, the water continued to gush down the road. Each step was a problem for horse as for rider. I marvelled at the ethnographer's control. Despite his horse's incessant sliding, he kept his dignity and . . . his gold-tipped cane. The same could not be said for my French companion. To begin with he had looked impeccable in his starched white canvas suit. Now the rain had dissolved the starch. Concerned above all with maintaining an uncertain balance, he kept a poor grip on the head of his horse, so that it fell, pulling its rider with it, who stood up looking like a pastry-chef dunked in a vat of chocolate. It was impossible to witness this spectacle without being overcome with laughter. Our two hounsies, the urchins and even the stately ethnographer could not contain themselves. Each of us thought to himself that a few yards on it would be his turn. The comic incident put an end to our horse ride.

What could we do? It was then that the officer had an inspired idea: obtain an ox cart. But as easy as it is in the Haitian countryside to hire horses in exchange for a few gourdes,[6] it is difficult to borrow oxen for a trip: these animals are rarer, they are kept for the transport of sugarcane consignments and the peasants are not keen to overwork them with useless tasks.

At first we had to put up with several polite refusals. They had no oxen, or those they had were penned too far away, and so on. Dieu-Loué, whose usefulness had not been notable in the course of the morning – perhaps fearing some punishment from the angered gods – roused himself. He discovered a young boy who was more intelligent and lively than the others and who, in exchange for a fairly high price, promised to supply us with the coveted means of transport. Indeed, after half an hour he returned with two oxen, and a cart borrowed from a neighbouring peasant. At rest it looked good even if simply constructed: it was a sort of tip-cart adapted to carting canes, whose very large solid wheels were more than six feet in diameter. We got in and set off. In motion, the vehicle proved to be much less stable than it had appeared. In fact it had no hubs, the wheels being simply threaded onto an iron bar; as they turned, they described a helical curve such that at certain moments they seemed to be lying completely underneath the floor of our cart. The latter did not stay horizontal for an instant: you would have thought it a raft on a wild sea, and standing upright became problematic. At the lowest point we were level with the mud, then we suddenly lurched towards the palms, which were heavy with water, and we were soaked all over again. The driver laughed loudly at our discomfort. To be fair, not many comedy routines work so successfully. He claimed that things would improve once we had left the muddy part of the track. Indeed, after a few hundred yards, the terrain was grassy and resistant and we moved forward in greater comfort.

The region we were entering was, of all those I know around the world, the closest to the idea one could have of Paradise: a sort of garden, wild and cultivated at the same time, planted with luxurious trees, great mapous with knotted grey trunks in the forms of animals, tall mango trees laden with strings of fruit, breadfruit trees with incised varnished leaves like acanthus, elegant palms and coconut palms with soaring stems. Emerging from large banana leaves at head height were bunches of red and purple flowers like bouquets of coral or mother-of-pearl. Hibiscus with their delicate crowns, white daturas, those flowers of sleep and, as in Persian miniatures, the golden fruits of orange and lemon trees shimmered in the setting of a dark-green foliage lacquered by rainwater. The latter had absorbed the excess heat and we dissolved into the world's euphoria.

Multicoloured hummingbirds moved, buzzing, from one flower to another; great blue birds flew high up in the tops of the mango trees. Now and again we passed groups of women who had resumed their walk to the distant town while peasants, machete in hand and trousers rolled up, made merry in this paradise; they replied ceremoniously and not without some fear to our friendly greetings.

I wanted this journey never to end. Unfortunately, here we were at a cluster of a few huts where the priestess lived, the one we had been seeking for two days. Not a soul stirred, silence. Dieu-Loué rushed inside. No doubt he wanted to prove to us that he really was part of the family. He soon emerged, crestfallen, accompanied by a puzzled man. Mrs Flampin was ill in bed. Nevertheless she rose to receive us. She and her husband swore by the gods that there never had been any celebration. We had been given false information. The unease that marked our arrival dissipated when we spoke of our respect for the voodoo cult and our interest in its ceremonies, and when our hounsies revealed that they were authentic initiates. We were then offered a glass of clairin. The maman loa agreed to show us her houmfor, a fairly rustic one at that: we paid homage to the earth and the ancestors by sprinkling a few drops of water on the four cardinal points.

We were then taken to the hut not far away where a large, very black woman, with sparkling eyes and worrying gestures, lived. Was she crazy, or a wild sorceress? The single room was full of ritual objects and, even more it seemed, with magic objects. I asked a few questions, but it was impossible for me to know who this strange person was, to the extent that I wondered if she was demented, a sort of zombi, taken in and cared for by the Flampin family, or if she was not the true, fearsome priestess who imposed her authority on the whole community. I was highly sceptical as to the ties uniting Dieu-Loué to these people who seemed not to know him. We had to be going; in the midst of a flood of confused words, we were assured that the sacrifice of the ox would take place shortly and we would be warned in time (although we never were).

What had happened? Had Dieu-Loué been misinformed? Had he set up the whole thing to give himself a pleasant day out? Was Mrs

Flampin really ill? All rather unlikely hypotheses. During the return journey, talking to the already less startled peasants, we believed we could grasp that it was we who had compromised everything. The unexpected arrival in the area of an officer accompanied by foreigners on the previous day had provoked a deep disquiet which had quickly spread. The ceremony, which had probably already started, was interrupted for reasons of prudence and everyone had dispersed before we got there. However, this too is no more than a conjecture.

Anyway, despite our failure, we had escaped the dangers. The hounsies were convinced that their presence had contributed to the fact that we had. The rest of us, recalling the secretary's nocturnal possession, were more thoughtful. We reflected a little sheepishly, some of us about Ogoun's powers, the others (my French friend and myself) about the difficulty of understanding Haitian psychology, made up as it is of astonishing intuitions and profound distrust redressed by the most affable smiles, all under the sway of the extreme fluctuations of the appearances and disappearances in the forest.

## Notes

1. Hounsie canzo: a woman belonging to the group of initiates which assists a hongan (papa loa or maman loa) in ritual ceremonies and participates in sacred dances and sacrifices.

2. The official language of Haiti is French. The entire population speaks Creole. This is a true language formed of old French, Spanish and English words, more or less deformed, and an African syntax. Creole is not only a language, it is a combination of adorned expressions expressing the peasant soul. You grasp it with difficulty in towns, and with much more difficulty in the countryside. It is the same for our regional patois.

3. The hut containing the altar and which acts as a temple.

4. Translator's note: *Barrière*: the entrance, which is protected by medicinal plants; it is also the door to the other world.

5. Rocking chairs popular in Haiti.

6. Haitian unit of currency: 5 gourdes are worth one dollar.

[published in Pierre Mabille, *Messages de l'étranger* (1981) Paris: Plasma]

PIERRE MABILLE

# The Haitian Panorama

T WENTY MILES OR SO from the towns and especially from the capital, in the escarpments of Kenscoff or the morne at Cabrits, you start to meet long lines of barefoot peasant women, balancing their heavy baskets on their heads. They go their way singing, chatting, laughing and even dancing, never setting down their enormous loads which do nothing to diminish the suppleness of their gait. They walk like this for hours, days, nights, years, for their whole lives. If I had to leave Haiti for good, the image I would retain of it would certainly be that of these women walking the length of eternity, descending the footpaths, effortlessly scaling the highest peaks, winding across the plain, taking with them mountains of herbs, carrots, sweet potatoes, cabbages, pineapples, baskets of poultry, piles of hats, stacks of chairs, cans of milk. Here, the procession is accompanied by a few asses, there by some thin Caribbean horses, bent under their excessive burdens.

Wherever you go there are people walking. They run in modern cities; they step with heavy tread in our own countryside; in North Africa they advance slowly in caravans which criss-cross the desert fleeing famine; but nothing compares with this possessed tramping of the Haitian peasant, a legacy of the African forest, possessed like the struggle of impoverished existence against the renewed assaults of poverty. This muttering old woman, a clay pipe between her teeth and her tinware on her head, climbs more than ten miles down the mountains each morning to carry milk to her customers. That one over there has travelled more than twelve miles to get to market so she can sell her basket of mangoes for no more than a gourde. Don't be surprised if in a few moments you see her crouched asleep in a shady corner, and don't speak too hastily of nonchalance. And if, retracing her path with rapid steps, the rain takes her by surprise, she will bundle up her sack-cloth dress, leaving only a shirt which the falling water will plaster against her black body. Then, tomorrow, perhaps you will hear coming from a hut the howls that accompany a death and which, according to tradition, succeed each other throughout the night over the corpse. Don't speak too hastily of a negro's sensitivity to pulmonary ailments.

[first published in *Tropiques*, no. 12 (January 1945); reprinted in *Messages de l'étranger* (1981)]

PIERRE MABILLE

# The Loas Speaking in Govis: Sorcery and Clairvoyance in Voodoo Religion

YESTERDAY MY FRIEND Dr Maximilien offered to take me to question the loas speaking in govis.[1] The problem worried him and he wanted my opinion. I accepted enthusiastically and at the end of the afternoon, with the heat already starting to lessen, we were on the road to Croix-aux-Bouquets, a small conglomeration beyond which lived the mambo[2] we were going to see.

Leaving Port-au-Prince, the first part of the road is asphalted. To our right stretched the air base with its new building, electric signals and uniformed employees, a base similar to those found throughout the American continent, for the departure and arrival of the great metal birds. To our left were hundreds of little wooden huts, rickety, swarming with half-naked children shouting, jabbering, living there joyfully in a poverty that is only tolerable in the tropics and which, in the surroundings of the European capitals, would be a sordid scourge.

We arrived at the plain where the road became a hot, dusty track again, bordered with tall palm trees whose languorous arms were rocked by the breeze. At the side of the road files of peasant men and women walked like ants, barefoot next to donkeys tottering under the most varied loads, returning to their mountain after having sold their meagre crop and bought a few morsels of salted fish and confectionery at the market. The women were dressed in white shirts, usually made from old flour sacks still bearing the printed trademark of the American manufacturer, the cloth tied around their supple loins by a string belt. On their heads they carried all their shopping piled up on a wooden tray which was held balanced despite their rapid step, or their athletic antics.

These people, who live in the mornes or at the end of the plain several hours' walk through the cane fields, are even more surrounded by worry, and their laughter will quickly turn to anguished cries if fever strikes them, if the child in the hut has writhed with convulsions all night, if the other one they left playing is found dead on the mat of dried banana leaves. Moreover, who knows if, when they come back down in a few days, the town policeman will be content with the two gourdes he demanded today to let them sell the little bag of coffee, the pile of mangoes, the three pairs of scrawny chickens outside the market? Perhaps, ill disposed, or on the evidence of malicious gossip, he will be brutal, so destroying the precarious household economy!

I love the gentleness of the heat at the end of these tropical afternoons. It seems as if there could be no greater physical happiness; it seems to be better than the voluptuousness of the most lukewarm baths: all the sharp, resinous, sweet smells mingle with the dark green of the giant trees. And yet the threat seems so close at hand! Storm and destruction are present, barely hidden, in this total beatitude. How little it would take to change these great outbursts of laughter into cries of pain or revolt! How little it would take to turn this heat, so perfectly agreeable, into catastrophe if it lasts too long, if it brings the drought which strikes every living thing with death.

In our temperate climates we are used to remarking on sequences of good fortune and on other, frankly sinister ones during which we lament a childhood illness, the loss of a job or a bereavement. We are in the habit of saying 'Bad luck comes in threes!' But, either because temperate climates discourage extremes, or because the social services are better established, it is very rare for an equilibrium not to be reached between fortunate and unfortunate events. What is more, personal responsibility seems more directly involved and the influence of natural forces weighs less heavily. What struck me in the tropical zone was the rapidity of the about-turn that casts a well-to-do family, successful in everything, into the most complete catastrophe. As soon as a death or a trial occurs in a household, it is rare for things to stop there and – within the space of a few weeks or a few months at most – for the number of misfortunes not to have increased, sometimes to the point of destroying the whole family. This sudden and implacable character is found in all the elements: it is the rain bucketing down, inundating, ravaging, destroying, washing away the harvest and the soil itself; it is the torrential downpour falling with such brutality that one often sees a house or a lorry carried off by the flood. It is the passage of a typhoon or a cyclone across a very narrow area, destroying some and sparing others. It is the attack of fever which suddenly erupts to cause the death of someone who had been in perfect health.

This insecurity, this ever-present and seemingly electively directed danger is one of the most striking features of the tropical atmosphere, calculated to increase fear. For, in the end, there seems to be nothing to explain the collapse: daily routine has not changed. What can have happened? If you ask a white priest, he invokes sin, or humanity's fate; but since nothing has altered, why this sudden change from a difficult life to terrible tragedies, and then if the God he professes is so great, so distant – the God of all mankind – how can he take part in the elaboration of such a specific, personal misfortune? No, the danger must be close by, familiar, it must know you and have directly hostile intentions. Perhaps in the course of Saturday night's ceremony, an incarnated loa will deign to speak and give the explanation you await so urgently. But will he come? Must you await the problematic disclosure, and isn't it better to force it out by interrogating the god personally? Not the god of everyone, but the one the mambo is devoted to, the one to whom she can speak directly. This is why the houngan[3] or the mambo is consulted, as witnesses to the unjust adversity that happens, to discover the sources of your misfortune. It is less a matter of interrogating the supernatural about the future than of elucidating the present and of knowing the intention of the events suddenly coming down around the heads of those who do not feel the pangs of bad conscience. And this is why we are observing the summoning of the loas in the govis tonight.

The govis, rather crude clay pots, are placed on the voodoo altar. They are consecrated to a god who will speak: his voice will issue from the vessel, as if he was contained inside the govi.

We approached the houmfor,[4] without crossing the threshold. The mambo had gone in near to the altar and was sitting on a low chair, holding the *açon*[5] and the bell.[6] She was concentrating and reciting prayers at length: an Ave, a Pater Noster and then Guinean prayers in an African tongue. She invoked the god she herself specifically served. She was hunched up, concentrating. It was then that a cavernous distant voice could be heard, speaking in Creole: it was the god's voice. He announced himself, introduced himself, greeted us, and the mambo told him of our presence. She asked him if he perhaps had a message to communicate to us.

The loa who had arrived was Ogoun Feraille. We put questions to him in French, he replied in Creole but did not venture any really precise prophesies. He seemed rather preoccupied with our state of health and the appropriate treatments to remedy it, for Ogoun, besides his functions as a blacksmith, is also a doctor and, with only a little prompting from us, would have dictated a complete prescription to his servant the mambo, including, besides the ingestion of plants, prayers and the execution of some ceremonies.

Neither Dr Maximilien nor myself could accept that it was the god speaking and we were alert for any hoax. We had heard that once a rubber pipe had been found passing under the earth, under the wall, and linking the houmfor to the outside. The replies would have been given by an accomplice who, in effect, would be using a sort of acoustic telephone similar to the systems in European apartments fifty years ago. We had spoken about this possibility to the mambo, who had invited us to look around the surroundings of the houmfor; there was nothing there and, for my part, I even believe this explanation had been given by 'strong-minded' people, always quick to offer rational solutions.

Was it a question of ventriloquy? Little is known about this phenomenon, but it is highly probable that those capable of it believe it to be a unique ability, and from there it is a short step to thinking that the internal voice is that of a divinity. In Paris I have been present during spiritualist seances, possessions expressed by changes in the voice and transformations of the face. These phenomena were exactly like those manifested by the Haitian mambo: she entered into a second state, and was under such nervous strain that she partially lost consciousness. She had reached that very specific phase of dissociation in which conscious and unconscious mechanisms coexist and express themselves without the subject being able to perceive exactly the value of one or the other. It is not at all a question of a deliberate hoax but of a state where the operator is at the same time simulating and duped. I am reminded of that seven-year-old girl who, wanting to scare her younger sister to keep her quiet, would cry 'Hey! It's the wolf!', at first straight-faced but gaily, but after four or five alarms she would burst into tears because she had fallen into her own trap and was genuinely afraid of the wolf. All the arguments raised by modern rationalists about the simulation or sincerity of spiritualists or fortune-tellers prove the extent to which the rationalist, logical, scientific mind, clumsily manipulating its principle of identity, is incapable of grasping all the subtleties of the mechanism of simulation and truth. The role that one man plays to another only has value if the one playing believes in it, even if he understands the technique that allows him to perform.

The state of the mambo was exactly comparable to that of the artist at the moment of creation, the actor during his performance and all those who feel themselves driven by an unknown mechanism they call inspiration and which is felt as a voice, as a force speaking within them, pushing them on, penetrating and moving them without their knowledge. The god, in the end, told us nothing of great interest, he withdrew and the mambo came out of the seance exhausted, regaining consciousness with some difficulty.

Several months later, in Port-au-Prince, I had the chance of a long meeting with an old woman who was not a mambo, and did not serve voodoo, but who had the power of clairvoyance. She was sitting in an armchair, her bright eyes lost in the distance, and she made predictions to the woman accompanying me and who was asking her about some events that would take place shortly afterwards. I considered these predictions inexact, for I possess the rather unique ability of being able to upset clairvoyants to the point of completely putting them off. The superiority of this woman over professional extrasensories is comparable to that of genuinely inspired artists over those who force inspiration using technique or artifice, or even more to the spontaneous outburst over the methodically controlled direction of all religious systems, whatever they might be. I accept the surrealist protest against the religions that have stifled and systematized what, within man, has the power to surpass him, something done with the fully conscious aim of exploitation.

I have seen a manifest example of this exploitation in Cuba. We had been taken to the far side of Marianao (a suburb of Havana) to see a sorcerer who interrogated the gods using seashells which he threw on the ground as many times as was necessary to obtain the figures and make predictions according to the laws of geomancy. He was a negro of commanding presence and still young; his house, comfortable and prepossessing, could perhaps have been that of a country doctor. What is more, our man was skilful in establishing a diagnosis, prognosis and treatment. I must say that, just this once, he was pretty brilliant as far as I was concerned, not that he could pinpoint my profession or the nature of my trip, but he announced that, during the voyage I was to undertake, a yellow paper would be missing and that this would put me in mortal danger. Moreover he appeared highly pessimistic in the explanations he gave to the person accompanying me, who was acting as my interpreter: he indicated to her that I was on the worst possible terms with Guemaya, the sea goddess, who was annoyed with me and demanded a sacrifice whose form he wrote on a sheet of paper. It was a question of sacrificing a white chicken and cockerel, a black chicken and cockerel, and of bringing several cakes, candles, bottles of rum and other ingredients whose alimentary value seemed less direct. As a favour he agreed, in exchange for twenty dollars or so, to celebrate this sacrifice which, if it was accepted by the goddess, could help me out of my present difficulties. This made me only too aware of the avid practitioner's know-how and how he could use his power to his own advantage, and I had no wish to pursue the idea.

My friend Lydia Cabrera, impressed by these worrying predictions, offered to take me to the house of a negress friend nearly a hundred years old, whose mother had come from Africa. We went that very evening to the district near Lydia's family property which, with poverty constantly swept away by the sun, is never dirty or sad. Our dear little old lady was not sad either, but she was solemn. I have never seen such nobility, such beauty as in that face. She received me from the hands of her Lydia, whom she had brought up, and welcomed me with nods of the head, considering my case with great interest. 'I must undertake a head-wash,' she said, making the appropriate actions, the way in which she could draw out of my head the hostile forces that had taken hold of it. She asked me to take my shoes off and put my bare feet in recept-acles filled with water. With my forearms bared, my head was annointed with an unction of spermaceti and castor oil. The old woman recited prayers, traced signs on me and bade me not to expose myself to the sun without a hat for three days, when the effects would be complete. Having ascertained the exact time of my departure from Havana, she would go to the seashore at that exact moment to offer flowers to Guemaya, and appease her wrath. I am obliged to relate that, upon entry to Mexico, I was asked for a paper which was in my file but which the immigration employee claimed not to have received, thus hoping for a substantial reward in the event of 'finding it again'. It took three weeks of administrative problems, and a large tip, to recover this document, *which was indeed yellow*. I finally left for Mexico City and the plane carrying me came within a whisker of crashing into the steep slopes of Orizaba, some thirteen hundred feet high. The goddess's anger had been narrowly averted, but just enough for the plane not to hit the peak, which had been masked until then by thick cloud.

What the faithful require is effectively a treatment whose therapy is almost always vegetal: the application of plants, bathing and infusions, to which are added ceremonies of reparation. The harm stems either

from the voluntary action of an individual whose hatred pursues you
and who has practised or had practised a spell, or from the anger of a
dead person to whom the duties necessary for his rest have not been
rendered and who thus finds himself in the state of a wandering, fam-
ished soul, or else because of the displeasure of a god whose rituals
have not been celebrated at the appropriate time or with due splendour.
Thus the reparation involves ceremonies that the houngan or mambo
will celebrate and which cost, as always, considerable sums: you will
have to sell or mortgage your few plots of land or your house to put an
end to the supernatural wrath and prevent the succession of catastrophes from carrying everything away. The cost of therapy, alas, often
manages to ruin the patient.

### Notes

1. The gods, speaking from the stoneware pot in which they are enclosed.
2. Voodoo priestess.
3. Voodoo priest.
4. The hut in which the voodoo altar is placed.
5. A sort of handled calabash covered in a network of snake vertebrae and
pearls, and which serves as an instrument during ceremonies.
6. A hand bell of bronze or cast iron.

· [first published in *Messages de l'étranger* (1981) Paris: Plasma]

MICHEL LEIRIS

# The Sacrifice of a Bull at the Home of the Houngan Jo Pierre-Gilles

THE FOLLOWING LINES are taken, almost without revision, from the notebooks I kept during a stay in Haiti, from 24 September to 26 October 1948, as a representative of the Ministry of Foreign Affairs (Department of Cultural Relations) as part of the activity of the French Institute directed by Simon B. Lando in Port-au-Prince.

I wish to take this opportunity to thank my friends Alfred Métraux, of the Department of Social Services at UNESCO, and Mrs Odette Mennesson-Rigaud for having given me an introduction to the practitioners of Haitian voodoo. Thanks to them, during too brief a period for more detailed study, I was able to make at least a few observations which offered me some interesting comparative elements in the study of African cults based on possession, cults that clearly reappear on several Caribbean islands and in many parts of the New World, where they represent a part of the cultural heritage brought by black slaves at the time of the slave trade.

To compile the commentary appended to these notes (which are not the result of any kind of systematic enquiry) I used the following two works, by Haitian authors, and in this way I could check and partially complete my own observations:

MARCELIN (Milo), *Mythologie vodou (rite aranda)*, two volumes, Port-au-Prince, Editions Haïtiennes, 1949 and Pétionville, Editions Canapé-Vert, 1950.

MAXIMILIEN (Louis), *Le Vodou haïtien (rite radas-canzo)*, Port-au-Prince, Imprimérie de l'Etat, 1945.

\*

Port-au-Prince, 19 October 1948

... Tomorrow Mrs Rigaud should take me to a place near the Mission Cross, to the home of a *houngan* who is giving a '*manger*' as part of a '*service*' which has already lasted a number of days and has included the launching at sea of a miniature boat consecrated to *Agwé*. This is a *houngan*, she says, who has become somewhat commercialized (as most of them are) but whose ceremony will certainly be of interest, because of his ostentation and the large number of other *houngans* and *mambos* who will take part along with their followers.[1]

20 October

... Around 9.30 Mrs Rigaud arrived, having come to collect me by car, a little late because of the rain (which threatened to delay the expected ceremony although it would not be postponed). She explained that the *houngan* we were to visit (whose *houmfor* adjoins that of Mrs Ildevert) is called Jo Pierre-Gilles. He possesses, besides the family *loa*, 'bought' *loa* and is considered to 'practise with both hands', not to say a little bit of a *loup-garou*.[2] Today's '*manger*' is for *Ogoun Badagri*, whose symbolic colour is red.[3]

We stopped in town to buy a bottle of rum for our hosts, then drove towards the Mission Cross and, passing it, took a left turn to come to a stop at the turn-off from the little road which runs between Mrs Ildevert's *houmfor* and her land. A man in his thirties, with uneven teeth and dressed in rags, was there waiting for us.

... The character in question took us, by an extremely muddy track which skirted the left-hand side of the land containing the Ildevert *houmfor* and crossed a series of fields or gardens, as far as Jo Pierre-Gilles's house, where as yet only a few people had gathered.

Mrs Rigaud introduced me to Pierre-Gilles, who was dressed in yellowish drill trousers with turn-ups and a shirt of the same colour, topped with an immense multicoloured peasant straw hat. He was a man of medium height, gaunt, with a little moustache, cold, shrewd eyes and prominent cheekbones. With fairly unwrinkled skin, he had that slightly mongoloid look one sees in a lot of people here. I am almost certain I recognized him as the *houngan* who presided at the inauguration at Clarzinie, along with the *houngan* François, who seemed to have an important role in the proceedings ...[4]

Around the place to which Mrs Rigaud had brought me I note, from memory, several *bagui*[5] containing various altars or *pè*, amongst which, in the same *caye*, separated only by a curtain, were on the left an altar consecrated to *Ayda* and *Damballah Wedo* (painted on the walls,

which met at a right angle, were a snake and a rainbow on each wall –
one for *Ayda*, the other for *Damballah* – and, between the two snakes,
an egg with its yolk clearly marked which was painted right in the
angle of the walls);[6] on the right, an altar consecrated to *Ogoun
Badagri*, its walls decorated on a red background; another *caye*, consecrated to *Agwé*: the left-hand side of the altar was covered in
seashells (like *lambi* shells, only smaller), and above it a trumpet was
placed against the left-hand wall against which two blue-painted '*zavi-
rons*' were leant; immediately to the right of the shell mosaic was a big
*lambi* conch painted blue;[7] a third *caye*, consecrated to *Zaka*: hung
from the left-hand wall were several peasant straw hats and wickerwork
satchels with tassels; on the end wall a white satchel of the same type
was drawn;[8] on the right-hand part of the altar, a vat had been hol-
lowed out: a middle-aged woman – no doubt a *hounsi* – standing there
with a decorated calabash, drew water from this vat so that first Mrs
Rigaud and then I could make the customary libations in front of the
altar: a little water towards the left, a little towards the right, a little
towards the centre; both of us did this twice, first in front of the left-
hand part of the altar, then in front of the right.[9]

In each of these *cayes*, a circular ditch had been dug in front of the
altar; several of these ditches contained the remains of food (notably
bones) and leaves.[10]

We also visited a bedroom devoted to *Erzulie*, with its dressing
table.[11]

I noticed, among the many reproductions decorating the different
*cayes*, a not in the least bit religious one showing two naked women by
a river, two copies of which were on one of the *cayes*.[12]

In Jo Pierre-Gilles's house there were two 'peristyles': one *rada*, the
one in which today's ceremony was taking place and whose back wall,
between two paintings representing Haiti's coat of arms with the device
'Union is Strength', bore, with a compass rose, the following inscription: 'Society of the Pole Star which dirrects (sic) the four cardinal
points. It is Agouet-Minfort Ayannan-Minfort Long Live Saint James
of the Holy Family.' On the right-hand part of the wall was a photo of
President Estimé; the whole ceiling was decorated with little paper
flags, some red, others blue. The other was *pétro* . . .[13]

As we looked around the place, Mrs Rigaud also showed me several
'resting places' surrounded by a stonework border and, in a sort of isolated niche, a cross of black wood recalling those normally consecrated
to Baron.[14]

Mrs Rigaud also took me to a hut where a large, very black woman,

still quite young and with an intelligent face, was living for a few days:
it was a certain Mrs . . ., a landowner of the Thomazeau region, who
had come to help with the series of '*services*' to thank Pierre-Gilles for
some trouble he had taken on her behalf.[15]

We returned to the *rada* peristyle. Against the wall by the entrance,
tables had been laden with the customary food (bread and biscuits) and
drinks.[16]

A man (who Mrs Rigaud told me was a *houngan* and who was later
to take charge of reciting the prayer, slaughtering the goat and running
the halter around the bull's neck) was busy tracing out a *vèvè* with
white flour. This *vèvè* consisted essentially of a huge equilateral triangle, the peak of which touched the 'middle post', the base facing the
entrance. In the centre of this triangle was a depiction of a bull, whose
body was decorated with vertical stripes alternating with the zigzag
motif so widespread in Africa; above the bull was the masonic symbol
of the superimposed compass and set-square; below it, a sabre painted
in a horizontal position.[17] Around the middle post was tied a yellowing
palm tree.

After 11 o'clock, with the *vèvè* complete, a man came to the middle
of the peristyle and rang a bell, seemingly a signal. Then another made
several circuits around the outside of the peristyle, banging in time on
an *ogan*.[18] Obeying the signal, the *hounsi* and guests began to gather.

Among the guests are several *houngans* and *mambos*, including Mrs
Ildevert, placid and majestic as ever, in a black dress with little white
flowers and a straw hat; Mrs Elie (formerly Mrs Henri), a famous
*mambo* who had been there from the beginning and seemed to occupy
an important position; and a colossus with a pot belly, very black and
with a full grey moustache. The *hounsi* were all dressed in short robes
of a very clean white fabric.[19] All of them, and many of the female
guests, had been given big knots of red material (the colour of Ogoun)
which they would attach to their chests. Some wore a red scarf across
their shoulders. Sitting beside the entrance I noticed a bourgeois couple, perhaps in their early thirties, he in a very formal khaki canvas suit,
she in a city dress with a red knot in her hair.

There were no drummers, since it was a weekday; the music would
consist of a chest with a circular hole in its front, next to which were
large metal blades like those of African *sanzas*. As one man set these
blades vibrating, another standing to his right would hit the left side of
the chest, as the spectators saw it, with two short drumsticks; a third
man carried an *ogan*.[20]

Most of the *hounsi* were standing behind the orchestra. In front of the orchestra was as usual the *hounguénikon*, a tall thin woman of fairly advanced years, and very dynamic.[21] There were perhaps fifty or so *hounsi*.

A first series of chants began, starting with 'Family, assemble!'[22]

Outside, by the right-hand entrance,[23] a fine flame coloured he-goat was tied; he would be draped with a crimson saddlecloth, and a pink scarf would be tied around his horns. Several (four?) large cockerels with motley plumage, but predominantly flame-coloured, were held by the *hounsi*.[24]

The '*la place*' (a young negro in a white shirt and trousers who was also a *houngan*, Mrs Rigaud said) and the two flag-bearers entered.[25] The customary greetings took place, kissing the ground and twists between two or three persons,[26] kissing the *la place*'s sabre, the staff, the flags and the middle post. Kisses were generally made three times.

The music fell silent and the prayers began: first invocations of Catholic saints, then of *loa*.

The music and chants began again. Various libations and offerings were made at several parts of the *vèvè*: water, Barbancourt Three Star rum, syrup, coffee, cereals and flour.

All present were then '*ventaillés*' with the cockerels, for different lengths of time: escorted by the two flag-bearers, the *la place* officiated the *ventaillage* himself, a cockerel in each hand, with both arms in a simultaneous gesture passing the cockerels along the bodies of the spectators, from top to bottom then from bottom to top.[27]

After the *ventaillage*, the cockerels were returned to Mrs Elie who let them all scratch about for offerings.

The adorned goat had been brought into the peristyle; he was tied to a post, on the left-hand side and in front of the orchestra. Rum was sprayed orally.[28] Tension mounted: the orchestra and chanting became more violent. Several *hounsi* fell into a trance, tottering, falling over into the arms of their companions and crying out. They all invaded the peristyle, dancing, leaping, singing, raising their arms, shouting and gesticulating.

. . . One of the *houngans* poured some rum near the middle post – by the orchestra – and set light to it. The *hounsi*, dancing, trampled the flames with their bare feet; one of the older ones walked across it, with exaggerated slowness . . .[29]

Looking towards the cockerels, I realized they had been put to death and now lay on the *vèvè*. Mrs Rigaud told me that they had been killed in the usual way: by breaking their limbs, pulling out their tongues and wringing their necks.[30]

Now it was the goat's turn. He was untied and brought next to the *vèvè*, sprinkled with rum and syrup, and covered in cornflour and grain ('*dior* food').[31] In order, each of the notables present stroked his head (in most cases from top to bottom then from left to right) with a branch and gave him a few leaves to chew.[32] All the *hounsi*, in a semi-circle, kissed the ground in front of the goat. (On the subject of the ground: during the prayer, when an important *loa* was named, each one touched the ground three times with the fingertips of the right hand . . .)

The *la place* and one of the *houngan* seized the goat, one of them holding the hind legs, the other the horns. They ran across the peristyle like this, holding the goat aloft. Twice they ran with it into the *caye* of *Ogoun Badagri* and came out again straight away. The goat, before being taken around like this, had been stripped of its attire. Armed with a machete, the sacrificer sliced off its genitals. The running parade continued a little longer and then, still held off the ground, the goat was brought next to the *vèvè* and the sacrificer cut its throat transversally with his machete. The goat struggled on the ground, held down, while its blood poured out.[33] Three men, leaning over, were busy doing something around it. The sacrificer, dipping his right hand in the blood, approached the three men in turn from behind and, passing his blood-soaked hand between their legs, touched them under their genitals. Everyone laughed at this joke, which Mrs Rigaud said was a 'modern' development which would not have been allowed in the past.

(Note that, during the veneration of the goat, an old *hounsi* or *mambo*, stroking it with the branch, had taken it by the horns and for an instant placed its forehead against her own.)

The bull (which until now had been penned up a few yards from the peristyle, to the right and a little behind it) was brought in: a reddish-brown bull, with its back covered in a pink or crimson saddlecloth and a scarf of similar colours around its horns.

It was tied to the middle post and a very old woman – quite small, very shrivelled and thin, with an ill-natured face, the nose and chin almost meeting (she was Jo Pierre-Gilles's mother, Mrs Rigaud told me) – came to dance in the centre of the peristyle. She soon began to stagger, 'drunkenly',[34] and emitted a few brief cries: she was possessed by *Ogoun Badagri*. She proceeded to the libations of rum and syrup and the pouring of solids over the bull's backbone. She poured Barbancourt Three Star on its head then, forcibly lifting its head, she put the mouth of the bottle into its neck and forced it to drink: the rum dripped down the bull's dewlap. Then the old woman, bottle in hand, leaned her back against the bull's right flank and fell backwards into him in a triumphant pose. She stayed like that for a moment, and then returned to the space between the middle post and the position of the *hounsi* and drank herself, a fairly long draught, straight from the bottle.

All the *hounsi* kissed the ground, in a semicircle around the bull.[35]

. . . During the consecration of the bull, the *la place* and the flag-bearers ran from the peristyle to the *barrière* and returned at a run from the *barrière* to the peristyle.[36]

Throughout the second part of the ceremony . . . – at least, from the consecration of the bull onwards – it was Pierre-Gilles himself (without an *asson* or hand bell) who played the role of *hounguénikon* . . .

The bull was stripped of its finery. He was untied and a halter was passed around his neck. The low wall on the right (a wooden wall, like that by the entrance and like the one on the left) had two exits: one near the entrance, the other near the orchestra. It was through the latter that the bull, like the goat, had been brought in, and through the former – first cleared of the people standing there – that he was rapidly led away, pulled by the halter and followed by a procession comprising the *la place*, the two flag-bearing *hounsi*, all the other *hounsi* and some of the spectators, myself included.

The bull, forced to run, was escorted by several men. The procession dispersed in the process into a disordered run with much gesticulation, laughter and shouting. After a few moments of total disorder, the bull could be seen, still pulled and running, being led away from the houses; all the members of the cortege, led by the *la place* and the flag-bearers, ran behind him. In this way we crossed a cane field . . . then we arrived at a piece of uncultivated land, with a large tree on one side and a building on the other. A man – having looked for the right spot – then pushed the blade of his machete almost vertically into the bull's neck, behind the horns, a little behind the place where matadors strike the thrust called the *descabello*. The bull fell, not yet conquered. Then the bottom of its throat was slit deeply with a knife. Its blood ran out onto the ground.[37]

During the dismemberment – which did not seem to be accompanied by any ritual (although one of the *houngan*, interrogated by Mrs Rigaud at my request, pronounced this to be a 'dangerous' moment and said that it was important for those dismembering to have drunk rum) – someone brought banana leaves to wipe up the blood.[38] In the same way, inside the peristyle, the goat's blood was covered with earth and then, with a broom, a woman was to sweep up this earth together with the remainder of the offerings, and take them outside. The cockerels and goat had already been taken away.

Here and there, kitchen fires were burning.[39]

I stayed for a moment at the spot where the bull had been sacrificed. The *hounsi* gradually dispersed. A few people, near the building, were pretending to squabble and, laughing, even pretended to be fighting. Two or three men joked with them. The tall thin *hounguénikon* was also there, full of cheer. For a moment I found myself next to the young bourgeois couple, who looked very happy.[40]

I went back to the peristyle, where Mrs Rigaud had already returned. An argument was taking place: Pierre-Gilles's mother, with a sour-looking face, was striding up and down the peristyle cursing and uttering recriminations, all the while chewing on a cigar that, already lit, she had been given. On our departure, Mrs Rigaud explained that *Ogoun Badagri* was complaining of not having received any '*service*' this year. The sacrifice that had just been made was actually not addressed, or only partly addressed, to him, since it was above all in *Ossangne Bakoulé*'s honour, who was a 'bought' *loa*.[41] Mrs Rigaud also told me that Pierre-Gilles wept because of *Ogoun Badagri*'s remonstrances. I noted – without telling Mrs Rigaud – that Pierre-Gilles's mother appeared to be drunk.

We left around 2.30pm, after bidding Pierre-Gilles farewell . . .

### Notes

1. *Houngan* and *mambo*: names given to the priests and priestesses of the voodoo cult. Their assistants are called *hounsi*. *Agwé*: god of the sea. Every year the *houngans* are obliged to make a series of sacrifices or '*mangers*' for the various *loas* or spirits they 'serve' (that is those by which they are regularly possessed, to whom they dedicate a cult and to whom they are in consequence permanently linked). According to Mrs Rigaud, the 'services' celebrated the previous year by Jo Pierre-Gilles were more sumptuous and brought together more people than those that I am nevertheless very grateful she made it possible for me to attend.

2. *Houmfor*: voodoo sanctuary, with its outbuildings (constructions and, on occasion, farmland) constituting the habitation of a priest, a priestess, or a household of priest and priestess. Mrs Ildevert was, at the time of my stay in Haiti, one of the richest *mambos* in the Port-au-Prince region. *Family loa*: an inherited spirit. '*Bought' loa*: a spirit that has been acquired so as to exercise magic. '*To practise with both hands*': to practise white magic (right hand, beneficient side) and black magic (left hand, malignant side). Jo Pierre-Gilles exercised the profession of healer like most *houngans* and had, on the other hand, the sinister reputation of being a sorcerer or *loup-garou*.

3. *Ogoun Badagri*: the war god. He is portrayed in military uniform, with a sabre in his hand; he likes rum and smokes large cigars.

4. Alfred Métraux (who was to attend with me on 23 October another sacrifice of a bull as part of the same series of *'mangers'*, this time given in honour of *Simbi*, the god of wells) has described Jo Pierre-Gilles thus: 'a cold, intelligent face, slightly cunning, very young in appearance'. When on 25 September I attended the inauguration of the *houmfor* which had just been opened at Port-au-Prince, in the Salines district, the aforementioned Clerzinie, I myself noted the remarkable elegance of this man who was nevertheless simply dressed and already middle-aged: 'Another *houngan* took the stage, a highly elegant character, also dressed in shirt-sleeves and wearing a straw hat with the brim turned up.' The large straw hat with coloured ribbons (or in multicoloured straw, like that of Jo Pierre-Gilles on 20 October, a very different hat from his city hat on 25 September) is an adornment worn by the 'inhabitants' of the mornes, and is amongst the attributes of the peasant god *Zaka*. Note that, according to Mrs Rigaud, Jo Pierre-Gilles 'covered' (in other words concealed) under the name of *Zaka* the 'evil *loa*' he used. 'Evil *loa*', that is the *loa* which – like those of the *Zaka* category – can be used more easily than others for evil doing but which cannot truly be regarded as bad in themselves (since a *loa*, in itself, is neither good nor evil).

5. *Bagui*: the part of the *houmfor* that constitutes the holy of holies and generally consists of a room situated behind the site called the 'peristyle', a sort of huge veranda; in each *houmfor* there are several *bagui*, which are also called *caye mystères* 'house of mysteries' (in other words of spirits).

6. *Damballah Wedo*: the god of fertility, whose emblems are the grass snake and the egg. His wife is *Ayda Wedo*, goddess of the rainbow.

7. The *lambi* conch is used as a trumpet in Haiti as in the French Caribbean; found in the sea, it symbolizes *Agwé*. A few days before the ceremony described here – on 5 October – navigating in a sailboat along the coast of the Ile de la Tortue, my companions and I had witnessed one of our sailors blowing into a *lambi* conch, in order to raise the wind and deliver us from the dead calm. Along with oars, the trumpet is one of the attributes of *Agwé*, whose emblems also include the boat and the fish and whose colour is blue.

8. Wickerwork satchels are part of the peasant's paraphernalia and for this reason are included among *Zaka*'s attributes. At Jo Pierre-Gilles's, the *caye* of Zaka is also consecrated to *Baron Samedi*, the god of graveyards. Alfred Métraux also notes that on 23 October (the day after a sacrifice to the *Guédé*, divinities of death which include *Baron*), 'the altar was painted black and bore a black cross with silvered trimmings (attributes of *Baron*). One side of the altar was taken up by a depression, a sort of basin. The cross was topped with peasant straw hats. A *vèvè* (sacred drawing) had been traced before the altar.' In this *caye* two flags were displayed whose staffs had at their tip a representation of a bird in place of the usual ornament in the form of a sideways *S*. The altar table was decorated, on the left, with *vèvè*-style drawings which might have represented birds with outstretched wings, on the right, on either side of the depression and a little in front of it, with two sorts of marker stones of irregular form – the one on the left larger – painted in fairly mottled colours but predominantly ochre; behind the left-hand stone,

standing up at the back, was a pebble (or weighty axe of polished stone?) whose base was embedded in the top of the altar. One of the *Zaka*, *Azaka Médé*, is called 'Azaka-Thunder', which may perhaps account for the presence of a polished axe recalling the 'lightning stones' so often used in African rituals for provoking rain.

9. Before every libation the pitcher is 'oriented', in other words it is presented to each of the assumed compass points in turn. The sacrificial victims (cockerels and goat) are 'oriented' in the same way.

10. The ditches to receive food would be filled in afterwards: the *'manger'* in the god's honour will thus have been buried.

11. *Erzulie*: goddess of love, who has *Damballah Wede*, *Agwé* and *Ogoun Badagri*, amongst others, as lovers. Her attributes are jewels and toiletries and her emblem is a heart.

12. The walls of the *caye mystère* are normally decorated with Catholic chromo-lithographic reproductions representing the saints with which the voodoo divinities are syncretically identified. I do not know which *loa* the picture with the two naked women was related to.

13. The *loa* are served following two principal rites: *rada* (the closest, it would seem, to African traditions, as its name, derived from 'Allada', a Dahomey town of great religious significance, would suggest), and *pétro* (probably more recent and tending towards black magic). With Jo Pierre-Gilles, the *caye* dedicated to *Damballah Wedo*, *Ayda Wedo* and *Ogoun Badagri* (as well as to *Ossangne*, another god in the *Ogoun* line, and to *Agassou*, divinity of fresh water) adjoined the peri-style reserved for the *rada* ceremonies, and the same went for the *Agwé caye*, whilst that of *Zaka* and *Baron*, as with another dedicated to the *Simbi* (in which numer-ous magic 'packages' are lined up) adjoined the *pétro* peristyle. The *houmfor* staff constitutes a 'society' whose inscription reproduces the name, along with the 'valiant name' or battle-name, of the *houngan* (in this case 'Agouet-Minfort Ayannan-Minfort'?). The 'Saint James' cited here is probably Saint James the Great, identified with the Lord of the *Ogoun*. The arms of the Haitian Republic and the portrait of the President are part of the habitual decoration of a *houmfor*.

14. Each spirit has its 'resting place', a tree or a plant considered to be its preferred dwelling place.

15. Mrs . . . offered us an excellent cup of coffee, prepared by a servant who accompanied her.

16. These tables constituted a sort of paid buffet where the faithful could eat during the ceremony.

17. Each *loa* has a *vèvè*, an emblematic drawing specific to it which is traced on the ground for each ceremony in which it is invoked. The *vèvè* described here is made up, apart from *Ogoun Badagri's* sword and the masonic symbols (common in this type of representation), of an effigy of the sacrificial victim, which constitutes the principal motif. The *houngan* drawing this *vèvè* having forgotten to draw the bull's genitalia, Mrs Rigaud jokingly observed to a *mambo* who was present (Mrs Elie, alias Mrs Henri): 'Are you going to sacrifice an ox?', upon which everybody laughed and the artist hurriedly rectified his omission. The 'middle post' is the cen-tral pillar, usually highly decorated, which holds up the roof of the peristyle. Its lower end is surrounded by a little circular stonework block, which forms a

pedestal and on which, during ceremonies, is placed – along with a lighted candle – the jug of water, the dish of flour and other ritual accessories.

18. The *ogan*, a little iron bell held in the left hand and hit with a short drumstick held in the right hand, is part of the orchestra of *rada* ceremonies, otherwise made up of three drums.

19. These short robes which the *hounsi* in today's *houmfor* wore were considered ugly by Mrs Rigaud, who preferred the long robes of previous fashion, still seen worn in certain country *houmfors*, which have remained more traditional. With the *houngan* André Baskia (who, at Port-au-Prince, in the Station Sans-Fil district, oversaw a relatively luxurious *houmfor* and who was known for his idiosyncratic interpretation of ritual) I myself saw three *hounsi* flag-bearers dressed in long robes made from apparently old material in a mixture of colours.

20. Voodoo meetings are only officially permitted in Port-au-Prince on Saturday and Sunday nights; this is why the drums (which are too loud) are replaced during the week by the instrument called a *manounba*. The musicians stood with their backs to the *caye mystère*, at the far side of the peristyle opposite the entrance.

21. *Hounguénikon*: leader of the chorus and coryphaeus, a man or a woman, who comes just below the *houngan* and the *mambo* in the hierarchy. He is equipped with an *asson* or gourd rattle.

22. According to Louis Maximilien (pp. 94–5, this chant:

> *La famille, semblez, agoe*
> *Eya! guinin va aider nous*

invites the community of initiates to assemble. '*Guinin*': Guinea, an expression designating Africa and the ancestral gods.

23. The peristyle, in this instance, was a rectangle adjoining the 'houses of mysteries' along one of its shorter sides, the principal entrance being opposite, that is in the middle of the other short side; it was covered by a roof supported by a certain number of pillars, including the 'middle post' and, on the two longer sides and that of the principal entrance, by thinner pieces of wood rising from an enclosing wall, about three feet high and including two exits to the right of the entrance. Here it is the closer of these two exits to the *caye mystère*.

24. The clothing (or plumage) and the ornaments of the victim are red, as this is the symbolic colour of the *Ogoun*.

25. The *la place* or master of ceremonies is escorted by two women, who bear emblematic flags of the spirits to be honoured.

26. The twisting greetings – an action expressed by the verb 'to turn' – are carried out by all the initiates and distinguished guests in order (invited by the *la place*, the *houngan*, the *mambo* or any initiate in an appropriate state of possession to greet them in this way). They are performed in the following way: the superior party who has himself greeted, holding with his raised right hand the left hand of the inferior person standing in front of him, slowly makes him execute a twirl (ending with a slight bending of the knees by the two partners facing each other), then a twirl in the opposite direction (concluded in the same way or by the prostration of the inferior, who kisses the ground near the superior's feet; the latter

makes him rise, his right hand still holding the other's left). One can also 'turn' two people at once, holding with the right hand the left of one and with the left the other's right. Everything is done in time, to the rhythm dictated by the orchestra.

27. An analogous action consists of passing the cockerels over the head and shoulders of the patient, each arm moved in turn. This is called 'passing', while one says '*ventailler*' when the two arms are deployed simultaneously in the manner described. According to Louis Maximilien (p. 107), this action is 'a symbolic means of establishing contact between humans and the animals to be sacrificed'. To '*ventailler*' or 'pass' – as for the dance that precedes either of these actions – the two cockerels were held by both feet in a single hand, heads down and with the wings flapping in the natural way.

28. These sprayings, called *foula*, are made in the following way: with his mouth previously filled with '*clairin*' (white rum) seasoned with pimento, the *houngan* (or other initiate of a certain rank) acts as a sort of vaporizer, blowing out of his inflated cheeks a spray of fine droplets, an action repeated several times and in all directions. When he blows in this way to his right, he throws his right forearm over his left shoulder in an arrogant gesture, then does the same with his left forearm thrown over the right when he blows to the left. A strong smell of alcohol and pimento thus pervades the peristyle.

29. Like all the *Ogoun* (and especially *Ogoun Feraille*, patron of blacksmiths), *Ogoun Badagri* is linked with fire.

30. Mrs Rigaud was not wrong to laugh at me – a professional ethnographer – when I let this important moment of the ceremony pass without noticing it; I was, it is true, entirely preoccupied with watching the behaviour of the *hounsi*.

On 23 October, the sacrifice of the bull was also preceded by that of several cockerels and by that of a goat; Alfred Métraux notes that the blood of the cockerels was collected in a dish full of syrup and that Mrs Henri, after stirring this beverage, drank a few spoonfuls of it.

31. The essential act of the consecration of the victims consists of '*croiciner*' (in other words, cross-signing). They are sprinkled, crosswise, with a few drops of various liquids (water, rum, syrup, coffee, etc), then a few pinches of sacred food called, in the *rada* rite, '*manger dior*'.

32. The branch in question was a branch of mombin, a plant whose leaves, according to Louis Maximilien (p. 108), might symbolize Africa.

33. On 23 October (according to Alfred Métraux's notes) the goat's blood was collected in a wooden trough, swiftly removed. We did not know what it was used for.

34. It is said that someone is 'drunk' when they undergo the beginnings of possession, which might remain at this stage or turn into a complete trance. Generally, the 'drunk' person jumps several times on one heel, as if losing balance and trying to regain it; often, after having tottered like this, they put their hand in front of their eyes for a moment, like someone trying to revive themselves, and go to sit down. The forms of complete trance – varying according to the spirits by which the subject is supposed to be possessed – are too diverse to be described here.

35. The victim, which had been consecrated and whose god (incarnated by Pierre-Gilles's mother) had just had it delivered to him, is venerated just as the god itself is.

36. The *barrière* – or door of the exterior enclosure which when passed leads to the *houmfor* properly speaking and to its peristyle – is placed under the guardianship of the god *Atibon Legba*, also called *Papa Legba*, master of crossroads and roads. According to Milo Marcellin (I, p. 15), 'it is he who allows men to enter into relations with other gods. In this way, before commencing any ceremony, any ritual dance, one must ask his permission. . . .'

37. On leaving the peristyle, the bull was first led rapidly towards the barrière, then those taking him made an about-turn and, at a run, led it to the place of sacrifice, followed by the initiates and assistants forming a procession, after a few moments of confusion. The killing took place immediately afterwards.

According to the notes taken by Alfred Métraux during the sacrifice on 23 October (which was carried out following a similar ritual) the sacrificer made a sign of the cross before dealing the blow. In the bullfight, the *descabello* is a *coup de grâce* carried out by the matador on a bull that has been struck a fatal blow by a surprise attack but which is still on its feet: it consists of thrusting the point of a special sword between the first two cervical vertebrae, which overwhelms the beast by severing its medulla oblongata. For the bull on 23 October, the blow was struck with a dagger and at the point where, in bullfights, the *coup de grâce* is normally given; thus it had an almost overwhelming effect, which was not the case for the bull on 20 October. On 23 as well as 20 October, the victim's throat was cut open after the first blow was struck. Note that neither Jo Pierre-Gilles nor his mother, nor any of the principal people of note, took part in the killing.

38. The *houngan* questioned by Mrs Rigaud was someone called Isena, a man in the prime of life who, it seemed, was fairly expert in his profession. Like the sacrifice, the dismemberment is considered dangerous because it is at the moment the blood flows out that the contact with sacred forces is most direct. This is why those officiating had to be sure to protect themselves fully. It is probably for similar reasons of safety that the absorption of rum is deemed advisable, in principle, by the *houngan* Isena.

39. The bull's flesh would be eaten by the participants, something which serves the function of a communion.

40. During this sacrifice (as well as during that of 23 October) I was surprised to see that, as soon as the bull had been put to death, a complete relaxation of the atmosphere succeeded, without transition, that of the agitation that had been increasing ceaselessly since the start of the ceremony. While in the other sacrifices (in the Caribbean and elsewhere, notably in Abyssinia) that I have been able to attend, the putting to death was just a culminating point preceded (according to the outline suggested by the late lamented Marcel Mauss) by a long period of progressive sacralization and followed by a no less important period of desacralization, everything happened on those two days as if the rites of desacralization had been reduced to a minimum, as if they were practically non-existent, at least as far as the participants I was able to observe were concerned. The reason for this is perhaps that these two ceremonies, events contributing to a series of sacrifices arranged over a considerable number of days, in all only represented the fragments of a vast ritual ensemble made up of the totality of the *services* celebrated consecutively by Jo Pierre-Gilles in that period of the year.

41. *Ossangne Bakoulé* belongs to the series of *Ogoun* and a victim of a colour appropriate for *Ogoun Badagri* can thus be suitable. Jo Pierre-Gilles's mother (or rather *Ogoun Badagri* himself, speaking through her) considered that by means of this possibility of the double destination of the victim, the family *loa*, the *loa* by which she was possessed, had been wronged to the benefit of the *loa* of the same series who Pierre-Gilles had acquired to carry out his trade and who was personal to him. This is a frequent type of dispute (as I was able to witness in Abyssinia) in cults where multiple spirits to whom one sacrifices are represented by people whom they are meant to possess.

[published in *Haïti, Poètes Noirs* (1951) as *Présence Africaine* 12]

# Biographical Notes

**Jacques Steven Alexis** (pseudonym Jacques la Colère) (Gonaïves, Haiti, 1922 – Port-au-Prince, 1961) After training as a doctor, his involvement in the 1946 revolution led to political commitment. He founded the oppositional, pro-communist PEP (Parti de l'Entente Populaire), and was a brilliant novelist whose works are among the most important to have been written in Haiti, though regrettably they have never been translated into English. He was murdered by Duvalier after leading an abortive invasion in 1961. Novels and stories: *Compère Général Soleil* (1955); *Les Arbres musiciens* (1957); *L'Espace d'un cillement* (1959); *Romancero aux étoiles* (1960).

**André Breton** (Tinchebray, 1896 – Paris, 1966) Pivot of the French Surrealist Group and a magnetic personality for surrealism worldwide, Breton was forced into exile in the Americas upon the capitulation of France to the Nazis. On route to New York in 1941, he spent three weeks in Martinique, a stay that had a profound effect upon him. In 1945 he was invited to Haiti to give the series of lectures described in this book. His complete works are being published in four volumes in the Pléiade series by Gallimard.

**Aimé Césaire** (Basse-Terre, Martinique, 1913) Author of *Cahier d'un retour au pays natal* (1939), conceived and first published in Europe and elaborated on in Martinique, which would become one of the most vital poetic documents of our time and which helped to initiate negritude and focus the anti-colonial struggle in the then French colonies. Founder with Suzanne Césaire and René Ménil of *Tropiques* in 1941. A magisterial poet of the contemporary age, his collected poetry has been published in English. As a politician, he was elected mayor of Fort de France and deputy in the French

Parliament in 1945. Volumes of poetry: *Les Armes miraculeuses* (1946); *Cahier d'un retour au pays natal* (1947); *Soleil cou coupé* (1948); *Corps perdu* (1949); *Ferrements* (1960); *Noria* (1976); Plays: *Toussaint Louverture* (1962); *La Tragédie du roi Christophe* (1964); *Une Saison au Congo* (1966); *Une Tempête* (1968).

**Suzanne Césaire** (Trois-Islets, Martinique, 1913 – ?) Founder of and theoretical writer for *Tropiques*, Suzanne Césaire seems to have assumed no public role after the Second World War.

**Hendrik Cramer** (Utrecht, 1884 – Neuengamme, 1944) An adventurer and amateur anthropologist, Cramer was a member of *Le Grand Jeu*. He visited Haiti on several occasions between 1923 and 1925 and wrote a short collection of stories based upon Haitian folklore. As a member of the Dutch resistance during the Second World War he was arrested by the Gestapo and died in a concentration camp. His collected works are published under the title *Vizioen en Geboorte* (1974).

**René Depestre** (Jacmel, 1926) One of those who welcomed Breton to Haiti in 1945, Depestre is a poet of scintillating images and powerful ideas. Without ever formally considering himself a surrealist, he has acknowledged the crucial importance surrealism has had in his life especially through the personal example given by Breton and Mabille. His great poem *A Rainbow for the Christian West* has been translated into English. Most of Depestre's adult life has been spent in exile, mainly in Cuba and France, where he lives today. His collections of poetry include: *Étincelles* (1945); *Gerbe de sang* (1946); *Végétations de clarté* (1951); *Traduit du grand large* (1952); *Minerai noir* (1957); *Journal d'un animal marin* (1964); *Un Arc-en-ciel pour l'occident chrétien* (1967). His novels and stories include: *Alléluia pour une femme-jardin* (1973); *Le Mât de cocagne* (1979); *Hadriana dans tous mes rêves* (1988).

**Wifredo Lam** (Sagua-La-Grande, 1902 – Paris, 1982) Cuban painter who participated in surrealist activities from 1939. Along with Breton and Masson, Lam travelled from France to the Americas fleeing the Nazis and was also interned in a concentration camp in Martinique for a few weeks, after which he returned home to Cuba. This gave him a fresh perspective on his art and he embarked on the research that led to his pathbreaking composition *The Jungle* (1943). His stay in Haiti during 1945 (when he participated in three exhibitions on the island) further deepened his work and gave him the opportunity to introduce voodoo mythology into his already rich imagery.

**Paul Laraque** (Jérémie, 1920) Haitian poet who participated in the 1946 revolution. He writes both in French and Creole. Forced into exile in the USA from 1961 until 1986 (and deprived of Haitian nationality in 1964), where he worked as a car-park attendant and as a lecturer in French. He was Secretary-General of the Association des ecrivains haïtiens à l'étranger from 1979. His book *Les Armes quotidiennes – poèsie quotidienne* was awarded the Casa de las America prize in 1979. His main collections of poetry are *Ce qui demeure* (1973); *Fistibal* (1974); *Les Armes quotidiennes – poèsie quotidienne* (1979); *Soldat mawon/Soldat* (1977); *Le Vieux Nègre et l'exil* (1988).

**Michel Leiris** (Paris, 1901 – Paris, 1990) Participant in surrealist activities from 1924, breaking with Breton in 1929, Leiris is one of the great stylists in contemporary French literature. A professional anthropologist, he took part in the momentous Dakar–Djibouti expedition (1931–33). In the late forties and early fifties he visited both Haiti and Martinique, writing his *Contacts de civilisation en Martinique et en Guadeloupe* for Unesco in 1955. Among his many important works are *L'Afrique fantôme* (1934); *L'Age d'Homme* (1939); *Biffures* (1948); *Fourbis* (1955); *Fibrilles* (1966); *Brisées* (1966); *Frèle brille* (1976); *Langage Tangage* (1985).

**Etienne Léro** (Lamentin, Martinique, 1910 – Lamentin, 1939) Founder of the Martiniquan Surrealist Group and animator of *Légitime défense*. The group's most original poet, but his early death in an airplane crash prevented his work from coming to full fruition.

**Pierre Mabille** (Paris, 1904 – Paris, 1952) Doctor and student of psychoanalysis and the hermetic sciences, Mabille participated in the Surrealist Group from 1936. He was one of the editors of *Minotaure*. Mabille is one of the most important writers to have emerged from the Surrealist Movement, advancing surrealist concerns into areas of medicine and the structure of human society. He first visited Haiti in 1940 and worked as a surgeon in Port-au-Prince. Becoming friends with the writer Jacques Roumain and the anthropologist Louis Maximilien, he helped them to establish the Haitian Bureau of Ethnology. He was appointed French Cultural Attaché to Haiti immediately after the Second World War and set up the journal *Conjonction* to examine issues of Haitian culture; it is still being published today. It was he who invited André Breton to visit Haiti in 1945, something that led to his recall after protests from the Haitian government. Main works: *La Construction de l'Homme* (1936); *Thérèse de Lisieux* (1937); *Égrégores ou la vie des* *civilisations* (1938); *Le Miroir du merveilleux* (1940); *Le Merveilleux* (1946); *Introduction à la connaisance de l'homme* (1949).

**Clément Magloire-Saint-Aude** (Port-au-Prince, 1912 – Port-au-Prince, 1971) One of the great poets of surrealism, Magloire-Saint-Aude was a participant in Les Griots, a movement of black consciousness that had a great impact in Haiti during the thirties. Magloire-Saint-Aude maintained a distance from literary circles and after the election of François Duvalier (who had once been a friend) in 1957, he increasingly assumed the status of a sort of internal exile, publishing nothing from then until his death. His main collections of poetry are *Dialogue de mes lampes* (1941); *Tabou* (1941); *Déchu* (1956); *Dimanche* (1973). His stories are published in *Parias* (1949); *Ombres et reflets* (1952); *Veillée* (1956).

**André Masson** (Balagny-sur-Thérain, 1896 – Paris, 1987) One of the most important painters of surrealism, he accompanied Breton across the Atlantic and during the stopover in Martinique. Although he was on the island for only a few weeks, the stay had a profound impact upon him, as witnessed by such works as *Antille* (1943). He was fascinated by the tropical landscape, and his suite of drawings inspired by Martinique are published in Breton's *Martinique, charmeuse de serpents*.

**René Ménil** (Fort-de-France, 1907) Founder member of *Légitime défense* and editor of *Tropiques*, René Ménil became a philosophy lecturer at the Lycée Schoelcher in Martinique and was cultural spokesman for the Martinique Communist Party. A writer on political theory and philosophy, his only book is *Tracées* (1981).

**Jules-Marcel Monnerot** (Fort-de-France, 1909) Founder member of *Légitime défense*, Monnerot also initiated, along with Georges Bataille and Roger Caillois, the College of Sociology. He is the author of what remains the most perceptive book on the sociological implications of surrealism, *La Poésie moderne et le sacré* (1946). After his powerful study *The Sociology of Communism*, he became an adviser to de Gaulle on communism and moved increasingly to the right. Other important works: *Les Faits sociaux ne sont pas des choses* (1946); *Sociologie du Communisme* (1949); *Inquisitions* (1974).

**Maurice-Sabas Quitman** Participant in *Légitime défense* about whom nothing else seems to be known.

**Pierre Yoyotte** (? – 1941?) Participant in *Légitime défense*, he contributed an excellent essay on fascism to *Documents 34*, published by the Belgian Surrealist Group in 1934. Active in the anti-fascist struggle, he is thought to have been shot by the Gestapo in 1941.

# Bibliography

Francis Affergan    *L'Anthropologie à la Martinique* (1983) Paris: Presses de Fondation National des Sciences Politiques

Régis Antoine    *La Littérature franco-antillaise: Haïti, Guadeloupe, Martinique* (1992) Paris: Karthala

A. James Arnold    *Modernism and Negritude: the Poetry and Poetics of Aimé Césaire* (1981) Cambridge, MA: Harvard University Press

René Bélance    'Une Sensationnelle interview de M. A. Breton' in *Haïti Journal*, 13 December 1945 (reprinted in André Breton, *Entretiens* (1952) Paris: Gallimard)

André Breton    *Martinique, charmeuse de serpents* (1972) Paris: Jean-Jacques Pauvert (original publication 1948, Paris: Sagittaire)

Richard D.E. Burton    'Between the Particular and the Universal: Dilemmas of the Martiniquan Intellectual' in Alistair Hennessy (ed.), *Intellectuals in the Twentieth-century Caribbean* (1981) Basingstoke: Macmillan Caribbean

Alejo Carpentier    *The Kingdom of This World* (1967) London: Victor Gollancz; (1991) London: André Deutsch

Aimé Césaire    *Discourse On Colonialism* (translated by Joan Pinkham) (1972) New York: Monthly Review Press

|  |  |
|---|---|
|  | *The Collected Poetry* (translated by Clayton Eschleman) (1983) Berkeley, CA: University of California Press |
| J. Michael Dash | *Literature and Ideology in Haiti 1915–1961* (1981) Basingstoke: Macmillan |
|  | *Haiti and the United States* (1988) Basingstoke: Macmillan |
|  | 'Blazing Mirrors: the Crisis of the Haitian Intellectual' in Alistair Hennessy (ed.), *Intellectuals in the Twentieth-century Caribbean* (1981) Basingstoke: Macmillan Caribbean |
| René Depestre | *Bonjour et adieu à la négritude* (1989) Paris: Robert Laffont |
|  | *A Rainbow For the Christian West* (translated by Jack Hirschman) (1972) Fairfax, CA: Red Hill Press |
| Frantz Fanon | *Black Skin, White Masks* (translated by Charles Lam Markmann) (1967) New York: Grove Press |
|  | *The Wretched of the Earth* (translated by Constance Farrington) (1968) New York: Grove Press |
| Roger Gaillard | 'André Breton et nous' in *Conjonction*, no. 103 (1966) |
| Edouard Glissant | *L'Intention poètique* (1978) Paris: Seuil |
|  | 'Creative Contradictions' in *Unesco Courier*, no. 11 (1981) |
|  | *Caribbean Discourse* (translated by J. Michael Dash) (1989) Charlotteville: University Press of Virginia |
|  | *Poétique de la rélation* (1990) Paris: Gallimard |
| Janheinz Jahn | *A History of Neo-African Literature* (1968) London: Faber |
| C.L.R. James | *The Black Jacobins* (1963) London: Allison & Busby |
| Ellen Conroy Kennedy | *The Negritude Poets* (1975) New York: Thunder's Mouth Press |
| Lilyan Kesteloot | *Les Écrivains noirs de langue française: Naissance d'une littérature* (1965) Brussels: Institut de Sociologie |

| | |
|---|---|
| Maximilien Laroche | *L'Image comme écho* (1978) Montreal: Nouvelle Optique |
| Jacqueline Leiner | *Imaginaire, langage, identité culturelle, négritude* (1980) Paris: Jean-Michel Place |
| Michel Leiris | *Contacts de civilisation en Martinique et en Guadeloupe* (1955) (1987) Paris: Gallimard/ Unesco |
| | *Zébrage* (1991) Paris: Gallimard |
| Pierre Mabille | *Messages de l'étranger* (1981) Paris: Plasma |
| Octave Manoni | *Prospero and Caliban: the Psychology of Colonialism* (1964) New York: Praeger (translated by Pamela Powesland; original edition, 1950, Paris: Seuil) |
| Albert Memmi | *The Colonizer and the Colonized* (1965) New York: Orion Press; (originally published 1957, Paris: Seuil) |
| René Ménil | *Tracées* (1981) Paris: Robert Laffont |
| Alfred Métraux | *Voodoo in Haiti* (translated by Hugo Charteris) (1972) New York: Schocken |
| Jean-Claude Michel | *Les Écrivains noirs et le surréalisme* (1982) Sherbrooke: Ed Naaman |
| Sidney W. Mintz | *Caribbean Transformations* (1974) Baltimore: Johns Hopkins |
| Jules Monnerot | *La Poésie moderne et le sacré* (1946) Paris: Gallimard |
| David Nicholls | *Haiti in Caribbean Context* (1985) Basingstoke: Macmillan |
| Jean Price-Mars | *Ainsi Parla l'Oncle* (1973) Ottawa: Leméac |
| Jacques Roumain | *Masters of the Dew* (translated by Langston Hughes) (1987) London: Heinemann |
| Shelton Williams | *Voodoo and the Art of Haiti* (1969) |

### Journals

*Légitime défense* (1932) reissued in facsimile by Jean-Michel Place (1979)

*Tropiques* (1941–46) reissued in facsimile by Jean-Michel Place (1978)

*Conjonction* nos 193–4 (April–June 1992) 'Surréalisme et révolte en Haïti'

# *Index*

# Also of interest from Verso

*Power in the Isthmus: A Political History of Modern Central America*
James Dunkerley

*The Pacification of Central America*
James Dunkerley

*The Black Atlantic: Modernity and Double Consciousness*
Paul Gilroy

*The Red Fez: Art and Spirit Possession in Africa*
Fritz Kramer
Translated by Malcolm Green

*The War of Gods: Religion and Politics in Latin America*
Michael Löwy

Printed in the United States
by Baker & Taylor Publisher Services